Imperium Press was founded in 2018 to supply students and laymen with works in the history of rightist thought. If these works are available at all in modern editions, they are rarely ever available in editions that place them where they belong: outside the liberal weltanschauung. Imperium Press' mission is to provide right thinkers with authoritative editions of the works that make up their own canon. These editions include introductions and commentary which place these canonical works squarely within the context of tradition, reaction, and counter-Enlightenment thought—the only context in which they can be properly understood.

ROBERT FILMER was the foremost English theoretician of the divine right of kings. Born in Kent, educated at Trinity College, Cambridge, knighted by Charles I, and imprisoned as a royalist, he was an important figure in the political life of the England of his time. His works were well received during his life, but his name was made posthumously with the publication of his *Patriarcha* in 1680, provoking liberal responses of widely varying quality.

PATRIⱭRCHA

THE COMPLETE
POLITICAL WORKS

ROBERT FILMER

PERTH
IMPERIUM PRESS
2021

Published by Imperium Press
www.imperiumpress.org

© Imperium Press, 2021

FIRST EDITION

A catalogue record for this
book is available from the
National Library of Australia

ISBN 978-1-922602-16-9 Paperback
ISBN 978-1-922602-17-6 EPUB
ISBN 978-1-922602-18-3 Kindle

Contents

Introduction

Sir Robert Filmer, born in 1588 to Sir Edward Filmer and Elizabeth Argall of East Sutton, Kent, was the eldest son of eighteen children. Filmer could trace his ancestry on his father's side back to at least the 14th century, while on his mother's side the ancestry was less ancient, yet still prestigious. Both families also shared an extensive involvement in the merchant ventures of the Virginia Company of London. It is within this dual world of Kent and London that Filmer would spend the majority of his life.

Filmer's education consisted of matriculating at Trinity College, Cambridge, followed by entry to Lincoln's Inn, however he did not practice law and instead seems to have spent his time managing his inherited estates.

Filmer maintained a rich and active interest in matters of politics and theology, but this remained a private endeavour prior to the First English Civil War. He did not publish any of his writing for the wider public and what he did write, including *Patriarcha*, was circulated within his sphere of intellectual acquaintances. Among those in this circle could be counted historians of the likes of Sir John Spelman, William Camden, and Sir Roger Twysden.

Filmer did not take an active part in the civil wars that washed over England in his lifetime, yet this did not stop him becoming a target of the parliamentary forces. His manor house was looted on numerous occasions, he was subject to punitive taxation by parliament, and ultimately he was imprisoned in Leeds Castle under what seems to have been the false charge of hiding arms for the royalist cause. It wasn't until sometime between 1647 and 1648 after his release from Leeds Castle that Filmer finally published some of his work.[1] It is at this time he made his political thoughts available to the wider public with the publication of *The Freeholder's Grand Inquest Touching our Soveraigne Lord the King and his Parliament,* a work developed from a section of the still unpublished *Patriarcha*. This work, as with all of his works published during his lifetime,

---

1   It appears that Filmer did not publish *Patriarcha* due to it being refused a printing license by the king who personally made the decision. See Stephen Orgel, Jennifer Andersen, and Elizabeth Sauer. *Books and Readers in Early Modern England Material Studies*. (Philadelphia: University of Pennsylvania Press, 2012), 233.

was published anonymously. Other works on politics that were published in his lifetime were *The Anarchy of a Limited or Mixed Monarchy*, and *The Necessity of the Absolute Power of all Kings, and in particular the King of England*, as well as *Observations concerning the Originall of Government, upon Mr. Hobbs Leviathan, Mr. Milton against Salmasius, H. Grotius "De Jure Belle"*, his final publication in 1652 being *Observation upon Aristotle's Politiques touching Forms of Government*. *Patriarcha*, his most famous work, was itself not published until 1680, long after his death in 1653. Why it was published at this point after his death is a question we will return to later, but first it is worth attending to the circumstances surrounding why he wrote when he did.

At the time Filmer wrote *Patriarcha* the question of parliament's status in relation to the monarchy had been a contentious issue for quite some time. The issue of taxation was central to this for the simple reason that kings would usually, if not always, call a parliament to sit for a limited time for the purpose of raising money. This is a point which the modern reader may not be aware of as this is very different to our modern parliament which sits almost every day and is a permanent fixture of the governmental apparatus. This dynamic was clearly burdensome for the kings as each attempt to raise finances led to counter demands from those being taxed, which is exactly the problem that Charles I faced.

In 1627, following setbacks in military engagements on the European mainland, Charles I required money and the option he chose was to appeal for parliamentary funding. This newly called parliament subsequently used Charles I's need for money to force his assent to the Petition of Rights in 1628. A key point of this petition was that it attempted to stop the king from trying to raise tax without parliamentary approval; end arbitrary arrests, as the King had been forcing loans and then arresting those who would not assent; and end the billeting of soldiers in civilian homes, something which the king seems to have done as a means of punishing his enemies.[2] The legal status of this petition was unclear and it was tested with the ship money controversy of 1634 when Charles I again attempted non-parliamentary approved taxation in direct opposition to the previously agreed petition. The premise for Charles I claiming he could tax the populace was an appeal to an archaic right allowing the king to demand coastal towns furnish ships for defence. This right included a provision that coastal towns could supply money in lieu of ships and on this basis Charles I's court pursued the money only. Not only did Charles I try

---

2   Reeve, L. J. *Charles I and the Road to Personal Rule*. (Cambridge University Press, 2002), 21.

to raise this money from coastal towns, but he also attempted to raise it from inland territories. This scheme resulted in a court case being brought against the king in 1637 which he won, but not convincingly. This court victory did not stop a large percentage of taxpayers refusing to pay subsequent attempts at levying the tax, which indicates that his position was weak. This pattern of using archaic rights to establish extra-parliamentary revenue streams was repeated with Charles I's fines for distraint of knighthood. This legally established punishment for failing to take up a knighthood had been resurrected after over 100 years of abeyance and was clearly a dubious scheme to raise money, but at least it was relatively subtler than the forced loans.

It is clear Charles I was attempting to govern without parliament as much as possible, and the attempt at removing the necessity of parliament came to a head with the Bishop's Wars of 1639, a war fought over the status of the monarchy in Scotland. The central question was about what form of church system would prevail, with the king favouring one including bishops who would obviously act as his deputies in governance of this territory. The Scottish system of Presbyterianism having been imported from Calvinist Geneva by John Knox proved to be a problem in that it placed the Kirk (Church) above the king. His failure to find adequate funding and subsequent military setbacks in this war required him to call parliament again after a period of eleven years without a single sitting. Funding from parliament was unsurprisingly not forthcoming, and instead this newly called parliament took the opportunity to bring into question the king's centralising attempts and extra-parliamentary money raising yet again. These disputes led to Charles I dissolving this parliament which came to be known as the "Short Parliament" due to the short time it sat. The resumption of hostilities with the Second Bishop's Wars of 1640 in which the Scottish forces invaded England resulted in the king having to pay an indemnity to the Scots for the return of Northumberland and County Durham. This led to the king having to call parliament once more. This "Long Parliament", so called for lasting from 3 November 1640 to 16 March 1660, took the chance to demand even more concessions from the king. It passed the Triennial Act of 1641 to try to ensure parliament would be convened with or without the king's permission every three years, and it again worked to remove the king's non-parliamentary sources of funding so as to rein in his attempts at governmental independence. The king, suspecting that members of parliament had encouraged the invasion of Northern England, chose to go to war with a rebellious parliament and the result was civil war, or rather three to be precise, from 1642–1646, 1648–1649, and finally 1649–1651.

THE CENTRALISATION OF POLITICAL STRUCTURES AND FILMER'S INNOVATION

Monarchy, as the name for a system of government, hides the bewildering array of specific relational patterns which can occur under it. In the case of Western European monarchy, the power which a monarch held varied by time and place. In its early beginnings in the Germanic kingdoms, kings held relatively little power in relation to their immediate followers. The lords, dukes, barons, and so on, who in the feudal system were granted land by the kings, and required by feudal relations to provide men and supplies in the case of war, were often able to refuse to do so. The kings were also often bound by the authority enjoyed by Church authorities who supplied the educated men that populated the king's court and could bring the kings to their knees by the act of excommunication.[3] This balance of power slowly shifted in favour of the king's court through a series of institutional developments facilitated by changes in technology.

In the field of military arrangements this trend is also found with the development of monetary payment for soldiers as opposed to feudal levies, and the shift in importance towards infantry and offensive capabilities which offset the military technology of armoured knights and castles.

As for the everyday structure of governance, writing and an expanding monetary system facilitated the establishment of permanent positions of government in capital cities and the creation of extensive taxation systems. With the Reformation and the removal of the Catholic Church from this dynamic, governance reached a tipping point as the king's court and his parliament took center stage. This new political arrangement—and it should be stressed that it was new—was in need of theological justification and in England the theology which developed in defence of this arrangement took the form of Anglican theological claims to the divine right of kings.

The claim that kings derived their political authority directly from their lineage from Adam does not have a place in Catholic theological schemes prior to this point. While traditionally Catholic doctrine has been supportive of monarchical authority in a very qualified way, it has always maintained an awkward relationship. This relationship has involved the developments of claims and counterclaims as to the nature of this relationship, and it is within this ever shifting dynamic that we find the papa-

---

3   In 1077 Henry IV, the Holy Roman Emperor sought absolution for his excommunication by Pope Gregory VII. Forced to wait at the gates of Canossa Castle for three days during a blizzard, this famous incident of penance has become known as the Road to Canossa.

cy itself innovating claims to divine right theories of supremacy. That the divine right theories of monarchy are in many ways an imitation of the Papacy's claims is only slightly less surprising than that the Church was also a source of modern theories regarding the consent of the governed. In response to the monarchical development, or imitation if you will, of divine right claims, the thinkers of the Church seem to have made cause to appeal to an elective or consensual basis for authority in an attempt to undermine it. Long before the advent of liberalism there existed claims that political authority is derived from a "people" who can choose their leader.[4] Through a winding and tortuous process this strain of Catholic theology would take a Protestant and then secular form in the state of nature arguments to come. This will likely come as something as a shock to the modern reader, steeped as they are in a Whig history where popular derived sovereignty is presented as a modern discovery. It is anything but, and it is this distorting Whig historiography to which we must now turn our attention.

THE DISTORTION OF WHIG HISTORIOGRAPHY AND THE ROLE OF JOHN LOCKE

Despite continual criticism of Whig history by historians and other academics, this form of history is so deeply ingrained that it permeates modern culture and education to such a degree that even the prime minister of Canada can refer to the current year as sufficient ethical justification for his actions.[5] The core of Whig history is the extravagant metaphysical claim that history is a rational and linear development to ever greater

---

4   A number of Catholic thinkers can be found arguing for government founded on the consent of the people; these include Nicholas of Cusa, Saint Thomas Aquinas, Robert Parsons, Francisco Suarez, and Robert Bellarmine, going as far back as at least Manegold of Lautenbach. This is not to say anything of the examples of this model of authority which date back to antiquity, such as the example of the Leges Regiae, the supposed donation of power by the people to the kings of Rome. For a detailed look at the connections between the Leges Regiae and Francisco Suarez's thought see Daniel Lee. *Popular Sovereignty in Early Modern Constitutional Thought.* (S.L.: Oxford University Press, 2018).

5   At the swearing in of his government on 4 November 2015, Canadian Prime Minister Justin Trudeau responded to reporter's question of why having a gender balanced cabinet was important to him with the response "because it's 2015." That such a remark could not only pass as acceptable but elicit chuckles from the audience at the expense of the journalist is quite revealing as to the nature of ethical thought in the modern world and the depth to which a Whig theology is imbued within the fabric of society.

freedom and liberty. The intellectual history of liberalism based on this thus requires that losers in this progress be set as the representative of an old world pushed aside by progress represented by the enlightened new world. In the case of Filmer, his place in this Whig scheme is to act as the symbol of an old patriarchal and monarchical world that is vanquished by the modern John Locke. This distorting narrative is rendered incoherent when it is understood that the contractual political thinking which Locke is famous for predates Locke and is a reaction to overt political centralisation which was itself the innovation. Locke's place in this narrative becomes even more suspect when we take into account that at the time Locke wrote he was not particularly influential and many of the themes he specifically wrote about were being advocated by others. Francis Bacon in *Atlantis* envisioned separation of Church and state in 1627, and pamphleteers such as Richard Overton were agitating for the same long before Locke. Even more strikingly, many of Locke's ideas such as religious tolerance were already in the process of occurring regardless of his input. Consider the fact that in 1687 King James II had attempted to extend religious tolerance to a degree *greater* than that supported by John Locke in his "A Letter Concerning Toleration" and greater than the Tolerance Act of 1689 introduced under William of Orange and his Glorious Revolution government. This all sits rather at odds with Whig history, or rather standard modern history.

If we reject this Whig history, then we are required to forward a further account that explains not only Filmer's subsequent obscurity but also the hegemonic success of Locke and the social contract theory tradition he belonged to. The alternative we can provide is that just as Filmer was writing in defence of a specific political arrangement of overt centralised monarchy, Locke and his contemporaries were likewise writing in defence of a specific political arrangement in the form of centralised parliamentary governance. The success of the relative institutions better explains the success of the theory than the other way around, and this success has less to do with some form of dialectical discussion or truth claims than it does with simple conflict. The winding and complicated thread of social contract theory demonstrates this well.

The origins of modern incarnations of social contract thinking clearly do not lie with John Locke, or even with Thomas Hobbes, but as has been previously noted, within Catholic theology and here we can see its underlying political function as well as its reliance on an extremely individualised version of Christian anthropology. The political function is demonstrated by the role of Francisco Suarez and the circumstances surrounding his *Defensio Fidei Catholicae*. In 1613 King James I, the author of *The True Law of Free Monarchies*, and a precursor to Filmer in divine right theology, had Suarez's book burned in public in London and forbade his subjects from reading it. The reason for this is that Suarez had provided a rejection of James' ideas on the divine rights of kings and he had based this rejection on the premise that authority initially rests with the people, something which the (initially) Catholic Scottish historian George Buchanan had also done in 1579 with the publication of *De Jure Regni apud Scotos*. Suarez had been asked to write this rejection of Anglican theology by Pope Paul V so any question to the orthodoxy of his ideas is answered by this.[6] Suarez's ideas would go on to be picked up by Hugo Grotius and incorporated into his *De Jure Belli ac Pacis*, a work devoted to his patron Louis XIII. It may seem incongruent that an argument which had once led to monarchs burning a book would subsequently be used in a book devoted to a king, but this merely foreshadows Hobbes' utilization of this thinking to justify absolute sovereignty. Far from contractual thinking proving destructive of sovereignty as Filmer feared, its placement of authority in the people would go on to justify extensive government centralization in the hands of a king, or even better, a parliament which could deflect this charge of centralisation very neatly by claiming to be the embodiment of the people. That conflict over political supremacy is at the heart of this contractual theory is observed astutely by Filmer himself, as he writes:

> Late writers have taken up too much upon trust from the subtle schoolmen, who to be sure to thrust down the king below the pope, thought it the safest course to advance the people above the king, that so the papal power may more easily take place of the regal.[7]

This is followed by the observation that this mode of thinking has been taken up by Calvinists (such as Grotius), again over political issues:

> Since the time that school divinity began to flourish, there hath been a common opinion maintained as well by divines as by divers other learned men, which affirms: 'Mankind is naturally endowed and born with freedom from all subjection, and at liberty to choose what form of government it please, and that the power which any one man hath over others was at the first by human right bestowed according to

6   Ellen Meiksins Wood. *Liberty and Property: A Social History of Western Political Thought from Renaissance to Enlightenment.* (London: Verso, 2012), 105.
7   See p. 4 below.

the discretion of the multitude.'

This tenet was first hatched in the schools, and hath been fostered by all succeeding papists for good divinity. The divines also of the reformed churches have entertained it, and the common people everywhere tenderly embrace it as being most plausible to flesh and blood, for that it prodigally distributes a portion of liberty to the meanest of the multitude, who magnify liberty as if the height of human felicity were only to be found in it—never remembering that the desire of liberty was the cause of the fall of Adam.

But howsoever this vulgar opinion hath of late obtained a great reputation, yet it is not to be found in the ancient fathers and doctors of the primitive church. It contradicts the doctrine and history of the Holy Scriptures, the constant practice of all ancient monarchies, and the very principles of the law of nature. It is hard to say whether it be more erroneous in divinity or dangerous in policy.

Yet upon the ground of this doctrine both Jesuits and some over zealous favourers of the Geneva discipline have built a perilous conclusion, which is 'that the people or multitude have power to punish or deprive the prince if he transgress the laws of the kingdom'. Witness Parsons and Buchanan. The first, under the name of Doleman, in the third chapter of his first book labours to prove that kings have been lawfully chastised by their commonwealths. The latter in his book *De Jure Regni apud Scotos* maintains a liberty of the people to depose their prince. Cardinal Bellarmine (book 3 *De Laicis*, chapter 6) and Calvin (*Institutes* book 4, chapter 10) both look asquint this way.[8]

Interestingly, it wasn't simply within the Catholic tradition directly that this pattern of thinking was developing, but we can also see it forming within the legal traditions of Europe at this time. Here it is less sophisticated and does not have a Christian metaphysics to base itself on which betrays its political purposes more clearly. J. G .A. Pocock in *The Ancient Constitution and the Feudal Law* claims that these, what he calls, "constitutionalist" movements included thinkers such as Francois Hotman in France, Pietro de Gregorio in Sicily, Francois Vrank in the Netherlands, and Erik Sparre in Sweden. All of these movements were driven by their

---

8   See p. 4 below.

respective positions to argue that the laws of their respective political orders were of "a practically infinite antiquity"[9] and that they had to revert to a "kind of historical obscurantism—compelled to attribute their liberties to more and more remote and mythical periods in the effort to prove their independence of the will of the king."[10]

This obscurantism is on full display in Filmer's *Patriarcha* where he struggles with the obvious incoherence of such a position. Filmer's broad argument against the claims of English constitutionalists is that the liberties granted by the Magna Carta were liberties granted by King John at the time it was drawn up. The purpose of Filmer establishing these liberties being granted by political authority was to argue against the obscurantist usage of the Magna Carta by these constitutionalist opponents of the monarchy. Sir Edward Coke's use of it as a basis for the Petition of Rights is relevant here. Coke's claims rested on a mythological narrative which somehow made the rights contained in the Magna Carta a rediscovery and continuation of ancient rights that predated William the Conqueror's invasion in 1066. This carries with it an implied societal spontaneity which Filmer was able to bring into question by simply pointing out that these previous laws would have been dependent on previous monarchical authority. The great hole in Coke's account, as noted by Pocock, is that there would need to be established a point of origin of law that put it prior to the existence of monarchical authority.

The structure of Filmer's *Patriarcha* should now be much clearer to the modern reader. The first half is devoted to a rebuttal of the natural rights theories being developed from the Christian tradition at the time, while the second half is directed against the constitutionalist theories being developed from the legal tradition, a pairing of arguments which otherwise would appear incongruent.

QUESTIONING LOCKE'S REJECTION OF FILMER

Despite the assumption that one would get from a modern education in politics, many of Filmer's criticisms of the anarchistic underpinnings of his opponents in *Patriarcha* have been woefully unanswered, or if they were provided with an answer they have either been weak or of dubious sincerity. No one demonstrates this better than Locke and his criticisms of Filmer in the *The Two Treatises of Government*. When comparing *Patriar-*

---

9   J. G. A. Pocock *The Ancient Constitution and the Feudal Law: A Study of English Thought in the Seventeenth Century* (Cambridge University Press, 1987) , 17.
10   Pocock, *The Ancient Constitution,* 17.

cha and *The Two Treatises of Government* it is worth noting that Filmer's work is not simply a biblical exegesis combined with a natural rights theory. It actually relies mostly on historical references and facts supported by documents, and is a genuine attempt to provide an accurate and truthful model of historical institutions and the working of authority. Locke's work on the other hand relies almost entirely on biblical exegesis, has no serious historical evidence to back up its claims, and when it does not rely on the bible for authority it turns Filmer's natural rights of the father on its head with the wielding of an individualistic state of nature argument which is the political theory equivalent of a *deus ex machina*.

Locke's dismissal of Filmer is contained in book one of the *Two Treatises* and it is almost entirely an attempt to dispute Filmer's biblical exegesis with recourse to biblically derived claims of the natural liberty granted to man by God. This is an argument which if one were to raise as a basis for liberalism in the present day would be met with confusion and derision. While we have no reason to agree directly with Locke or Filmer on the Biblical exegesis, what we can instead do is extract the underlying claims and compare them. Locke's ultimate underlying claim is that authority inheres in the individual as a result of man's nature as given by God. Filmer meanwhile asserts that man's nature is inherently structured and marked by authority in the form of patriarchal relationships, again, as determined by God. These are both natural law bases for their respective positions but underlying these natural rights is an issue of simple logic relating to the direction of authority, and we can see that Locke's account is deeply unreasonable.[11]

Both writers argue from the observed nature of humans, but the manner of their reasoning from human nature takes very different turns. We can see this in the case of dependency and inheritance. In the *Two Treatises* §89, Locke writes the following of the nature of childhood dependency:

> For children being by the course of nature, born weak, and unable to provide for themselves, they have by the appointment of God himself, who hath thus ordered the course of nature, a right to be nourished and maintained by their par-

---

11   On the issue of both Filmer and Locke sharing a connection in their respective usage of natural rights for a basis of political theory see Figgis, *The Divine Right of Kings*, 158-160. For Figgis, Filmer represents a trailblazer in setting his political theory on the inalienable rights of the father. This led the way for Locke to simply take this natural right and supplant it with his own individualistic conception. This in Figgis' opinion makes Locke's theory a version of divine right governance in disguise.

ents; nay, a right not only to a bare subsistence, but to the conveniencies and comforts of Life, as far as the conditions of their parents can afford it. Hence it comes, that when their parents leave the world, and so the care due to their children ceases, the effects of it are to extend as far as possibly they can, and the provisions they have made in their life-time, are understood to be intended, as nature requires they should, for their children, whom, after themselves, they are bound to provide for: though the dying parents, by express words, declare nothing about them, nature appoints the descent of their property to their children, who thus come to have a title, and natural right of inheritance to their fathers goods, which the rest of mankind cannot pretend to.

The reader should be immediately struck by the close interaction of God or Nature on affairs here, and the reliance on rights which derive from God's will. Locke's rejection of primogeniture and his assertion of the natural requirement for parents to provide property for their children equally is framed as the ordination of "God himself" who has granted the "right of being nourished and maintained by their parents" to children and has obliged parents to do so "as a duty." God is inescapably required in an immediate sense for the individual and this need culminates in the flight to the state of nature argument which is the only way to set such a system of natural law in motion. We have to have the individuals simply appear *ex nihilo* as if made by God, which is what we see in §4, ch. 2:

To understand political power right, and derive it from its original, we must consider, what State all Men are naturally in, and that is, a *State of Perfect* freedom to order their Actions, and dispose of their Possessions and Persons, as they think fit, within the bounds of the Law of Nature, without asking leave, or depending upon the Will of any other Man.

To defend the validity of this state of nature as being theologically sound he makes an appeal to authority in the form of the theologian Richard Hooker in §5:

This *equality* of Men by Nature, the judicious *Hooker* looks upon as so evident in it self, and beyond all question, that he makes it the Foundation of that Obligation to mutual Love amongst Men, on which he Builds the Duties they owe one another, and from whence he derives the great Maxims of *justice* and *charity.*

It is a remarkable fact that the document which we are told triumphantly rejected the succession of authority from Adam does so by forwarding a claim which makes exponentially less sense, is even more dependent on naked biblical arguments than Filmer's succession of authority from Adam, and which demands tortuous logic and a fantastical state of nature.

Clearly there is something very strange occurring here for this to still be counted as a serious political tract. It must have served a purpose and still serves a purpose and one such purpose is observable in the way in which Locke uses the natural right system to divorce authority from property. This is best seen in his famous labor theory of property which made property a matter of individual interaction with nature and not a social convention. In the *Two Treatises* the political purpose of this is evident in the following passage found in §91:

> But no one could pretend to the whole inheritance, or any sovereignty supposed to accompany it; since a right of inheritance gave every one of the rest, as well as any one, a title to share in the goods of his father. Not only upon this account, I say, have I been so particular in examining the reason of children's inheriting the property of their fathers, but also because it will give us farther light in the inheritance of *rule* and *power,* which in countries where their particular municipal laws give the whole possession of land entirely to the first-born, and descent of power has gone so to men by this custom, some have been apt to be deceived into an opinion, that there was a natural or divine right of primogeniture, to both *estate* and *power;* and that the inheritance of both *rule* over men, and *property* in things, sprang from the same original, and were to descend by the same rules.

Locke's disconnect of "*rule* over men, and *property* in things" as being inheritable serves two purposes. On the one hand it preserves the property rights of his particular class, and on the other hand, it undermines the claims to monarchical inheritance of authority.

In contrast to Locke's tortuous theory, Filmer's theory based on the observable dependency of children is very straightforward. This relationship is inherently asymmetrical and cannot be anything but, as it is the nature of childhood and the dependency that this creates that children are subject to the authority of parents. Filmer does not offer a deeper anthropological account for this, simply being content to note this relationship. In contrast, Locke does, but Locke's reasoning is exceptionally bad in this regard. For Locke the footing of this relationship is a mix of God/Nature given rights and duties to the individual directly, combined with a sort of strange generational debt as can be seen in the following section at §90:

> But that having been done in obedience to the same law, whereby he received nourishment and education from his own parents; this score of education, received from a man's father, is paid by taking care, and providing for his own children; is paid, I say, as much as is required of payment by alteration of property, unless present necessity of the parents require a return of goods for their necessary support and subsistence: for we are not now speaking of that reverence, acknowledgment, respect and honour, that is always due from children to their parents; but of possessions and commodities of life valuable by money. But though it be incumbent on parents to bring up and provide for their children, yet this debt to their children does not quite cancel the score due to their parents; but only is made by nature preferable to it: for the debt a man owes his father takes place, and gives the father a right to inherit the son's goods, where, for want of issue, the right of children doth not exclude that title.

We can see here the great lengths to which Locke has to go in order to account for society on the basis of individuals.

The final point to which I wish to draw the reader's attention is the differing consideration of political freedom inherent in both Locke and Filmer. For Filmer, this freedom can only be granted by authority and the only one who can have complete freedom is the sovereign of society. To see what Filmer was pointing towards, we can first take a small detour in the historical usage of the word "freedom".

In England during the middle ages and up until the early modern period, to gain one's freedom was to be made free from local feudal obligations and to become a subject of the king directly.[12] This is its origin. So here we have a relationship involving three parties: the central power of the king, then the subject, and finally the intermediaries to whom the subject

---

12   For a detailed look at the actions of the king's court in applying negative liberties to undermine franchise holder in medieval England, see Nicholas Szabo's "Jurisdiction as Property: Franchise Jurisdiction from Henry III to James I" (April 21, 2006). Available at SSRN: https://ssrn.com/abstract=936314.

was initially also subject to, be this local lords, the Church, or some other corporate entity. The king removed the intermediaries, who were his competitors within the power structure, by raising the station of the individual with claims of granting him freedom. Filmer is very much aware of this passive nature of the linguistic construct of "freedom" wherein an individual is granted their freedom from a specific relationship *by a greater political authority*. We see this in his criticisms of Grotius whom he catches in the act of turning this word into an active linguistic construct. Citing Aristotle on the issue of a child gaining their freedom from parental authority Grotius translates it as *until they do separate*. In response, Filmer writes:

> But Aristotle speaks only of a passive separation. For he doth not say that children are subject to parents until they *do separate*, but he saith until they *be separated*, χωρισθῇ, in the verb of the passive voice. That is, until *by law* they be separated. For the law (which is nothing else but the will of him that hath the power of the supreme father) doth in many cases, for the public benefit of society, free children from subjection to the subordinate parent. So that the natural subjection by such emancipation of children is not extinguished, but only assumed and regulated by the parent paramount.[13]

By altering this from passive to active what Grotius is doing is not altering the fact that this freedom from parents is being granted by a government, but hiding the role of government in this act. The value of this in advancing the expansion of a centralised power is astronomical, as the populace can be enlisted in the process of political conflict between the intermediaries and the centralising power without being aware they are being enlisted by this power. Centralising power can now expand exponentially and undermine all relationships within society that come between it and the individual, and it does this by hiding itself and focusing all attention on the concepts of liberty and freedom. In Locke's case this is no different. He may frame the rights of the individuals as being from God, but in reality this God is none other than the centralised government under the control of parliament.

13   See p. 147 below.

FILMER AND THE ENLIGHTENMENT

As we no longer talk of these rights of modernity which give the individual his shape as being God granted, and given that we no longer consider the state of nature argument as being a valid basis of liberal theory, the question now turns to why Locke is placed forward as the father of liberalism and as being a formative influence on the Enlightenment.

The beginning of the move towards the *Two Treatises of Government* becoming influential appears to be connected with the Irish writer William Molyneux and constitutional issues that arose around the status of Ireland's parliament. Molyneux's argument centred around the concept of consent of the governed which he claimed was a relationship that existed between the Irish people (seemingly expressed through the Irish Parliament) and the King[14]. This brought into dispute the claims of the English parliament to pass laws affecting Ireland. Yet again we see political conflict at the scene of intellectual history and the wielding of the concept of consent as a means to undermine one political relationship in favour of another.

While Molyneux's attempts to use Locke against the English parliament came to nothing, Locke's influence would nonetheless receive another great boost with the French Revolution and the American Revolution where he was cited and promoted by such figures as Voltaire and Thomas Jefferson. However, could it be said that these events would have occurred regardless of Locke? Was Locke a significant cause? Or was he merely someone whose polemic proved popular at this point in time? As we have seen so far in this introduction, the concepts which Locke outlined were far from being original; rather, they show all the signs of being a structurally influenced development. Individuals caught in the same broad background and facing the same institutional changes respond in generally similar ways and it could so easily be the case that due to mere chance, we could have been faced with the constant invocation of Algernon Sydney by modern political theorists instead,[15] another writer who wrote in response

14   Martyn P. Thompson, "The Reception Of Locke's Two Treatises Of Government 1690-1705," *Political Studies Association*, vol 24, Issue 2, (1976): 184-191.
15   Martyn P. Thompson makes much the same criticism as the one put forward here, noting that Locke's ideas were neither original nor particularly important upon their release. I agree with Thompson that it would be very rewarding to understand how and when Locke became such a dominant figure within this tradition of thought, as from a strictly theoretical position it is rather inexplicable. Thompson, "The Reception Of Locke's Two Treatises Of Government 1690-1705," 184-191.

to Filmer, rather than the ubiquitous references to Locke.

Regardless of whether Locke was really all that important to events, it is still the case that he was popular among the thinkers of the Enlightenment period. The actors on mainland Europe and the United States evidently saw in his work concepts which accorded with their specific experiences and which lent support to their philosophical and political reactions. In a broad sense what we can note is that throughout this period there was a general and sustained trend towards systemising Protestant ideas centred on the radical individual within a non-theological setting. This occurred not just in the realm of politics but also epistemology and ethics, all concepts which are invariably tied in with the nature of authority. To assist in this criticism we can turn to the work of Alasdair MacIntyre whose work charting and explaining the failure of modern philosophers to achieve this overall goal is exceptionally helpful in this regard.

In the field of epistemology, for MacIntyre, the Enlightenment's interpretation of first principles is a foundationalist one where first principles had to supply two functions: first, they had to "warrant an immediate justified certitude on the part of any rational person who uttered it in the appropriate way, perhaps in the appropriate circumstances"[16], and second, they had to be able to furnish the basis of all further knowledge. Central to this modern first principle is a rejection of authority evident by placing the start point of epistemology on the individual abstracted from context. The ground from which epistemology is being launched in this sense is the radical individual who, like the Protestant working from scripture alone, has no need for authority to provide him with a basis from which to understand what is before him. This project has failed and has led to these systems becoming what they originally were supposed to transcend—traditions.

This general pattern of individual-based thought continues in the area of ethics in which again the radical autonomous individual is seen as the starting point, and the given tradition of the individual is rejected as a valid basis from which to reason—as is any sort of authority. As a result, ethics, MacIntyre contends, has been stripped of teleology and appeals to a shared scheme within which the actions of an individual can be measured. By shifting the basis of ethics to the abstracted individual, the possibility of measuring an action against a standard to which it should accord has robbed words such as "good" and "bad" of their role as evaluative concepts. To be a good man requires there be some standard of what a man

16   Alasdair C. MacIntyre. *First Principles Final Ends and Contemporary Philosophical Issues.* (Milwaukee: Marquette University, 1990), 11.

should be, a standard which we can assess someone as moving towards so that we can say he is a good man, or failing to do so and therefore being a bad man. Ethics has subsequently devolved into a state of confusion that has culminated in emotivism where ethical pronouncements really do amount to little more than assertions of personal feelings.[17]

As for the realm of political thought, the abject failure to provide a justification for basing political thought on the autonomous individual is exemplified in the form of human rights which have evolved from the very same natural rights used by Locke and his contemporaries. In MacIntyre's words, these rights are so baseless that belief in them is no better than belief in witches and unicorns.[18]

If this entire modern philosophical structure based on the individual has failed so badly, then we are left with the task of providing an explanation for its continual hegemonic dominance and the dogmatic adherence of modern thinkers to it despite the persistent and clearly insurmountable intellectual problems which it presents. The unpleasant answer we can again provide is that this form of thinking is, and has always been, inescapably linked to political conflict and the interests of a specific political configuration. This is something which again MacIntyre points out:

> Liberalism, beginning as a repudiation of tradition in the name of abstract, universal principles of reason, turned itself into a politically embodied power, whose inability to bring its debates on the nature and context of those universal principles to a conclusion has had the unintended effect of transforming liberalism into a tradition.[19]

The nature of this embodied power is that of a centralising center of power ranged against a society comprised of newly liberated individuals. A window into this is interestingly provided by none other than Immanuel Kant in his essay *What is Enlightenment?* In this essay, Kant declares that the meaning of enlightenment is:

> man's emergence from his self-imposed immaturity. Immaturity is the inability to use one's understanding without guidance from another. This immaturity is self-imposed

---

17   For an extended exposition of MacIntyre's criticism of modern ethics the reader is recommended to turn to Alasdair C. MacIntyre, *After Virtue: A Study in Moral Theory* (Notre Dame, IN: University of Notre Dame Press, 1980),

18   MacIntyre, *After Virtue*, 83.

19   MacIntyre, *After Virtue*, 349.

when its cause lies not in lack of understanding, but in lack
of resolve and courage to use it without guidance from another. *Sapere Aude!* ["dare to know"] "Have courage to use
your own understanding!"—that is the motto of enlightenment.[20]

How it is that these individuals are liberated from this "immaturity" they
are held in becomes evident as Kant celebrates the actions of Frederick II
as:

A prince who does not find it beneath him to say that he
takes it to be his duty to prescribe nothing, but rather to
allow men complete freedom in religious matters—who
thereby renounces the arrogant title of tolerance—is himself
enlightened and deserves to be praised by a grateful present
and by posterity as the first, at least where the government is
concerned, to release the human race from immaturity and
to leave everyone free to use his own reason in all matters of
conscience.[21]

It is clear that Kant is describing liberation of the people by a centralising
monarch being conducted at the expense of intermediary structures. It is
unlikely that Kant and his contemporaries saw themselves as apologists
for centralising political power but instead evidently saw themselves as
champions of the enlightenment of the individual.[22] The reader may at
this point be reminded of Filmer's previously quoted complaints of the
connection between social contract theory and the political aims of the
Papacy and Calvinists to undermine kings. Advocacy of the individual is
invariably a symptom of the expansion of a centralising center of power
and the advocates are always found in the company of these same centers
of power.

20   Immanuel Kant, "What Is Enlightenment?", http://www.columbia.edu/acis/
ets/CCREAD/etscc/kant.html
21   Kant,   "What   Is   Enlightenment?",   http://www.columbia.edu/acis/ets/
CCREAD/etscc/kant.html
22   This relationship of Enlightenment figures and the centralisation of society
has largely been expunged from common understanding of the Enlightenment
due to its use in polemical debates surrounding the role of democracy. The major
figures such as Kant and Voltaire, and even such thinkers as Francois Quesnay
of the Physiocratic school were proponents of centralized governmental control.

FILMER'S THEORY ON HIS OWN GROUNDS

Central to Filmer's theory is that authority is uni-directional. This is best expressed in his claim that "kings are either fathers of their people, or heirs of such fathers or usurpers of the right of such fathers."[23] The problem which this claim faces is that it appears from the standpoint of modernity that this has been falsified. We have political systems which are based on elections and while there still may be monarchies in most cases these are utterly powerless. Patriarchal descent in a strict sense is not a justifiable basis of political theory. The advent of modernity and democracy would *seem* to undermine Filmer fatally.

In Filmer's later works, such as the *Observation upon Aristotle's Politiques touching Forms of Government*, Filmer interestingly gives us a deeper look into the theoretical rigor of his thinking when he begins to disconnect sovereignty from the specific institution of monarchy and the act of biological inheritance. In doing so he still confusingly calls this culmination of government in a single sovereign position "monarchy," but this is really a result of him not having the required vocabulary to express his point. Take for example Filmer's claim that the Roman innovation of having consuls after the expulsion of kings was a mere name change only.[24] Likewise, in the case of Venice he likens the position of Duke to a king in everything but name only, going as far as to dismiss the republican governments of Venice and the United Provinces with the claim that "Whatsoever is either good or tolerable in either of their governments, is borrowed or patched up of broken and distracted monarchy."[25] Filmer even speculates that representative parliamentary governments in general are nothing more than "petty monarchies" wherein their governments "hath the liberty to have many kings by turns."

For Filmer, it is obvious that democratic government by parliament is nothing more than a variant of monarchy in that, regardless of its grand claims, its structure always terminates in hierarchy with a single person, or we could say entity of some kind or position, be it occupied or not by a physical person. This has clear echoes in the more recent claims of the

23   See p. 2 below.
24   See p. 176.
25   See p. 189.

political theorist Carl Schmitt with the theory of the state of exception.[26] The culmination of Filmer's thought along these lines resulted in the following axioms:

1. That there is no form of government, but monarchy only.

2. That there is no monarchy, but paternal.

3. That there is no paternal monarchy, but absolute or arbitrary.

4. That there is no such thing as an aristocracy or democracy.

5. That there is no such form of government as a tyranny.

6. That the people are not born free by nature.[27]

As Filmer has already established that even democracies are monarchical in structure in that they culminate in a single point of sovereignty, his reference here to paternal inheritance surely cannot mean literal paternal inheritance of father to son. If, instead, Filmer meant authority being derived from previous authority then a great deal of the criticism he has faced disappears very quickly. In this case, we can even consider the supremacy of Parliament in relation to the King as transference of power in an abstract paternal sense. Parliament, having been created by the King, surpassed it in a conflict and in a sense inherited its position in a paternal way. It was itself born of authority and did not rise up out of the ground spontaneously and it did not attain power as a result of popular consent.

One of the greatest problems faced by an account like this is the modern insistence on the validity of popular revolutions which Locke so famously sanctioned. For Filmer to be fully vindicated we would need to provide an historical and social account of regime change and revolution which specifically models these developments as being patriarchal in the same sense as the succession of parliament. Luckily just such an account is presented

---

26   Schmitt's highly influential concept of the state of exception rests on a consideration of sovereignty which Filmer would no doubt recognise, both having been influenced by Jean Bodin. Both writers are working on the principle that the king never dies which is also implicit in Bertrand de Jouvenel's political theory. Having set up the juridical structures of government which makes sovereignty in the Bodinian sense a reality, removing the official king from a position of sovereignty does not alter the fact that this point of sovereign control remains and can be occupied by another, even if that other actor denies that they are in such a position.

27   See p. 196 below.

by the unlikely figure of Bertrand de Jouvenel.[28]

For Jouvenel, the revolutions which wracked the world from Filmer's time onwards, and which were harbingers of popular government, were not spontaneous uprisings, but the actions of centralising centers of power encouraging elements of society to rebellion. As we have seen already it was the kings who did so much to raise the individuals of society into direct relationship with them; this process, as with the development of "freedom" we saw before, represented a growth of the state under the stewardship of monarchs:

> The growth of its authority strikes private individuals as being not so much a continual encroachment on their liberty as an attempt to put down various tyrannies to which they have been subject. It looks as though the advance of the state is a means to the advance of the individual.[29]

The Reformation represents a great leap forward in this process, and the later parliamentary and colonial government-led revolutions directed against these monarchs are a result of the monarch's expansion of liberty being turned against them. Unhappy with the centralisation attempted by kings, these authorities instigated popular uprisings of their own in response, and in doing so they made appeals to calls of popular sovereignty that move beyond the conception of freedom promoted by monarchs. That this freedom based on natural law or some other such scheme is impossible is far from being a problem—it is a positive benefit. Under this cover of freedom and popular sovereignty the centralisation of power was advanced to levels which the so-called absolute monarchs, such as Charles I, could only dream of. Where Charles I could barely raise an army without begging and scratching for money, the governments of modernity centered on parliaments or republican structures could, and did, conscript the entire masses of the populace in total wars. As Jouvenel writes of the French Revolution:

> Is not the revolution which overthrows the king going to pull down this structure, attack the apparatus of command[…]? By no means; instead it will introduce the conscription

---

28   A liberal writer and a member of the Mount Pelerin Society, Jouvenel nonetheless produced an account of the development of power which is inescapably within the monarchical divine right tradition.

29   Bertrand de Jouvenel, *On Power: Its Nature and the History of Its Growth*, (USA: Beacon Press Boston, 1962), 130.

which the monarch long desired but never had the strength to realize.[30]

Wherever we see a revolution, what we are seeing is not a spontaneous organisation of the people; instead, what we are really seeing are the results of a power center of society raising and directing masses at another center of power. The cries of freedom and liberty that get these masses moving are happily encouraged and mouthed by these elites and the elites may even come to believe them wholeheartedly, but it is these elites manning institutions that direct these revolutions, and it is they who benefit in the end. The people are unable to organise themselves spontaneously, a point on which Filmer has been endlessly vindicated. With the Glorious Revolution this was the English Parliament, with the French Revolution it was the French Parliament, with the American Revolution it was the colonial governments, and so on.

Quite why these governing institutions are needed at all after the revolution (or even during the revolution) is a point that has never been explained adequately by modernity and it has been the task of the likes of Locke, Hobbes, and Rousseau to provide excuses. This conflict between the supposedly natural and possible anarchism of the individual and the presence of governments is demonstrated in Filmer's confusion with the state of nature argument of Bellarmine. In *Patriarcha*, Filmer raises an issue with this that still stands against modernity. Filmer notes that "[Bellarmine] saith that by the law of God, power is immediately in the people; hereby he makes God the author of a democratical estate," only for him to then conclude that the people are unable to organise as such and thus need to "give their power to one man, or to some few," which they may change back into a democracy "if there be a lawful cause."[31] The incoherence is palpable—why would God grant natural liberty and equality to the individual who must then give it away? Likewise, why would a people who had risen up in revolution to overthrow their kings then grant a right of governance to parliaments? It seems obvious that parliaments and the American colonial authorities needed some intellectual narrative to simultaneously explain their undermining of monarchs with calls to anarchism, as well as simultaneous justification of their own *inheritance* of governance on these terms, and it is in this environment that Hobbes, Locke, and the rest auditioned with their respective works. These theorists were picked up and championed when they were needed in political conflict.

---

30   Jouvenel, *On Power*, 128.
31   See pp. 4–5 below.

Filmer, the famed defender of absolutism, ironically, was of no use as a provider of intellectual justification for the expansive absolute governments of modernity, but this says nothing about the inherent validity of Filmer's ideas. For far too long the accepted assumption has been that the thought of modern theorists is *prima facie* correct and that it has triumphed over Filmer's account due to some process of reason. Filmer was not proved wrong; he was sidelined by a centralizing political structure because he was of no use to them.

A revival of Filmer's thought has much to recommend it, not least of which is the potential insight such a different view of society can provide in understanding the flaws and limitations of our current political theories. The thought of modern political theorists has proven utterly incapable of providing explanations of political phenomena, and that this is so can be determined from the sorry state that political science and the social sciences find themselves. Premised on deep seated methodological individualism, these disciplines have taken the individual as their scientific bedrock, an individual which the philosopher Charles Taylor has correctly traced back to the thought of Filmer's opponents.[32] Filmer points towards a correction of this by making the connection between this individual's liberty and the overarching political order of a society a constant of human existence. This gives us a far more accurate point of departure for political theory and helps to unmask the ultimately liberal ideological nature of the social sciences as well as their role as apologetics of the liberal political order of centralised power.

---

32 Taylor's broad attack on the social sciences consists of his realisation that underpinning these naturalistic research programs is an ideological system derived from social contract theory based political thought. The individual that forms the basis of political science and which is taken as the scientific atom from which political scientists believe they can form extensive models, is itself a product of the structure which it supposedly makes.

Note on the Text

All of Filmer's political works have been included in this volume save one, *The Necessity of the Absolute Power of All Kings*, which is a series of extracts of Richard Knolles' 1606 translation of Jean Bodin's *Les Six livres de la République* entitled *The Six Bookes of a Commonweale*. This has been excluded because Imperium Press will release a modern translation of Bodin's superior Latin edition which will include everything in the *Necessity* and more, and because Filmer simply reprinted the material without adding any commentary.

The text has been slightly modernized and harmonized between the works and manuscripts, e.g. "lib." = "book", "20 *H*. 3" = "20 Henry III", etc. Filmer's works exist in various editions which do not always agree with each other. *Patriarcha* was never published in his lifetime, and so no definitive edition exists—all modern editions of his works, especially *Patriarcha*, are to a degree compilations. So it is with the present edition. The sources for each of the included works are as follows:

Patriarcha:

Copy-text is the 1680 Chiswell edition. Transcription is based on the Chicago manuscript (MS 413, ca. 1631), with some Chiswell and the Cambridge manuscript (MS 7078, ca. 1635) as required for completeness. The Cambridge manuscript has additional material which has been re-inserted:

- A part of ch. 2, §1, after which the section resumes as per the Chicago MS.
- A part of ch. 3, §2.
- A part of ch. 3, §9.
- Two sentences at the end of ch. 3, §15.

The chapters on Grotius and Selden are omitted from *Patriarcha*, being present in the *Observations on Grotius*.

The Anarchy:

Copy-text is the 1696 edition. Transcription is based on the 1648 edition, with some 1679.

Observations on Hobbes, Milton, Grotius:

Copy-text is the 1696 edition. Transcription is based on the Harleian manuscript (MS 6867) up to second paragraph of §12 of Hobbes, then on the Cambridge manuscript for the rest.

Observations on Aristotle:

Copy-text is the 1696 edition. Transcription is based on the 1652 edition, with some 1679.

Directions for Obedience:

Copy-text is the 1696 edition. Transcription is based on the 1652 edition, with some Harleian MS.

Free-Holders Inquest:

Copy-text is 1696 edition. Transcription is based on the 1679 edition.

Patriarcha;
or the Natural Power of KINGS.

By the Learned
Sir ROBERT FILMER Baronet.

Libertas populi, quem regna coercent libertate perit.

> ["The liberty of the people, whom power restrains unduly, perishes through liberty."]

Lucanus
—*Pharsalia 3.146*

Fallitur egregio quisquis sub Principe credit servitium; nunquam libertas gratior extat quam sub rege pio.

> ["Whoever thinks it is slavery to serve under an eminent prince is mistaken; liberty is never more gracious than under a pious king."]

Claudian
—*De Consulatu Stilichonis 3.113*

CHAP. I: That the first kings were fathers of families.

(1) The tenet of the natural liberty of mankind new, plausible, and dangerous; (2) the question stated out of Bellarmine; some contradictions of his noted; (3) Bellarmine's argument answered out of Bellarmine himself; (4) the royal authority of the patriarchs before the Flood; (5) the dispersion of nations over the world after the confusion of Babel, was by entire families over which the fathers were kings; (6) and from

them all kings are descended; (7) all kings are either fathers
of their people, (8) or heirs of such fathers or usurpers of the
right of such fathers; (9) of the escheating of kingdoms; (10)
of regal and paternal power and of their agreement.

(1) Since the time that school divinity began to flourish, there hath been a
common opinion maintained as well by divines as by divers other learned
men, which affirms: 'Mankind is naturally endowed and born with freedom from all subjection, and at liberty to choose what form of government it please, and that the power which any one man hath over others
was at the first by human right bestowed according to the discretion of the
multitude.'

This tenet was first hatched in the schools, and hath been fostered by
all succeeding papists for good divinity. The divines also of the reformed
churches have entertained it, and the common people everywhere tenderly embrace it as being most plausible to flesh and blood, for that it prodigally distributes a portion of liberty to the meanest of the multitude, who
magnify liberty as if the height of human felicity were only to be found in
it—never remembering that the desire of liberty was the cause of the fall
of Adam.

But howsoever this vulgar opinion hath of late obtained a great reputation, yet it is not to be found in the ancient fathers and doctors of the primitive church. It contradicts the doctrine and history of the Holy Scriptures,
the constant practice of all ancient monarchies, and the very principles of
the law of nature. It is hard to say whether it be more erroneous in divinity
or dangerous in policy.

Yet upon the ground of this doctrine both Jesuits and some over zealous
favourers of the Geneva discipline have built a perilous conclusion, which
is 'that the people or multitude have power to punish or deprive the prince
if he transgress the laws of the kingdom'. Witness Parsons and Buchanan.
The first, under the name of Doleman, in the third chapter of his first book
labours to prove that kings have been lawfully chastised by their commonwealths. The latter in his book *De Jure Regni apud Scotos* maintains a liberty of the people to depose their prince. Cardinal Bellarmine (book 3
De Laicis, chapter 6) and Calvin (*Institutes* book 4, chapter 10) both look
asquint this way.

This desperate assertion, whereby kings are made subject to the censures
and deprivations of their subjects, follows (as the authors of it conceive)
as a necessary consequence of that former position of the supposed natural equality and freedom of mankind, and liberty to choose what form of
government it please.

And though Sir John Hayward, Adam Blackwood, John Barclay, and some others have learnedly confuted both Buchanan and Parsons, and bravely vindicated the right of kings in most points, yet all of them, when they come to the argument drawn from the natural liberty and equality of mankind, do with one consent admit it for a truth unquestionable, not so much as once denying or opposing it. Whereas if they did but confute this first erroneous principle, the whole fabric of this vast engine of popular sedition would drop down of itself.

The rebellious consequence which follows this prime article of the natural freedom of mankind may be my sufficient warrant for a modest examination of the original truth of it. Much hath been said, and by many, for the affirmative. Equity requires that an ear be reserved a little for the negative.

In this discourse I shall give myself these cautions:

First, I have nothing to do to meddle with mysteries of state. Such *arcana imperii*, or cabinet councils, the vulgar may not pry into. An implicit faith is given to the meanest artificer in his own craft. How much more is it then due to a prince in the profound secrets of government. The causes and ends of the greatest politic actions and motions of state dazzle the eyes and exceed the capacities of all men, save only those that are hourly versed in the managing public affairs. Yet since the rule for each man to know in what to obey his prince cannot be learnt without a relative knowledge of those points wherein a sovereign may command, it is necessary when the commands and pleasures of superiors come abroad and call for an obedience that every man inform himself how to regulate his actions or his sufferings. For according to the quality of the thing commanded an active or passive obedience is to be yielded, and this is not to limit the prince's power, but the extent of the subject's obedience, by giving to Caesar the things that are Caesar's, etc.

Secondly, I am not to question or quarrel at the rights or liberties of this or any other nation. My task is chiefly to enquire from whom these first came, not to dispute what or how many they are, but whether they were derived from the law of natural liberty or from the grace and bounty of princes. My desire and hope is that the people of England may and do enjoy as ample privileges as any nation under heaven. The greatest liberty in the world (if it be duly considered) is for a people to live under a monarch. It is the Magna Carta of this kingdom. All other shows or pretexts of liberty are but several degrees of slavery, and a liberty only to destroy liberty.

If such as maintain the natural liberty of mankind take offence at the liberty I take to examine it, they must take heed that they do not deny by retail that liberty which they affirm by wholesale. For if the thesis be true, the hypothesis will follow, that all men may examine their own charters, deeds, or evidences by which they claim and hold the inheritance or freehold of their liberties.

Thirdly, I must not detract from the worth of all those learned men who are of a contrary judgment in the point of natural liberty. The profoundest scholar that ever was known hath not been able to search out every truth that is discoverable: neither Aristotle in philosophy, nor Hooker in divinity. They are but men, yet I reverence their judgments in most points, and confess myself beholding to their errors too in this. Something that I found amiss in their opinions guided me in the discovery of that truth which (I persuade myself) they missed. A dwarf sometimes may see that which a giant looks over, for whilst one truth is curiously searched after, another must necessarily be neglected. Late writers have taken up too much upon trust from the subtle schoolmen,[1] who to be sure to thrust down the king below the pope, thought it the safest course to advance the people above the king, that so the papal power may more easily take place of the regal. Thus many an ignorant subject hath been fooled into this faith, that a man may become a martyr for his country by being a traitor to his prince; whereas the new-coined distinction of subjects into royalists and patriots is most unnatural, since the relation between king and people is so great that their well-being is reciprocal.

(2) To make evident the grounds of this question about the natural liberty of mankind, I will lay down some passages of Cardinal Bellarmine, that may best unfold the state of this controversy. 'Secular or civil power', saith he

> is instituted by men. It is in the people unless they bestow it on a prince. This power is immediately in the whole multitude, as in the subject of it. For this power is by the divine law, but the divine law hath given this power to no particular man. If the positive law be taken away, there is left no reason why amongst a multitude (who are equal) one rather than another should bear rule over the rest. Power is given by the multitude to one man, or to more by the same law of nature, for the commonwealth itself cannot exercise this power, therefore it is bound to bestow it upon some one man, or some few. It depends upon the consent of the multitude to ordain over themselves a king, or consul, or other magistrate; and if there be a lawful cause, the multitude may

1   See introduction, p. xiii.

change the kingdom into an aristocracy or democracy. (*De Laicis*, book 3, chapter 4)[2]

Thus far Bellarmine, in which passages are comprised the strength of all that ever I have read or heard produced for the natural liberty of the subject.

Before I examine or refute these doctrines, I must a little make some observations upon his words.

First, he saith that by the law of God power is immediately in the people. Hereby he makes God to be the immediate author of a democratical estate. For a democracy is nothing else but the power of the multitude. If this be true, not only aristocracies, but all monarchies are altogether unlawful, as being ordained (as he thinks) by men, when as God himself hath chosen a democracy.

Secondly, he holds that although a democracy be the ordinance of God, yet the people have no power to use the power which God hath given them, but only power to give away their power; whereby it follows that there can be no democratical government, because the people, he saith, 'must give their power to one man, or to some few'; which maketh either a regal or aristocratical estate, which the multitude is tied to do, even by the same law of nature which originally gave them the power. And why then doth he say, the multitude may change the kingdom into a democracy?

Thirdly, he concludes that 'if there be a lawful cause the multitude may change the kingdom into an aristocracy or democracy'. Here I would fain know who shall judge of this lawful cause? If the multitude (for I see nobody else can) then this is a pestilent and dangerous conclusion.

(3) I come now to examine that argument which is used by Bellarmine, and is the one and only argument I can find produced by any author for the proof of the natural liberty of the people. It is thus framed: that God hath given or ordained power is evident by Scripture; but God hath given it to no particular man, because by nature all men are equal; therefore he hath given power to the people or multitude.

To answer this reason, drawn from the equality of mankind by nature, I will first use the help of Bellarmine himself, whose very words are these: 'if many men had been together created out of the earth, they all ought to have been princes over their posterity' (book 1, *De Romano Pontifice*, chapter 2). In these words we have an evident confession that creation made man prince of his posterity. And indeed not only Adam, but the succeeding patriarchs had, by right of fatherhood, royal authority over their children. Nor dares Bellarmine deny this also. 'That the patriarchs', saith he, 'were endowed with kingly power, their deeds do testify'.[3] For as Adam was lord of his children, so his children under him, had a command and power over their own children, but still with subordination to the first parent, who is lord paramount over his children's children to all generations, as being the grandfather of his people.

I see not then how the children of Adam, or of any man else, can be free from subjection to their parents. And this subjection of children is the fountain of all regal authority, by the ordination of God himself. It follows that civil power not only in general is by divine institution, but even the assignment of it specifically to the eldest parent, which quite takes away that new and common distinction which refers only power universal as absolute to God, but power respective in regard of the special form of government to the choice of the people. Nor leaves it any place for such imaginary pactions between kings and their people as many dream of.

(4) This lordship which Adam by creation had over the whole world, and by right descending from him the patriarchs did enjoy, was as large and ample as the absolutest dominion of any monarch which hath been since the creation. For power of life and death we find that Judah, the father, pronounced sentence of death against Thamar his daughter-in-law, for playing the harlot. 'Bring her forth', saith he, 'that she may be burnt'.[4] Touching war, we see that Abraham commanded an army of 318 soldiers of his own family; and Esau met his brother Jacob with 400 men at arms. For matter of peace, Abraham made a league with Abimilech, and ratified the articles by an oath. These acts of judging in capital crimes, of making war, and concluding peace, are the chiefest marks of sovereignty that are found in any monarch.

(5) Not only until the Flood, but after it, this patriarchal power did continue—as the very name of patriarch doth in part prove. The three sons of Noah had the whole world divided amongst them by their father, for of them was the whole world overspread, according to the benediction given to him and his sons: 'Be fruitful and multiply, and replenish the Earth'.[5] Most of the civillest nations in the world labour to fetch their original from some one of the sons or nephews of Noah, which were scattered abroad after the confusion of Babel. In this dispersion we must certainly find the establishment of regal power throughout the kingdoms of the world.

3   Robert *Bellarmine, De Romano Pontifice*, book 1, ch. 2.
4   Genesis 38:24.
5   Genesis 9:1.

It is a common opinion that at the confusion of tongues there were seventy-two distinct nations erected, all which were not confused multitudes, without heads or governors, and at liberty to choose what governors or government they pleased, but they were distinct families, which had fathers for rulers over them. Whereby it appears that even in the confusion God was careful to preserve the fatherly authority, by distributing the diversity of languages according to the diversity of families. For so plainly it appears by the text. First, after the enumeration of the sons of Japhet, the conclusion is: 'By these were the isles of the gentiles divided in their lands; every one after his tongue, after their families, in their nations'.[6] So it is said: 'These are the sons of Ham after their families, after their tongues, in their countries, and in their nations'.[7] The like we read: 'These are the sons of Shem after their families, after their tongues, in their lands, after their nations. These are the families of the sons of Noah after their generations in their nations, and by these were these nations divided in the earth, after the Flood'.[8]

In this division of the world, some are of opinion that Noah used lots for the distribution of it. Others affirm he sailed about the Mediterranean sea in ten years and as he went about, appointed to each son his part, and so made the division of the then known world into Asia, Africa, and Europe, according to the number of his sons, the limits of which three parts are all found in that midland sea.

(6) But howsoever the manner of this division be uncertain, yet it is most certain the division itself was by families from Noah and his children, over which the parents were heads and princes.

Amongst these was Nimrod, who no doubt (as Sir Walter Raleigh affirms) was by good right lord or king over his family.[9] Yet against right did he enlarge his empire by seizing violently on the rights of other lords of families, and in this sense he may be said to be the author and first founder of monarchy. And all those that do attribute unto him the original regal power do hold he got it by tyranny or usurpation, and not by any due election of the people or multitude, nor by any paction with them.

As this patriarchal power continued in Abraham, Isaac, and Jacob, even until the Egyptian bondage, so we find it amongst the sons of Ismael and Esau. It is said: 'These are the sons of Ismael, and these are their names by

6 Genesis 10:5.
7 Genesis 10:20.
8 Genesis 10:32.
9 Sir Walter Raleigh, *The History of the World*, book 1, ch. 10.

their castles and towns, twelve princes of their tribes or families.'[10] 'And these are the names of the dukes that came of Esau, according to their families and their places by their nations.'[11] ⌐

(7) Some, perhaps, may think that these princes and dukes of families were but some petty lords under some greater kings, because the number of them are so many that their particular territories could be but small, and not worthy the title of kingdoms. But they must consider that at first kings had no such large dominions as they have nowadays. We find in the time of Abraham, which was about 300 years after the Flood, that in a little corner of Asia nine kings at once met in battle, most of which were but kings of cities apiece, with the adjacent territories, as of Sodom, Gomorrha, Shinar, etc. In the same chapter is mention of Melchisedek king of Salem, which was but the city of Jerusalem. And in the catalogue of the kings of Edom, the name of each king's city is recorded as the only mark to distinguish their dominions. In the land of Canaan, which was but of a small circuit, Joshua destroyed thirty one kings, and about the same time, Adonibezeck had seventy kings whose fingers and toes he had cut off, and made them feed under his table. A few ages after this, thirty-two kings came to Benhadad king of Syria, and about seventy kings of Greece went to the wars of Troy. Caesar found more kings in France than there be now provinces there, and at his sailing over into this island he found four kings in our county of Kent. These heaps of kings in each nation are an argument that their territories were but small, and strongly confirms our assertion that erection of kingdoms came at first only by distinction of families.

By manifest footsteps we may trace this paternal government unto the Israelites coming into Egypt, where the exercise of supreme patriarchal jurisdiction was intermitted because they were in subjection to a stronger prince. After the return of these Israelites out of bondage, God, out of a special care of them, chose Moses and Joshua successively to govern as princes in the place and stead of the supreme fathers, and after them likewise for a time He raised up Judges to defend his people in times of peril. But when God gave the Israelites kings, He re-established the ancient and prime right of lineal succession to paternal government. And whensoever He made choice of any special person to be king, He intended that the issue also should have benefit thereof, as being comprehended sufficiently in the person of the father—although the father only was named in the grant.

---

10 Genesis 25:16.
11 Genesis 36:40.

(8) It may seem absurd to maintain that kings now are the fathers of their people, since experience shows the contrary. It is true, all kings be not the natural parents of their subjects, yet they all either are, or are to be reputed the next heirs to those progenitors who were at first the natural parents of the whole people, and in their right succeed to the exercise of supreme jurisdiction. And such heirs are not only lords of their own children, but also of their brethren, and all others that were subject to their fathers. And therefore we find that God told Cain of his brother Abel: 'His desires shall be subject unto thee, and thou shalt rule over him'.[12] Accordingly, when Jacob bought his brother's birthright, Isaac blessed him thus: 'Be Lord over thy Brethren, and let the Sons of thy Mother bow before thee'.[13] So we find that at the offering of princes at the dedication if the tabernacle the princes of Israel are said to be the heads of the houses of their fathers, as Eliab the son of Helon was prince of the children of his father Zebulun.

As long as the first fathers of families lived, the name of patriarchs did aptly belong unto them. But after a few descents, when the true fatherhood itself was extinct and only the right of the father descended to the true heir, then the title of prince or king was more significant to express the power of him who succeeds only to the right of that fatherhood which his ancestors did naturally enjoy. By this means it comes to pass that many a child, by succeeding a king, hath the right of a father over many a grey-headed multitude, and hath the title of *pater patriae* ["father of the country"].

(9) It may be demanded what becomes of the right of fatherhood in case the crown do escheat for want of an heir, whether doth it not then devolve to the people? The answer is:

1. It is but the negligence or ignorance of the people to lose the knowledge of the true heir, for an heir there always is. If Adam himself were still living, and now ready to die, it is certain that there is one man, and but one in the world, who is next heir, although the knowledge who should be that one man be quite lost.

2. This ignorance of the people being admitted, it doth not by any means follow that for want of heirs the supreme power is devolved to the multitude, and that they have power to rule, or choose what rulers they please. No, the kingly power escheats in such cases to the princes and independent heads of families, for every kingdom is resolved into those parts whereof at first it was made. By the uniting of great families or petty princedoms, we find the greater monarchies were at the first erected, and into such

12   Genesis 4:7.
13   Genesis 28:29.

again—as into their first matter—many times they return again. And because the dependency of ancient families is oft obscure or worn out of knowledge, therefore the wisdom of all or most princes hath thought fit to adopt many times those for heads of families and princes of provinces whose merits, abilities, or fortunes, have enabled them, or made them fit and capable of such royal favours. All such prime heads and fathers have power to consent in the uniting or conferring of their fatherly right of sovereign authority on whom they please. And he that is so elected claims not his power as a donative from the people, but as being substituted properly by God, from whom he receives his royal charter of an universal father, though testified by the ministry of the heads of the people.

If it please God, for the correction of the prince, or punishment of the people, to suffer princes to be removed and others placed in their rooms, either by the factions of the nobility or rebellion of the people, in all such cases the judgment of God—who hath power to give and to take away kingdoms—is most just. Yet the ministry of men who execute God's judgments without commission is sinful and damnable. God doth but use and turn men's unrighteous acts to the performance of His righteous decrees.

(10) In all kingdoms and commonwealths in the world, whether the prince be the supreme father of the people or but the true heir of such a father, or whether he come to the crown by usurpation, or by election of the nobles or of the people, or by any other way whatsoever, or whether some few or a multitude govern the commonwealth: yet still the authority that is in any one, or in many, or in all these, is the only right and natural authority of a supreme father. There is, and always shall be continued to the end of the world, a natural right of a supreme father over every multitude, although, by the secret will of God, many at first do most unjustly obtain the exercise of it.

To confirm this natural right of regal power, we find in the decalogue that the Law which enjoins obedience to kings is delivered in the terms of 'honour thy father',[14] as if all power were originally in the father. If obedience to parents be immediately due by a natural law, and subjection to princes but by the mediation of a human ordinance, what reason is there that the law of nature should give place to the laws of men, as we see the power of the father over his child gives place and is subordinate to the power of the magistrate?

If we compare the natural duties of a father with those of a king, we find them all one, without any difference at all but only in the latitude or extent

14   Exodus 20:12.

of them. As the father over one family, so the king, as father over many families, extends his care to preserve, feed, clothe, instruct and defend the whole commonwealth. His wars, his peace, his courts of justice, and all his acts of sovereignty tend only to preserve and distribute to every subordinate and inferior father, and to their children, their rights and privileges, so that all the duties of a king are summed up in an universal fatherly care of his people.

CHAP. II. It is unnatural for the people to govern or choose governors.

(1) Two passages in the civil law cleared; Aristotle examined about the freedom of the people and justified; (2) Suarez disputing against the regality of Adam; (3) families diversely defined by Aristotle, Bodin and others; (4) Suarez contradicting Bellarmine; (5) of election of kings, (6) by the major part of the people, (7) by proxy, and by silent acceptation; (8) no example in Scripture of the people's choosing their king; Mr. Hooker's judgment therein; (9) God governed always by monarchy; (10) Bellarmine's and Aristotle's judgment of monarchy; (11) imperfection of the Roman democracy; (12) Rome began her empire under kings, and perfected under emperors; (13) in danger the people of Rome always fled to monarchy; (14) whether democracies were invented to bridle tyrants, or rather that they came in by stealth; (15) democracies vilified by their own historians; (16) popular government more bloody than tyranny; (17) of a mixed government of the king and people; (18) the people may not judge or correct their king; (19) no tyrants in England since the Conquest.

(1) By conferring these proofs and reasons drawn from the authority of Scripture, it appears to be little less than a paradox which Bellarmine and others affirm of the freedom of the multitude to choose what rulers they please.

Had the patriarchs their power given them by their own children? Bellarmine does not say it, but the contrary. If then, the fatherhood enjoyed this authority for so many ages by the law of nature, when was it lost, or when forfeited, or how is it devolved to the liberty of the multitude?[15]

<There are two places cited out of the civil law which do seem much to strengthen the opinion of Grotius about natural community. Though they be not alleged by him, yet they are fit to be considered because they are authorities of the greatest antiquity in this point, and the foundation upon which the late schoolmen have built. In the digests there is first this principle: *'Jure naturali omnes homines liberi nascuntur'*[16] ["all men are born free by the natural law"]. Secondly, the law there, speaking of the prince, saith: *'Populus ei et in eum omne suum imperium et potestatem confert'* ["the people grants all its power and imperium unto him and upon him"]. For a general answer to these two texts of the civil law, it must be remembered that the grounds of the law are but the opinions and sayings of heathens that knew not, or at least believed not, the history of the Scriptures or of the creation, and that this law was fitted properly for the commonwealth and empire of the Romans. For these causes it is no great wonder if the principles of the Roman laws vary from the rules of Scripture, and customs of other nations.

To answer in particular to the first text, it may be said the sense of these words, 'by the law of nature all are born free', must needs mean a freedom only that is opposite to such subjection as was between *master* and *servant*, and not a freedom from such subjection as is between *father* and *son*. This is made manifest by the text of the law, for Ulpian in that place speaketh only of manumission, which is setting at liberty of servants from servitude, and not of emancipation, which is the freeing of children from their fathers' tuition. 'Servitude', as the law teacheth, 'is a constitution of the law of nations, by which a man is subjected to the dominion of any other man against nature'.[17] So not every subjection is servitude, but subjection contrary to the law of nature. No man is born a servant, or subject to the power of a master by the law of nature, yet every man is born subject to the power of a father. This the law itself saith: *'In potestate nostra liberi nostri sunt'* ["our children are in our power"]. And Ulpian teacheth that the education of children is by the law of nature, so that *'qui ex me et uxore mea nascitur in potestate mea est'*[18] ["who is born of me and my wife is in my power"].

For answer to the second text, 'that the people bestow all the power upon

---

15   Subsequent section in angled brackets included from Cambridge manuscript. In that manuscript, §2–4 follow, then the remainder of §1.
16   *Corpus Iuris Civilis, Digestorum et Pandectorum*, i, 4.
17   *Digest*, v, 4.
18   *Digest*, vi, 4.

the prince', certainly the law there intends no more than to note *the partic-ular fact* of the people of Rome, and not *a general right* of all other people. When Julius and Augustus had successively taken the power into their hands, the people of Rome very bountifully, by a royal law, bestowed that power upon Augustus which he before had taken upon him. This act of the people the law mentioned, not to prove the right of all people to give power to princes, but produceth it against the people, to show them that by their own act the prince was free from all laws. And therefore in the very same place the civil law doth conclude that 'what pleaseth the prince had the vigour of law, or whatsoever the emperor ordained by his epistles, or rescripts, or commanded upon mature deliberation, or by edict, was a law'. The title of the law *De constitutione principium* ["concerning the ordaining of princes"] is not concerning the ordaining of princes by the people, but the ordaining of laws by the princes.>

Because the Scripture is not favourable to the liberty of the people, therefore many fly to natural reason and to the authority of Aristotle. I must crave liberty to examine or explain the opinion of this great philosopher.

I find this sentence in the third of his *Politics*, chapter 16: 'It seems *to some* not to be natural for one man to be lord of all the citizens, since a city consists of equals'.[19] These words seem to favour the equality of mankind. Lambin, in his Latin interpretation of this text, hath omitted the translation of this word 'τισιν' ["to some"]. By that means he maketh that to be the opinion of Aristotle which Aristotle allegeth to be the opinion but of some. This negligent or wilful escape of Lambin, in not translating a word so material, hath been an occasion to deceive many, who, looking no further than this Latin translation, have concluded, and made the world now of late believe, that Aristotle here maintains a *natural equality of men.* And not only our English translator of Aristotle's *Politics* is in this place misled by following Lambin; but even the learned Monsieur Duval in his analytical *Synopsis* bears them company. And yet this version of Lambin's is esteemed the best, and printed with Causabon's corrected Greek copy, though in the rendering of this place the other translations have been more faithful. And he that shall compare the Greek text with the Latin shall find that Causabon had just cause in his preface to Aristotle's works to complain that the best translations of Aristotle did need correction.

To prove that in these words, which seem to favour the equality of mankind, Aristotle doth not speak according to his own judgment but recites only the opinion of others, we find him clearly deliver his own opinion that the power of government did originally arise from the right of father-

---

19   Aristotle, *Politics*, 1287[a] 10–12.

hood, which cannot possibly consist with that natural equality which men dream of. For in the first of his *Politics* he agrees exactly with the Scripture, and lays this foundation of government: 'The first society made of many houses is a village, which seems most naturally to be a colony of families or foster brethren of children and children's children. And therefore, at the beginning, cities were under the government of kings, for the eldest in every house is king. And so for kindred sake it is in colonies'.[20] And in the fourth of his *Politics*, chapter 2, he gives the title of the 'first and divinest sort of government to the institution of kings',[21] by defining tyranny to be a digression from the first and divinest.

Whosoever weighs advisedly these passages will find little hope of natural reason in Aristotle to prove the natural liberty of the multitude. Also, before him the divine Plato concludes 'a commonweal to be nothing else but a large family'.[22] I know that for this position Aristotle quarrels with his master, but most unjustly. For therein he contradicts his own principles, for they both agree to fetch the original of civil government from the prime government of families. No doubt but Moses' history of the creation guided these two philosophers in finding out of this lineal subjection, deduced from the loins of the first parents, according to that rule of St. Chrysostom: 'God made all mankind of one man, that he might teach the world to be governed by a king, and not by a multitude'.[23]

The ignorance of the creation occasioned several errors amongst heathen philosophers. Polybius, though otherwise a most profound philosopher, and judicious historian, yet here he stumbles. For in searching out the original of civil societies he conceited that 'multitudes of men after a deluge, a famine, or a pestilence, met together like herds of cattle without any dependency, until the strongest bodies and boldest minds got the mastery of their fellows, even as it is', saith he, 'among bulls, bears and cocks'.[24]

And Aristotle himself, forgetting his first doctrine, tells us the first heroical kings were chosen by the people for their deserving well of the multitude, 'either by teaching them some new arts, or by warring for them, or by gathering them together, or by dividing land amongst them'.[25] Also Aristotle had another fancy, that those men 'who prove wise of mind were by nature intended to be lords and govern, and those which were strong

20 Aristotle, *Politics*, 1252ᵇ 15–21.
21 Aristotle, *Politics*, 1289ᵃ 39–40.
22 Plato, *Statesman*, 259b.
23 Bellarmine, *De Romano Pontifice*, book 1, ch. 2; Francisco Suarez, *Tractatus De Legibus ac Deo Legislatore*, book 3, ch. 2.
24 Polybius, *Histories*, book 6, ch. 5.
25 Aristotle, *Politics*, 1285ᵇ 4–11.

of body were ordained to obey and be servants'.[26] But this is a dangerous and uncertain rule, and not without some folly. For if a man prove both wise and strong, what will Aristotle have done with him? As he was wise, he could be no servant, and as he had strength, he could not be a master. Besides, to speak like a philosopher, nature intends all men to be perfect both in wit and strength. The folly or imbecility proceeds from some error in generation or education, for nature aims at perfection in all her works.

(2) Suarez the Jesuit riseth up against the royal authority of Adam, in defence of the freedom and liberty of the people; and thus argues: 'by right of creation', saith he,

> Adam had only economical power, but not political. He had a power over his wife, and a fatherly power over his sons, whilst they were not made free. He might also, in process of time, have servants and a complete family, and in that family he might have complete economical power. But after that families began to be multiplied, and men to be separated and become the heads of several families, they had the same power over their families. But political power did not begin until families began to be gathered together into one perfect community. Wherefore, as the community did not begin by the creation of Adam, nor by his will alone, but of all them which did agree in this community, so we cannot say that Adam naturally had political primacy in that community. For that cannot be gathered by any natural principles, because by the force of the law of nature alone it is not due unto any progenitor to be also king of his posterity. And if this be not gathered out of the principles of nature, we cannot say 'God by a special gift or providence gave him this power'. For there is no revelation of this, nor testimony of Scripture. (*De Legibus* book 3, chapter 2)

Hitherto Suarez.

Whereas he makes Adam to have a fatherly power over his sons, and yet shuts up this power within one family, he seems either to imagine that all Adam's children lived within one house and under one roof with their father; or else as soon as any of his children lived out of his house, they ceased to be subject, and did thereby become free. For my part I cannot believe that Adam, although he were sole monarch of the world, had any

26 Aristotle, *Politics*, 1252ᵃ 34–6.

such spacious palace as might contain any such considerable part of his children. It is likelier that some mean cottage or tent did serve him to keep his court in; it were a hard case he should lose part of his authority because his children lay not within the walls of his house. But if Suarez will allow all Adam's children to be of his family, howsoever they were separate in dwellings, if their habitations were either contiguous or at such distance as might easily receive his fatherly commands, and that all that were under his commands were of his family—although they had many children or servants married, having themselves also children—then I see no reason but that we may call Adam's family a commonwealth, except we will wrangle about words. For Adam living 930 years, and seeing seven or eight descents from himself, he might live to command of his children and their posterity a multitude far bigger than many commonwealths and kingdoms.

(3) I know the politicians and civil lawyers do not well agree about the definition of a family, and Bodin doth seem in one place to confine it to a house. Yet in his definition he doth enlarge his meaning to 'all persons under the obedience of one and the same head of the family', and he approves better of the propriety of the Hebrew word for a family, which is derived from a word that signifies a head, a prince, or lord, than the Greek word for a family, which is derived from 'οἶκος', which signifies a house. Nor doth Aristotle confine a family to one house, but esteems it to be made of those 'that daily converse together', whereas, before him, Charondas called a family 'homosypioi', those that feed together 'out of one common pannier', and Epimenides, the Cretan, terms a family 'homocapnoi', 'those that sit by a common fire or smoke'. But let Suarez understand what he please by Adam's family. If he will but confess, as he needs must, that Adam and the patriarchs had absolute power of life and death, of peace and war and the like, within their houses or families, he must give us leave at least to call them kings of their houses or families. And if they be so by the law of nature, what liberty will be left to their children to dispose of?

Aristotle gives the lie to Plato and those that say political and economical societies are all one, and do not differ *specie* ["in kind"], but only *multitudine et paucitate* ["in greatness and smallness"], as if there were no difference betwixt a great house and a little city. All the argument I find he brings against them is this:

> The community of man and wife differs from the community of master and servant, because they have several ends. The intention of nature, by conjunction of male and female, is generation. But the scope of master and servant is only

preservation, so that a wife and a servant are by nature distinguished. Because nature does not work like the cutlers of Delphos, for she makes but one thing for one use. (*Politics,* 1252^b 1–4)

If we allow this argument to be sound, nothing doth follow but only this, that conjugal and despotical communities do differ. But it is no consequence that therefore economical and political societies do the like. For though it prove a family to consist of two distinct communities, yet it follows not that a family and a commonwealth are distinct, because, as well in the commonwealth as in the family, both these communities are found.

And as this argument comes not home to our point, so it is not able to prove that little which it shows for. For if it should be granted (which yet is false) that generation and preservation differ about the *individuum*, yet they agree in the *general*, and serve both for the conservation of mankind. Even as several servants differ in their particular ends or offices, as one to brew, and another to bake, yet they agree in the general preservation of the family. Besides, Aristotle himself confesseth that amongst the barbarians (as he calls all them that are not Grecians)

a wife and a servant are the same, because by nature no barbarian is fit to govern. It is fit the Grecians should rule over the barbarians, for by nature a servant and a barbarian is all one. Their family consists only of an ox for a manservant and a wife for a maid, so they are fit only to rule their wives and their beasts. (*Politics,* 1252^b 4–21)

Lastly, Aristotle, if it had pleased him, might have remembered that nature doth not always make *one thing but for one use*. He knows the tongue serves both to speak, and to taste.

(4) But to leave Aristotle and return to Suarez. He saith that 'Adam had fatherly power over his sons whilst they were not made free'.[27] Here I could wish that the Jesuit had taught us how and when sons become free. I know no means by the law of nature. It is the favour, I think, of the parents only, who, when their children are of age and discretion to ease their parents of part of their fatherly care, are then content to remit some part of their fatherly authority. Therefore the customs of some countries doth in some cases enfranchise the children of inferior parents, but many nations have no such custom, but on the contrary have strict laws for the obedience of

27 Suarez, *Tractatus*, book 3, ch. 2.

children. The judicial law of Moses giveth full power to the father to stone his disobedient son, so it be done in presence of a magistrate. And yet it did not belong to the magistrate to enquire or examine the justness of the cause, but it was so decreed lest the father should in his anger suddenly or secretly kill his son.

Also, by the laws of the Persians and of the people of the Upper Asia, and of the Gauls, and by the laws of all the West Indies, the parents have power of life and death over their children. The Romans, even in their most popular estate, had this law in force, and this power of parents was ratified and amplified by the laws of the twelve tables, to the enabling of parents to sell their children two or three times over. By the help of this fatherly power Rome long flourished, and oftentimes was freed from great dangers. The fathers have drawn out of the very assemblies their own sons, when, being tribunes, they have published laws tending to sedition.

Memorable is the example of Cassius, who 'threw his son headlong out of the consistory, publishing the law *agraria* for the division of lands in the behoof of the people. And afterwards, by his own private judgment put him to death'[28] by throwing him down from the Tarpeian rock, the magistrates and people standing thereat amazed and not daring to resist his fatherly authority, although they would with all their hearts have had that law for the division of land. By which it appears it was lawful for the father to dispose of the life of his child contrary to the will of the magistrates or people. The Romans also had a law that what the children got was not their own but their father's, although Solon made a law which acquitted the son from the nourishing of his father if his father had taught him no trade whereby to get his living.

Suarez proceeds, and tells us that 'in process of time, Adam had complete economical power'.[29] I know not what this 'complete economical power' is, nor how or what it doth really and essentially differ from political. If Adam did or might exercise in his family the same jurisdiction which a king doth now in a commonweal, then the kinds of power are not distinct, and though they may receive an accidental difference by the amplitude or extent of the bounds of the one beyond the other, yet since the like difference is also found in political estates, it follows that economical and political power differ no otherwise than a little commonweal differs from a great one.

---

28   Jean Bodin, *The Six Bookes of a Commonweale*, tr. Richard Knolles, book 1, ch. 4.

29   Suarez, *Tractatus*, book 3, ch. 2.

Next, saith Suarez, 'community did not begin at the creation of Adam'.[30] It is true—because he had nobody to communicate with. Yet community did presently follow his creation, and that by his will alone, for it was in his power only, who was Lord of all, to appoint what his sons should have in proper, and what in common. So that *property* and *community* of goods did follow originally from him, and it is the duty of a father to provide as well for the common good of his children as for their particular.

Lastly, Suarez concludes that 'by the law of nature alone it is not due unto any progenitor to be also king of his posterity'. This assertion is confuted point blank by Bellarmine, who expressly affirmeth that 'the first parents ought to have been princes of their posterity'.[31] And until Suarez bring some reason for what he saith, I shall trust more to Bellarmine's proofs than to his bare denials.

(5) But let us condescend a while to the opinion of Bellarmine and Grotius and Suarez, and of all those who place supreme power in the whole people, and ask them if their meaning be that there is but one and the same power in all the people of the world, so that no power can be granted, except all the people upon the earth meet and agree, to choose a governor? An answer is here given by Suarez, that:

> It is scarce possible nor yet expedient that all men in the world should be gathered together into one community. It is likelier that either never, or for a very short time, that this power was in this manner in the whole multitude of men collected; but a little after the creation men began to be divided into several commonwealths, and this distinct power was in each of them.[32]

This answer of 'scarce possible, nor yet expedient'—'it is likelier', begets a new doubt how this distinct power comes to each particular community when God gave it to the whole multitude only, and not to any particular assembly of men. Can they show or prove that ever the whole multitude met and divided this power, which God gave them in gross, by breaking into parcels and by apportioning a distinct power to each several commonwealth? Without such a compact, I cannot see, according to their own principles, how there can be any election of a magistrate by any commonwealth, but by a mere usurpation upon the privilege of the whole world. If any man think that particular multitudes, at their own discretion, had

30 Suarez, *Tractatus*, book 3, ch. 2.
31 Bellarmine, *De Romano Pontifice*, book 1, ch. 2.
32 Suarez, *Tractatus*, book 3, ch. 2.

power to divide themselves into several commonwealths, those that think so have neither reason nor proof for so thinking, and thereby a gap is opened for every petty factious multitude to raise a new commonwealth, and to make more commonweals than there be families in the world.

But let this also be yielded them, that in each particular commonwealth there is a distinct power in the multitude; was a general meeting of a whole kingdom ever known for the election of a prince? Is there any example of it ever found in the whole world? To conceit such a thing is to imagine little less than an impossibility, and so by consequence no one form of government or king was ever established according to this supposed law of nature.

(6) It may be answered by some that if either the greatest part of a kingdom, or if a smaller part only by themselves and all the rest by proxy, or if the part not concurring in election do after by a tacit assent ratify the act of others, that in all these cases, it may be said to be the work of the whole multitude.

As to the acts of the *major* part of a multitude, it is true that by politic human constitutions it is oft ordained that the voices of the most shall overrule the rest. And such ordinances bind, because where men are assembled by an human power, that power that doth assemble them can also limit and direct the manner of the execution of that power. And by such derivative power, made known by law or custom, either the greater part, or two thirds, or three parts of five or the like, have power to oversway the liberty of their opposites. But in assemblies that take their authority from the law of nature it cannot be so. For what freedom or liberty is due to any man by the law of nature, no inferior power can alter, limit or diminish. No one man, nor a multitude, can give away the natural right of another. The law of nature is unchangeable, and howsoever one man may hinder another in the use or exercise of his natural right, yet thereby no man loseth the right itself. For the right and the use of the right may be distinguished, as right and possession are oft distinct. Therefore, unless it can be proved by the law of nature that the major, or some other part, have power to overrule the rest of the multitude, it must follow that the acts of multitudes not entire are not binding to all but only to such as consent unto them.

(7) As to the point of proxy, it cannot be showed or proved that all those that have been absent from popular elections did ever give their voices to some of their fellows. I ask but one example out of the history of the whole world. Let the commonweal be but named wherever the multitude, or so much as the greatest part of it, consented either by voice or by procuration

to the election of a prince. The ambition sometimes of one man, sometimes of many, or the faction of a city or citizens, or the mutiny of an army, hath set up or pulled down princes. But they have never tarried for this pretended order by proceeding of the whole multitude.

Lastly, if the silent acceptation of a governor by part of the people be an argument of their concurring in the election of him, by the same reason the tacit assent of the whole commonwealth may be maintained. From whence it follows that every prince that comes to a crown, either by succession, conquest, or usurpation, may be said to be elected by the people. Which inference is too ridiculous, for in such cases the people are so far from the liberty of *specification* that they want even that of *contradiction*.

(8) But it is vain to argue against the liberty of the people in the election of kings as long as men are persuaded that examples of it are to be found in Scripture. It is fit, therefore, to discover the grounds of this error. It is plain by an evident text that it is one thing to choose a king, and another thing to set a king over the people. This latter power the children of Israel had, but not the former. This distinction is found most evident in Deut. 17:15, where the law of God saith: Him shalt thou set king over thee whom the lord shall choose'. So God must *eligere* ["choose"], and the people only do *constituere* ["establish"]. Mr. Hooker, in his eighth book of *Ecclesiastical Polity*, clearly expounds this distinction. His words are worth the citing:

> Heaps of scripture (saith he) are alleged concerning the solemn coronation or inauguration of Saul, David, Solomon and others, by nobles, ancients, and the people of the commonwealth of Israel; as if these solemnities were a kind of deed, whereby the right of dominion is given. Which strange, untrue, and unnatural conceits are set abroad by seedmen of rebellion, only to animate unquiet spirits, and to feed them with possibilities of aspiring unto the thrones, if they can win the hearts of the people, whatsoever hereditary title any other before them may have; I say these unjust and insolent positions I would not mention, were it not thereby to make the countenance of truth more orient. For unless we will openly proclaim defiance unto all law, equity and reason, we must (there is no other remedy) acknowledge that in kingdoms hereditary, birthright giveth right unto sovereign dominion, and the death of the predecessor putteth the successor by blood in seisin.[33] Those public solemnities before

33   Into legal possession by freehold.

mentioned do either serve for an open testification of the inheritor's right, or belongeth to the form of inducing of him into possession of that thing he hath right unto.[34]

This is Mr. Hooker's judgment of the Israelites' power to set a king over themselves. No doubt but if the people of Israel had had power to choose their king, they would never have made their choice of Joas, a child but of seven years old, nor of Manasses, a boy of twelve, since, as Solomon saith, 'Woe to the land whose king is a child'.[35] Nor is it probable they would have elected Josias, but a very child, and a son to so wicked and idolatrous a father as that his own servants murdered him. And yet all the people set up this young Josias and slew the conspirators of the death of Ammon his father, which justice of the people God rewarded, by making this Josias the most religious king that ever that nation enjoyed.

(9) Because it is affirmed that the people have power to choose as well what form of government as what governors they please, of which mind is Bellarmine in those places we cited at first, therefore it is necessary to examine the strength of what is said in defence of popular commonweals against this natural form of kingdoms which I maintained. Here I must first put the Cardinal in mind of what he affirmeth in cold blood in other places, where he saith 'God, when He made all mankind of one man, did seem openly to signify that He rather approved the government of one man than of many'.[36] Again, 'God showed His opinion, when He endued not only men, but all creatures, with a natural propensity to monarchy. Neither can it be doubted but a natural propensity is to be referred to God, who is author of nature'.[37] And again in a third place, 'what form of government God confirmed by His authority may be gathered by that commonweal, which He instituted amongst the Hebrews, which was not aristocratical, (as Calvin saith) but plainly monarchichal'.[38]

(10) Now if God (as Bellarmine saith) have taught us by natural instinct, signified to us by the creation, and confirmed by His own example the excellency of monarchy, why should Bellarmine or we doubt but that it is natural? Do we not find that in every family the government of one alone is most natural? God did always govern His own people by monarchy only.

34   Richard Hooker, *Of the Laws of Ecclesiastical Polity*, book 8, ch. 2.
35   Ecclesiastes 10:16.
36   Bellarmine, *De Romano Pontifice*, book 1, ch. 2.
37   Bellarmine, *De Romano Pontifice*, book 1, ch. 2.
38   Bellarmine, *De Romano Pontifice*, book 1, ch. 2.

The patriarchs, dukes, Judges, and kings were all monarchs. There is not in all Scripture mention and approbation of any other form of government. At the time when Scripture saith 'There was no king in Israel, but that every man did that which was right in his own eyes',[39] even then, the Israelites were under the kingly government of the fathers of particular families. For in the consultation after the Benjamitical war for providing wives for the Benjamites, we find the elders of the congregation bare only sway, Judges 21:16. To them also were complaints to be made, as appears by verse 22. And though mention be made of 'all the children of Israel', 'all the congregation', and 'all the people', yet by the term of '*all*' the Scripture means only all the fathers, and not all the whole multitude, as the text plainly expounds itself in 2 Chronicles 1:2, where Solomon speaks unto *all* Israel, to the captains, the judges, and to every governor, the chief of the fathers. So the elders of Israel are expounded to be the chief of the fathers of the children of Israel, 1 Kings 8:12; 2 Chronicles 5:2.

At that time also, when the people of Israel begged a king of Samuel, they were governed by kingly power. God, out of a special care and love to the house of Israel, did choose to be their king Himself, and did govern them at that time by His viceroy Samuel and his sons. And therefore God tells Samuel: 'they have not rejected thee but Me, that I should not reign over them'. It seems they did not like a king by deputation, but desired one by succession like all the nations. All nations belike had kings then, and those by inheritance, not by election. For we do not find the Israelites prayed that they themselves might choose their own king; they dreamt of no such liberty, and yet they were the elders of Israel gathered together. If other nations had elected their own kings, no doubt but they would have been as desirous to have imitated other nations as well in the electing as in the having of a king.

Aristotle, in his book of *Politics*, when he comes to compare the several kinds of government, he is very reserved in discovering what form he thinks best. He disputes subtly to and fro of many points, and judiciously confutes many errors, but concludes nothing himself. In all those books I find little in commendation of monarchy. It was his hap to live in those times when the Grecians abounded with several commonwealths, who had then learning enough to make them seditious. Yet in his *Ethics* he hath so much good manners as to confess in right down words that 'monarchy is the best form of government, and a popular estate the worst'.[40] And though he be not so free in his *Politics*, yet the necessity of truth hath here

---

39   Judges, 21:25.
40   Aristotle, *Politics*, 1160[a] 36.

and there extorted from him that which amounts no less to the dignity of monarchy. He confesseth it to be the 'first, the natural, and the divinest form of government',[41] and that the gods themselves did live under a monarchy. What can a heathen say more?

Indeed, the world for a long time knew no other sort of government but only monarchy. The best order, the greatest strength, the most stability, and easiest government, are to be found all in monarchy, and in no other form of government. The new platforms of commonweals were first hatched in a corner of the world, amongst a few cities of Greece, which have been imitated by very few other places. Those very cities were first for many years governed by kings, until wantonness, ambition, or faction made them attempt new kinds of regiment. All which mutations proved most bloody and miserable to the authors of them, happy in nothing but that they continued but a small time.

(11) A little to manifest the imperfection of popular government, let us but examine the most flourishing democracy that the world hath ever known. I mean that of Rome.

1. First, for the durability; at the most, it lasted but 480 years (for so long it was from the expulsion of Tarquin, to Julius Caesar), whereas both the Assyrian monarchy lasted, without interruption, at the least twelve hundred years, and the empire of the East continued 1495 years.

2. Secondly, for the order of it, during those 480 years, there was not any one settled form of government in Rome. For after they had once lost the natural power of kings, they could not find upon what form of government to rest. Their fickleness is an evidence that they found things amiss in every change. At the first they choose two annual consuls instead of kings. Secondly, these did not please them long but they must have tribunes of the people to defend their liberty. Thirdly, they leave tribunes and consuls, and choose them ten men to make them laws. Fourthly, they call for consuls and tribunes again; sometimes they choose dictators, which were temporary kings, and sometimes military tribunes, who had consular power. All these shiftings caused such notable alteration in the government, as it poseth historians to find out any perfect form of regiment in so much confusion: one while the senate made laws, another while the people. The dissensions which were daily between the nobles and the commons bred those memorable seditions about usury, about marriages, and about magistrates. Also the Gracchian, the Apulian, and the Drusian seditions filled the market-places, the temples, and the capitol itself with blood

---

41   Aristotle, *Politics*, 1289ᵃ 39–40.

of the citizens. The Social War was plainly civil; the wars of the slaves and the other of the fencers, the civil wars of Marius and Sulla, of Cataline, of Caesar and Pompey, the triumvirate of Augustus, Lepidus and Antonius, all these shed an ocean of blood within Italy and the streets of Rome.

3. Thirdly, for their government, let it be allowed that for some part of this time it was popular, yet was it popular as to the city of Rome only, and not as to the dominions, or whole empire of Rome. For no democracy can extend further than to one city. It is impossible to govern a kingdom, much less many kingdoms, by the whole people, or by the greatest part of them.

(12) But you will say, yet the Roman empire grew all up under this kind of popular government, and the city became mistress of the world. It is not so. For Rome began her empire under kings, and did perfect it under emperors; it did only increase under that popularity. Her greatest exaltation was under Trajan, as her longest peace had been under Augustus. Even at those times when the Roman victories abroad did amaze the world, then the tragical slaughter of citizens at home deserved commiseration from their vanquished enemies.

(13) What though in that age of her popularity she bred many admired captains and commanders (each of which was able to lead an army, though many of them were but ill requited by the people) yet all of them were not able to support her in times of danger, but she was forced in her greatest troubles to create a dictator (who was a king for a time), thereby giving this honourable testimony of monarchy, that the last refuge in perils of states is to fly to regal authority. And though Rome's popular estate for a while was miraculously upheld in glory by a greater providence than her own, yet in a short time, after manifold alterations, she was ruined by her own hands. 'Suis et ipsa Roma viribus ruit' ["and Rome herself plunges into ruin by her own might"]. for the arms she had prepared to conquer other nations were turned upon herself, and civil contentions at last settled the government again into a monarchy.

(14) The vulgar opinion is that the first cause why the democratical government was brought in was to curb the tyranny of monarchs. But the falsehood of this doth best appear by the first flourishing popular estate of Athens, which was founded not because of the vices of their last king, but for that his virtuous deserts were such as the people thought no man worthy enough to succeed him—a pretty wanton quarrel to monarchy! For when their king Codrus understood by the oracle that his country could not be saved unless the king were slain in the battle, he in disguise

entered his enemy's camp and provoked a common soldier to make him a sacrifice for his own kingdom. And with his death ended the royal government, for after him was never any more kings of Athens. As Athens thus for the love of her Codrus changed the government, so Rome, on the contrary, out of hatred to her Tarquin, did the like. And though these two famous commonweals did for contrary causes abolish monarchy, yet they both agreed in this, that neither of them thought it fit to change their state into a democracy. But the one chose archontes and the other consuls to be their governors, both which did most resemble kings, and continued until the people, by lessening the authority of these their magistrates, did by degrees and stealth bring in their popular government. And I verily believe, never any democratical state showed itself at first fairly to the world by any elective entrance, but they all secretly crept in by the back door of sedition and faction.

(15) If we will listen to the judgment of those who should best know the nature of popular government, we shall find no reason for good men to desire or choose it. Xenophon, that brave scholar and soldier, disallowed the Athenian commonweal, for that they followed that form of government wherein 'the wicked are always in greatest credit',[42] and virtuous men kept under. They expelled Aristides the just; Themistocles died in banishment, Miltiades in prison; Phocion, the most virtuous and just man of his age, though he had been chosen forty-five times to be their general, yet he was put to death with all his friends, kindred and servants by the fury of the people, without sentence, accusation, or any cause at all. Nor were the people of Rome much more favourable to their worthies. They banished Rutilius, Metellus, Coriolanus, the two Scipios and Tully. The worst men sped best—for, as Xenophon saith of Athens, so Rome was a sanctuary for all turbulent, discontented and seditious spirits. The impunity of wicked men was such that upon pain of death it was forbidden all magistrates to condemn to death, or banish any citizen, or to deprive him of his liberty, or so much as to whip him, for what offence soever he had committed, either against the gods or men.

The Athenians sold justice as they did other merchandise, which made Plato call a popular state 'a fair, where everything is to be sold'.[43] The officers, when they entered upon their charge, would brag they went to a golden harvest. The corruption at Rome was such that Marius and Pompey durst carry bushels of silver into the assemblies to purchase the

---

42   Bodin, *Six Bookes*, book 6, ch. 4.
43   Plato, *Republic*, 8.557e.

voices of the people. Many citizens under their grave gowns came armed unto the public meetings, as if they went to war. Often, contrary factions fell to blows, sometimes with stones and sometimes swords. The blood hath been sucked up in the market-place with sponges: the river Tiber hath been filled with the dead bodies of citizens, and the common privies stuffed full with them.

If any man think these disorders in popular states were but casual, or such as might happen under any kind of government, he must know that such mischiefs are unavoidable and of necessity do follow all democratical regiments. The reason is given: because the nature of all people is to desire liberty without restraint, which cannot be but where the wicked bear rule. And if the people should be so indiscreet as to advance virtuous men, they lose their power, for that good men would favour none but the good, which are always the fewer in number; and the wicked and vicious (which is still the greatest part of the people) should be excluded from all preferment, and in the end, by little and little, wise men should seize upon the state and take it from the people.

I know not how to give a better character of the people than can be gathered from such authors as lived among or near to popular states. Thucydides, Xenophon, Livy, Tacitus, Cicero, and Sallust, have set them out in their colours. I will borrow some of their sentences.

'There is nothing more uncertain than the people. Their opinions are as variable and sudden as tempests. There is neither truth nor judgment in them. They are not led by wisdom to judge of anything, but by violence and rashness, nor put they any difference between things true and false. After the manner of cattle they follow the herd that goes before. With envious eyes they behold the felicity of others. They have a custom always to favour the worst and weakest. They are most prone to suspicions, and use to condemn men for guilty upon any false suggestion. They are apt to believe all news, especially if it be sorrowful, and like Fame, they make it more in the believing. When there is no author, they fear those evils which themselves have feigned. They are most desirous of new stirs and changes, and are enemies to quiet and rest. Whatsoever is giddy or headstrong they account manlike and courageous, but whatsoever is modest or provident, seems sluggish. Each man hath a care of his particular, and thinks basely of the common good. They look upon approaching mischiefs as they do upon thunder, only every man wisheth it may not touch his own person. It is the nature of them, they must either serve basely or domineer proudly, for they know no mean.'

Thus do their own friends paint to the life this beast of many heads. Let me give you the cypher of their form of government. As it is begot by sedition, so it is nourished by arms; it can never stand without wars, either with an enemy abroad, or with friends at home. The only means to preserve it is to have some powerful enemy near, who may serve instead of a king to govern it, that so, though they have not a king among them, yet they may have as good as a king over them, for common danger of an enemy keeps them in better unity than the laws they make themselves.

(16) Many have exercised their wits in paralleling the inconveniencies of regal and popular government. But if we will trust experience before speculations philosophical, it cannot be denied but this one mischief of sedition, which necessarily waits upon all popularity, weighs down all the inconveniences that can be found in monarchy, though they were never so many. It is said: 'Skin for skin, yea, all that a man hath will he give for his life';[44] and: 'A man will give his riches for the ransom of his life'.[45] The way then to examine what proportion the mischiefs of sedition and tyranny have one to another, is to enquire in what kind of government most subjects have lost their lives. Let Rome, which is magnified for her popularity and vilified for those tyrannical monsters the emperors, furnish us with examples. Consider whether the cruelty of all the tyrannical emperors that ever ruled in this city, did spill a quarter of that blood that was poured out in the last hundred years of her glorious popular commonwealth. The murders by Tiberius, Caligula, Nero, Domitian and Commodus, put all together, cannot match that civil tragedy which was acted in that one sedition between Marius and Sulla. Nay, even by Sulla's part alone (not to mention the acts of Marius) were fourscore and ten senators put to death, fifteen consuls, two thousand and six hundred gentlemen, and a hundred thousand others.

This was the height of the Roman liberty: any man might be killed that would, a favour not fit to be granted under a royal government. The miseries of these licentious times are briefly touched by Plutarch in these words. 'Sulla', saith he,

> fell to the shedding of blood, and filled Rome with infinite and unspeakable murders. And this was not only done in Rome, but in all the cities of Italy throughout. There was no temple of any god whatsoever, no altar in anybody's house, no liberty of hospital, no father's house, which was not imbrued with blood and horrible murder. The husbands were slain in the wives' arms and the children in the mothers' laps,

44   Job 2:4.
45   Proverbs, 13:8.

and yet they that were slain for private malice were nothing in respect of those that were murdered only for their
goods... He openly sold their goods by the crier, sitting so
proudly in his chair of state that it grieved the people more
to see their goods packed up by them to whom he gave or
disposed them than to see them taken away. Sometimes he
would give a whole country or the whole revenues of certain
cities unto women for their beauty, or to pleasant jesters,
minstrels or wicked slaves made free. And to some he would
give other men's wives by force, and make them to be married against their wills.[46]

Now let Tacitus and Suetonius be searched, and see if all their cruel emperors can match this popular villain in such an universal slaughter of citizens
or civil butchery. God only was able to match him, and overmatched him
by fitting him with a most remarkable death, just answerable to his life.
For as he had been the death of many thousands of his countrymen, so, as
many thousands of his own kindred in the flesh were the death of him, for
he died of an imposthume,[47]

which corrupted his flesh in such sort that it turned all to
lice. He had many about him to shift him continually night
and day, yet the lice they wiped from him were nothing to
them that multiplied upon him. There was neither appar-
el, linen, baths, washings, nor meat itself, but was presently
filled with swarms of this vile vermin.[48]

I cite not this to extenuate the bloody acts of any tyrannical princes, nor
will I plead in defence of their cruelties. Only in the comparative I maintain the mischiefs to a state to be less universal under a tyrant king. For the
cruelty of such tyrants extends ordinarily no further than to some particular men that offend them, and not to the whole kingdom. It is truly said
by his late majesty King James, 'A king can never be so notoriously vicious
but he will generally favour justice, and maintain some order, except in
the particulars wherein his inordinate lust carries him away'.[49] Even cruel
Domitian, Dionysius the tyrant, and many others are commended by historians for great observers of justice. A natural reason is to be tendered for

---

46   Plutarch, *Parallel Lives, Sulla*, chs. 31 & 33.
47   An abscess.
48   Plutarch, *Sulla*, ch. 36.
49   James I, *The True Law of Free Monarchies*, ch. 2.

it. It is the multitude of people and the abundance of their riches which are the only strength and glory of every prince. The bodies of his subjects do him service in war, and their goods supply his public wants. Therefore, if not out of affection to his people, yet out of natural love to himself, every tyrant desires to preserve the lives and protect the goods of his subjects, which cannot be done but by justice, and if it be not done, the prince's loss is the greatest.

On the contrary, in a popular state every man knows the public good doth not depend wholly on his care, but the commonwealth may well enough be governed by others though he tend only his private benefit. He never takes the public to be his own business. Thus, as in a family, where one office is to be done by many servants, one looks upon another, and every one leaves the business for his fellow until it is quite neglected by all. Nor are they much to be blamed for their negligence, since it is an even wager their ignorance is as great. For the magistrates among the people, being for the most part annual, do always lay down their office before they understand it, so that a prince though of a duller understanding, by use and experience must needs excel them.

Again, there is no tyrant so barbarously wicked but his own reason and sense will tell him that though he be a god, yet he must die like a man, and that there is not the meanest of his subjects but may find a means to revenge himself of the injustice that is offered him. Hence it is that great tyrants live continually in base fears, as did Dionysius the elder. And Tiberius, Caligula, and Nero are noted by Suetonius to have been frighted with panic fears. But it is not so where wrong is done to any particular person by a multitude. He knows not who hurt him, or who to complain of, or to whom to address himself for reparation. Any man may boldly exercise his malice and cruelty in all popular assemblies. There is no tyranny to be compared to the tyranny of a multitude.

(17) What though the government of the people be a thing not to be endured, much less defended, yet many men please themselves with an opinion that though the people may not govern, yet they may partake and join with a king in government, and so make a state mixed of popular and regal power, which they take to be the best tempered and equallest form of government. But the vanity of this fancy is too evident. It is a mere impossibility or contradiction. For if a king but once admit the people to be his companions, he leaves to be a king, and the state becomes a democracy. At least, he is but a titular and no real king, that hath not the sovereignty to himself. For the having of this alone, and nothing but this, makes a king to be a king. As for that show of popularity which is found in such

kingdoms as have general assemblies for consultation about making public laws, it must be remembered that such meetings do not share or divide the sovereignty with the prince, but do only deliberate and advise their supreme head, who still reserves the absolute power in himself. For if in such assemblies the king, the nobility, and people have equal shares in the sovereignty, then the king hath but one voice, the nobility likewise one, and the people one, and then any two of these voices should have power to overrule the third. Thus the nobility and commons together should have power to make a law to bind the king, which was never yet seen in any kingdom, but if it could, the state must needs be popular and not regal.

(18) If it be unnatural for the multitude to choose their governors, or to govern, or to partake in the government, what can be thought of that damnable conclusion which is made by too many, that the multitude may correct or depose their prince if need be? Surely the unnaturalness and injustice of this position cannot sufficiently be expressed. For admit that a king make a contract or paction with his people, either originally in his ancestors, or personally at his coronation (for both these pactions some dream of but cannot offer any proof for either) yet by no law of any nation can

> a contract be thought broken, except that first a lawful trial be had by the ordinary judge of the breakers thereof, or else every man may be both party and judge in his own case, which is absurd once to be thought. For then it will lie in the hands of the headless multitude when they please to cast off the yoke of government (that God hath laid upon them) to judge and punish him by whom they should be judged and punished.[50]

Aristotle can tell us what judges the multitude are in their own case, ʹοἱ πλεῖστοι φαῦλοι κριταὶ περὶ τῶν οἰκείωνʹ, 'the multitude are ill judges in their own cause.'[51]

The judgment of the multitude in disposing of the sovereignty may be seen in the Roman history, where we may find many good emperors murdered by the people, and many bad elected by them. Nero, Heliogabalus, Otho, Vitellius, and such other monsters of nature were the minions of the multitude, and set up by them. Pertinax, Alexander Severus, Gordianus, Gallus, Aemilianus, Quintilius, Aurelianus, Tacitus, Probus, and Numerianus, all of them good emperors in the judgment of all historians, yet murdered by the multitude.

---

50   James I, *True Law*, ch. 2.
51   Aristotle, *Politics*, 1280ª 15.

(19) Whereas many out of an imaginary fear pretend the power of the people to be necessary for the repressing of the insolencies of tyrants, herein they propound a remedy far worse than the disease. Neither is the disease indeed so frequent as they would have us think. Let us be judged by the history even of our own nation. We have enjoyed a succession of kings from the Conquest now near about 600 years (a time far longer than ever yet any popular state could continue). We reckon to the number of twenty-five of these princes of the Norman race, and yet not one of these is taxed by our histories for tyrannical government. It is true, two of these kings have been deposed by the people and barbarously murdered, but neither of them for tyranny. But, as a learned historian of our age saith, Edward II and Richard II were not insupportable either in their nature or rule, and yet the people more upon wantonness than for any want, did take an unbridled course against them:

> Edward II, by many of our historians is reported to be of a good and virtuous nature, and not unlearned. They impute his defects rather to fortune than either to council or carriage of his affairs. The deposition of him was a violent fury, led by a wife both cruel and unchaste, and can with no better countenance of right be justified than may his lamentable both indignities and death. Likewise the deposition of King Richard II was a tempestuous rage, neither led nor restrained by any rules of reason or of state. Examine his actions without distempered judgment, and you will not condemn him to be exceeding either insufficient or evil; weigh the imputations that were objected against him, and you shall find nothing either of any truth or of great moment. Holinshed writeth that he was most unthankfully used by his subjects; for, although through the frailty of his youth he demeaned himself more dissolutely than was agreeable to the royalty of his estate, yet in no king's days were the commons in greater wealth, the nobility more honoured, and the clergy less wronged, who, notwithstanding, in the evil-guided strength of their will, took head against him, to their own headlong destruction afterwards, partly during the reign of Henry his next successor, whose greatest achievements were against his own people in executing those who conspired with him against King Richard, but most especially in succeeding times, when, upon occasion of this disorder, more English blood was spilt than was in all the foreign wars which had

been since the Conquest.[52]

Twice hath this kingdom been miserably wasted with civil war, but neither of them occasioned by the tyranny of any prince. The cause of the barons' wars is by good historians attributed to the stubbornness of the nobility, as the bloody variance of the houses of York and Lancaster, and the late rebellion, sprang from the wantonness of the people. These three unnatural wars have dishonoured our nation amongst strangers, so that in the censures of kingdoms the king of Spain is said to be the king of men, because of his subjects' willing obedience; the king of France, king of asses, because of their infinite taxes and impositions; but the king of England is said to be the king of devils, because of his subjects' often insurrections against, and depositions of their princes.

CHAP. III. Positive laws do not infringe the natural and fatherly power of kings.

(1) Regal authority not subject to the positive laws; kings were before laws; the king of Judah and Israel not tied to laws: (2) of Samuel's description of a king, 1 Samuel 8; (3) the power ascribed to kings in the New Testament; (4) whether laws were invented to bridle tyrants; (5) the benefit of laws; (6) kings keep the laws though not bound by the laws; (7) of the oaths of kings; (8) of the benefit of the king's prerogative over laws; (9) the king the author and interpreter and corrector of the common laws; (10) the king judge in all causes both before the Conquest and since; (11) the king and his council anciently determined causes in the Star Chamber; (12) of parliaments; (13) the people when first called to parliament; (14) the liberty of parliament not from nature but from grace of princes; (15) the king alone makes laws in parliament, (16) governs both Houses as head by himself, (17) by his council, (18) or by his judges.

(1) Hitherto I have endeavoured to show the natural institution of regal authority, and to free it from subjection to an arbitrary election of the people. It is necessary also to enquire whether human laws have a superiority over princes, because those that maintain the acquisition of royal jurisdiction from the people do subject the exercise of it to human positive laws.

52　Sir John Hayward, *An Answer to the First Part of a Certaine Conference.*

But in this also they err. For as kingly power is by the law of God, so it hath no inferior law to limit it.

The father of a family governs by no other law than by his own will, not by the laws and wills of his sons or servants. There is no nation that allows children any action or remedy for being unjustly governed; and yet for all this every father is bound by the law of nature to do his best for the preservation of his family. But much more is a king always tied by the same law of nature to keep this general ground, that the safety of his kingdom be his chief law. He must remember that the profit of every man in particular, and of all together in general, is not always one and the same, that the public is to be preferred before the private, and that the force of laws must not be so great as natural equity itself—which cannot fully be comprised in any laws whatsoever, but is to be left to the religious arbitrament of those who know how to manage the affairs of state, and wisely to balance the particular profit with the counterpoise of the public, according to the infinite variety of times, places, persons.

A proof unanswerable for the superiority of princes above laws is this, that there were kings long before there were any laws. For a long time the word of a king was the only law. 'And if practice', as saith sir Walter Raleigh, 'declare the greatness of authority, even the best kings of Judah and Israel were not tied to any law, but they did whatsoever they pleased in the greatest matters'.[53]

(2) The unlimited jurisdiction of kings is so amply described by Samuel that it hath given occasion to some to imagine that it was but either a plot or trick of Samuel to keep the government in himself and family by frighting the Israelites with the mischiefs in monarchy, or else a prophetical description only of the future ill government of Saul. But the vanity of these conjectures are judiciously discovered in that majestical discourse of *The True Law of Free Monarchy*, wherein it is evidently showed that the scope of Samuel was to teach the people a dutiful obedience to their king, even in those things which themselves did esteem mischievous and inconvenient. For, by telling them what a king would do, he indeed instructs them what a subject must suffer, yet not so that it is right for kings to do injury, but it is right for them to go unpunished by the people if they do it. So that in this point it is all one whether Samuel describe a king or a tyrant, for patient obedience is due both. No remedy in the text against tyrants, but in crying and praying unto God in that day. But howsoever in a rigorous construction Samuel's description be applied to a tyrant, yet the words by a benign

interpretation may agree with the manners of a just king, and the scope and coherence of the text doth best imply the more moderate or qualified sense of the words. For, as Sir Walter Raleigh confesseth, 'all those inconveniences and miseries' (which are reckoned by Samuel as belonging to kingly government) 'were not intolerable, but such as have been borne, and are still borne, by free consent of subjects towards their princes'.[54] Nay, at this day and in this land, many tenants by their tenures and services are tied to the same subjection, even to subordinate and inferior lords. To serve the king in his wars and to till his ground is not only agreeable to the nature of subjects but much desired by them, according to their several births and conditions. The like may be said for the offices of women servants, confectioners, cooks, and bakers. For we cannot think that the king would use their labours without giving them wages, since the text itself mentions a liberal reward of his servants. As for the taking of the tenth of their seed, of their vines, and of their sheep, it might be a necessary provision for their king's household, and so belong to the right of tribute. For whereas is mentioned the taking of the tenth, it cannot agree well to a tyrant, who observes no proportion in fleecing his people.

Lastly, the taking of their fields, vineyards, and olive trees, if it be by force or fraud, or without just recompense to the damage of private persons only, it is not to be defended. But if it be upon the public charge and general consent, it might be justified as necessary at the first erection of a kingdom. For those who will have a king are bound to allow him royal maintenance by providing revenues for the crown, since it is both for the honour, profit, and safety of the people to have their king glorious, powerful, and abounding in riches. Besides, we all know the lands and goods of many subjects may be ofttimes legally taken by the king, either by forfeitures, escheat, attainder, outlawry, confiscation, or the like. Thus we see Samuel's character of a king may literally well bear a mild sense. For greater probability there is that Samuel so meant, and the Israelites so understood it, to which this may be added: Samuel tells the Israelites 'this will be the manner of the king that shall reign over you',[55] 'and ye shall cry because of your king which ye shall have chosen you'.[56] That is to say, thus shall be the common custom or fashion or proceeding of Saul your king. Or, as the vulgar Latin renders it, this shall be the right or law of your king, not meaning, as some expound it, the casual event or act of some *individuum vagum* ["vague individual"], or indefinite king, that might happen one

---

54 Raleigh, *History*, book 2, pt. 1, ch. 16.
55 1 Samuel 8:11.
56 1 Samuel 8:18.

day to tyrannize over them. So that Saul, and the constant practice of Saul, doth best agree with the literal sense of the text.

Now that Saul was no tyrant, we may note that the people asked a king as all nations had. God answers, and bids Samuel to hear the voice of the people in all things which they spake, and appoint them a king. They did not ask a tyrant, and to give them a tyrant when they asked a king had not been to hear their voice in all things, but rather when they asked an egg to have given them a scorpion, unless we will say that all nations had tyrants. Besides, we do not find in all Scripture that Saul was punished, or so much as blamed, for committing any of those acts which Samuel describes. And if Samuel's drift had been only to terrify the people, he would not have forgotten to foretell Saul's bloody cruelty in murdering eighty-five innocent priests, and smiting with the edge of the sword the city of Nob, both man, woman, and child. Again, the Israelites, it seems, never shrank at these conditions proposed by Samuel, but accepted of them as such as all other nations were bound unto. For their conclusion is: 'Nay, but we will have a king over us, that we also may be like all the nations, and that our king may judge us, and go out before us to fight our battles'[57]—meaning he should earn his privileges by doing their work for them, by judging them, and fighting for them. Lastly, whereas the mention of the people's complaints and cries unto the Lord argues they should be under some tyrannical oppression, we may remember that the people's complaints and cries are not always an argument of their living under a tyrant. No man can say king Solomon was a tyrant, yet all the congregation of Israel complained that Solomon made their yoke grievous, and therefore their prayer to Rehoboam is, 'Make thou the grievous service of thy father Solomon, and his heavy yoke which he put upon us, lighter, and we will serve thee.'[58] To conclude, it is true Saul lost his kingdom, but not for being too cruel or tyrannical to his subjects, but by being too merciful to his enemies. His sparing Agag when he should have slain him was the cause why the kingdom was torn from him.[59]

<It was objected that when Saul was made king, Samuel gave him a written law by which he was to govern, so that Saul was subject to that law. The answer is, the law which Samuel writ was to instruct the people in their duty, not to teach the king his office. For the text saith 'That Samuel told

---

57 1 Samuel 8:19–20.

58 2 Chronicles 10:4.

59 Subsequent section in angled brackets included from Cambridge manuscript. In that manuscript, §3 follows as usual.

the people the manner of the kingdom'.[60] There is no speech of reading to the king what Samuel had formerly told the people when they desired a king. Of the manner of the king and the things they must suffer he now writes, and leaves it to remain upon record to all posterity, and laid it up before the Lord. Thus saith Josephus, who should best know the Jewish records. Those err that think that the law in Deuteronomy xvii concerning the duty of a king was the same law that Samuel writ and laid up. If it had been the same, what need Samuel have writ and laid it up?—since that was writ and laid up long before in the ark, Deuteronomy xxxi. Secondly, the law in Deuteronomy concerns properly the king, and should have been read to him rather than to the people. Thirdly, the law itself in Deuteronomy xvii was but some few general precepts which did properly concern the particular kings of the Jews, as the not multiplying of horses or wives, not returning into Egypt. And though there be no question but that God may give laws to all kings, though the people may not, yet the laws in Deuteronomy xvii were only laws for the kings of the particular commonwealth of the Hebrews>.

(3) If any desire the direction of the New Testament, he may find our Saviour limiting and distinguishing royal power, 'By giving to Caesar those things that were Caesar's, and to God those things that were God's'.[61] Let St. Basil expound this text: *Obediendum est in quibus mandatum Dei non impeditur*: we must obey princes in those things wherein the commandment of God is not hindered'. There is no other law but God's law to hinder our obedience. It was the answer of a Christian to the emperor: 'We only worship God, in other things we gladly serve you'. And it seems Tertullian thought whatsoever was not God's was the emperor's, when he saith: '*Bene apposuit Caesari pecuniam, te ipsum Deo, alioqui quid erit Dei, si omnia Caesaris*: our Saviour hath well apportioned our money for Caesar, and ourselves for God, for otherwise what shall God's share be if all be Caesar's?' The Fathers mention no reservation of any power to the laws of the land, or to the people. St. Ambrose, in his *Apology for David*, expressly saith: 'He was a king, and therefore bound to no laws, because kings are free from the bonds of any fault'. St. Augustine also resolves: '*Imperator non est subjectus legibus, qui habet in potestate alias leges ferre*: the emperor is not subject to laws, who hath power to make other laws'. For, indeed, it is the rule of Solomon that, 'We must keep the king's commandment, and not to say to him, what dost thou? Because where the word of a king is,

---

60 1 Samuel 10:25.
61 Matthew 22:21.

there is power, and all that he pleaseth he will do'.[62]

If any dislike this divinity in England, let him but hearken to Bracton, chief justice in King Henry III's days, which was since the institution of parliaments. His words are, speaking of the king: '*Omnes sub eo, et ipse sub nullo, nisi tantum sub Deo*', &c:

> all are under him, and he under none but God only. If he offend, since no writ can go against him, their remedy is by petitioning him to amend his fault. Which, if he shall not do, it will be punishment sufficient for him to expect God as a revenger. Let none presume to search into his deeds, much less to oppose them.[63]

When the Jews asked our blessed Saviour whether they should pay tribute, He did not first demand what the law of the land was, or whether there was any statute against it, nor enquired whether the tribute were given by act of parliament, nor advised them to stay their payment until a parliament should grant it. He did no more but look upon the superscription, and concluded, 'This image you say is Caesar's, therefore give it to Caesar'. Nor must it here be said that Christ taught this lesson only to the conquered Jews, for in this He gave direction for all nations, who are bound as much in obedience to their lawful kings as to any conqueror or usurper whatsoever.

Whereas St. Paul bids us 'be subject to the higher powers', some have strained these words to signify the laws of the land, or else to mean the highest power, as well aristocratical and democratical as regal. It seems St. Paul looked for such interpreters, and therefore thought fit to be his own expositor, and to let it be known that by power he understood a monarch that carried a sword: 'Wilt thou not be afraid of the power?' that is the ruler that carrieth the sword, for 'he is the minister of God to thee, for he beareth not the sword in vain'. It is not the law that is the 'minister of God', or that 'carries the sword', but the ruler or magistrate. So they that say the law governs the kingdom may as well say that the carpenter's rule builds the house and not the carpenter, for the law is but the rule or instrument of the ruler. And St. Paul concludes: 'For this cause pay you tribute also, for they are God's ministers, attending continually upon this very thing. Render therefore tribute to whom tribute is due, custom to whom custom'.[64]

---

62   Ecclesiastes 8:2–4.
63   Henry de Bracton, *Henrici de Bracton De Legibus et Consuetudinibus Angliae, libri quinque*, folios 5b–6a.
64   Romans 13:6–7.

He doth not say, give tribute as a gift to God's minister, but ἀπόσυτε, render or restore tribute as a due. Also, St. Peter doth most clearly expound this place of St. Paul, where he saith: 'Submit yourselves to every ordinance of man for the Lord's sake, whether it be to the king as supreme or unto governors, as unto them that are sent by him'.[65] Here the very self same word 'supreme', or 'ὑπερέχοντι' which St. Paul coupleth with power, St. Peter conjoineth with the king, 'βασιλεῖ ὡς ὑπερέχον', thereby to manifest that king and power are both one. Also St. Peter expounds his own words of human ordinance to be the king, who is the *lex loquens*—a speaking law. He cannot mean that kings themselves are an human ordinance, since St. Paul calls the supreme power the ordinance of God, and the wisdom of God saith 'By me kings reign'.[66] But his meaning must be that the commands or laws of kings are human ordinances. Next, the governors that are sent by him: that is, by the king, not by God, as some corruptly would wrest the text to justify popular governors as authorised by God, whereas in grammatical construction 'him', the relative, must be referred to the next antecedent, which is 'the king'. Besides, the antithesis between 'supreme' and 'sent' proves plainly that the governors were sent by kings. For, if the governors were sent by God and the king be an human ordinance, then it follows that the governors were supreme and not the king. Or, if it be said that both king and governors are sent by God, then they are both equal, and so neither of them 'supreme'. Therefore St. Peter's meaning is in short: 'Obey the laws of the king or of his ministers'. By which it is evident, that neither St. Peter nor St. Paul intended other form of government than only monarchical, much less any subjection of princes to human laws.

That familiar distinction of the schoolmen,[67] whereby they subject kings to the *directive* but not to the *coactive* power of laws, is a confession that kings are not bound by the positive laws of any nation—since the compulsory power of laws is that which properly makes laws to be laws, by binding men by rewards or punishment to obedience; whereas the direction of the law is but like the advice and direction which the kings council gives the king, which no man can say is a law to the king.

(4) There want not those who believe that the first invention of laws was to bridle and moderate the over-great power of kings. But the truth is, the original of laws was for the keeping of the multitude in order. Popular states could not subsist at all without laws, whereas kingdoms were governed many ages without them. The people of Athens, as soon as they

65   1 Peter 2:13–14.
66   Proverbs 8:15.
67   See introduction p. whatever.

gave over kings, were forced to give power to Draco first, then to Solon, to make them laws not to bridle kings but themselves. And though many of their laws were very severe and bloody, yet for the reverence they bare to their lawmakers they willingly submitted to them. Nor did the people give any limited power to Solon, but an absolute jurisdiction at his pleasure to abrogate and confirm what he thought fit, the people never challenging any such power to themselves. So the people of Rome gave to the ten men, who were to choose and correct their laws for the twelve tables, an absolute power without any appeal to the people.

(5) The reason why laws have been also made by kings was this: when kings were either busied with wars or distracted with public cares, so that every private man could not have access to their persons to learn their wills and pleasure, then of necessity were laws invented, that so every particular subject might find his prince's pleasure deciphered unto him in the tables of his laws, that so there might be no need to resort to the king but either for the interpretation or mitigation of obscure or rigorous laws, or else in new cases, for a supplement where the law was defective. By this means both king and people were in many things eased:

1. The king, by giving laws, doth free himself of great and intolerable troubles, as Moses did himself by choosing elders.

2. The people have the law as a familiar admonisher and interpreter of the king's pleasure, which being published throughout the kingdom doth represent the presence and majesty of the king.

Also the judges and magistrates (whose help in giving judgment in many causes kings have need to use) are restrained by the common rules of the law from using their own liberty to the injury of others, since they are to judge according to the king's laws, and not follow their own opinions.

(6) Now albeit kings who make the laws be, as King James teacheth us, above the laws, yet will they rule their subjects by the law; 'And a king, governing in a settled kingdom, leaves to be a king and degenerates into a tyrant so soon as he seems to rule according to his laws'.[68]

> Yet where he sees the laws rigorous or doubtful he may mit-
> igate and interpret. General laws made in parliament may,
> upon known respects to the king, by his authority be mit-
> igated or suspended upon causes only known to him. And
> although a king do frame all his actions to be according to

---

68　James I, *A Speech to the Lords and Commons of the Parliament at White-Hall, on Wednesday the XII of March, Anno 1609.*

the laws, yet he is not bound thereto but at his good will and for good example,[69]

or so far forth as the general law of the safety of the commonweal doth naturally bind him. For in such sort only positive laws may be said to bind the king, not by being positive but as they are naturally the best or only means for the preservation of the commonwealth. By this means are all kings, even tyrants and conquerors, bound to preserve the lands, goods, liberties, and lives of all their subjects, not by any municipal law of the land, but by the natural law of a father, which binds them to ratify the acts of their forefathers and predecessors in things necessary for the public good of their subjects.

(7) Others there be that affirm that although laws of themselves do not bind kings, yet the oaths of kings at their coronations tie them to keep all the laws of their kingdoms. How far this is true, let us but examine the oath of the kings of England at their coronation, the words whereof are these: 'Art thou pleased to cause to be administered in all thy judgments, indifferent and upright justice, and to use discretion with mercy and verity? Art thou pleased that our upright laws and customs be observed, and dost thou promise that those shall be protected and maintained by thee?'[70] These two are the articles of the king's oath which concern the laity or subjects in general, to which the king answers affirmatively, being first demanded by the Archbishop of Canterbury, 'Pleaseth it you to confirm and observe the laws and customs of ancient times, granted from God by just and devout kings unto the English nation, by oath unto the said people, specially the laws, customs, and liberties granted unto the clergy and laity by the famous King Edward?'[71] We may observe, in these words of the articles of the oath, that the king is required to observe not *all* the laws, but only the *upright laws*, and that with discretion and mercy. The word *upright* cannot mean *all* laws, because in the oath of Richard II, I find 'evil and unjust laws' mentioned, which the king swears to abolish. And in the old abridgment of statutes set forth in Henry VIII's days, the king is to swear wholly to 'put out evil laws', which he cannot do if he be bound to keep *all* laws. Now what laws are upright and what evil, who shall judge but the king, since he swears to administer upright justice with discretion and mercy, or as Bracton hath it, '*aequitatem praecipiat, et misericordiam*'[72]

---

69 James I, *True Law*, p. 63.
70 Thomas Milles, *The Catalogue of Honor or Treasury of True Nobility*, p. 53.
71 Milles, *Catalogue of Honor*, p. 53.
72 Bracton, *De Legibus*, folio 107a.

["let him command justice and mercy"]. So that in effect the king doth swear to keep no laws but such as in his judgment are upright, and those not literally always, but according to the equity of his conscience joined with mercy, which is properly the office of a chancellor rather than of a judge. And if a king did strictly swear to observe all the laws, he could not without perjury give his consent to the repealing or abrogating of any statute by act of parliament, which would be very mischievable to the state.

But let it be supposed for truth that kings do swear to observe all the laws of their kingdoms, yet no man can think it reason that kings should be more bound by their voluntary oaths than common persons are by theirs. Now if a private person make a contract either with oath or without oath, he is no further bound than the equity and justice of the contract ties him. For a man may have relief against an unreasonable and unjust promise, if either deceit, or error, or force, or fear induced him thereunto, or if it be hurtful or grievous in the performance. Since the laws in many cases give the king a prerogative above common persons, I see no reason why he should be denied the privilege which the meanest of his subjects doth enjoy.

Here is a fit place to examine a question which some have moved, whether it be a sin for a subject to disobey the king if he command anything contrary to his laws? For satisfaction in this point we must resolve that not only in human laws, but even in divine, a thing may be commanded contrary to law, and yet obedience to such a command is necessary. The sanctifying of the sabbath is a divine law, yet if a master command his servant not to go to church upon a sabbath day, the best divines teach us, that the servant must obey this command, though it may be sinful and unlawful in the master; because the servant hath no authority or liberty to examine and judge whether his master sin or no in so commanding, for there may be a just cause for a master to keep his servant from church, as appears Luke 14:5. Yet it is not fit to tie the master to acquaint his servant with his secrets, counsels, or present necessity, and in such cases the servant's not going to church becomes the sin of the master, and not of the servant. The like may be said of the king's commanding a man to serve him in the wars. He may not examine whether the war be just or unjust, but must obey, since he hath no commission to judge of the titles of kingdoms or causes of war, nor hath any subject power to condemn his king for breach of his own laws.

(8) Many will be ready to say it is a slavish and dangerous condition to be subject to the will of any one man who is not subject to the laws. But such men consider not:

1. That the prerogative of a king is to be above all laws, for the good only of them that are under the laws, and to defend the people's liberties—as his majesty graciously affirmed in his speech after his last answer to the Petition of Right.[73] Howsoever some are afraid of the name of prerogative, yet they may assure themselves the case of subjects would be desperately miserable without it. The court of chancery[74] itself is but a branch of the king's prerogative to relieve men against the inexorable rigour of the law, which without it is no better than a tyrant, since *summum jus* is *summa injuria* ["supreme law" is "supreme injustice"]. General pardons at the coronation and in parliaments are but the bounty of the prerogative.

2. There can be no laws without a supreme power to command or make them. In all aristocracies the nobles are above the laws, and in all democracies the people. By the like reason, in a monarchy the king must of necessity be above the laws. There can be no sovereign majesty in him that is under them. That which giveth the very being to a king, is the power to give laws; without this power he is but an equivocal king. It skills not which way kings come by their power, whether by election, donation, succession, or by any other means, for it is still the manner of the government by supreme power that makes them properly kings, and not the means of obtaining their crowns. Neither doth the diversity of laws, nor contrary customs—whereby each kingdom differs from another—make the forms of commonweal different, unless the power of making laws be in several subjects.

For confirmation of this point, Aristotle saith that 'a perfect kingdom is that wherein the king rules all things according to his own will, for he that is called a king according to the law, makes no kind of kingdom at all'. This it seems, also the Romans well understood to be most necessary in monarchy. For though they were a people most greedy of liberty, yet the senate did free 'Augustus from all necessity of laws, that he might be free of his own authority, and of absolute power over himself and over the laws to do what he pleased and leave undone what he list. And this decree was made while Augustus was yet absent'. Accordingly we find that Ulpian, that great lawyer, delivers it for a rule of the civil law: '*princeps legibus solutus est*, the prince is not bound by the laws'.[75]

---

73 See introduction p. whatever.
74 The Court of Chancery was a court of equity in England and Wales charged with relaxing the rigour of English common law in cases where the law was seen to produce an "unfair" outcome. Refer to Henry Sumner Maine's *Ancient Law* for an in-depth discussion of the legal concept of equity.
75 *Digest*, iii, 31.

(9) If the nature of laws be advisedly weighed, the necessity of the prince's being above them may more manifest itself. We all know that a law in general is the command of a superior power. Laws are divided (as Bellarmine divides the word of God) into written and unwritten. 'τῶν νόμον οἱ μεν ἐγγραφοι οἱ δε ἀγραφοι,' saith Ulpian in the Civil Law, 'The common law unwritten and the statute law written'.[76] The common law is called unwritten not for that it is not written at all, but because it was not written by the first devisers or makers of it. The common law (as the lord chancellor Egerton teacheth us) is the 'common custom of the realm'.[77] Now concerning customs, this must be considered, that for every custom there was a time when it was no custom, and the first precedent we now have, had no president when it began. When every custom began, there was something else than custom that made it lawful, or else the beginning of all customs were unlawful. Customs at first became lawful only by some superior which did either command or consent unto their beginning. And the first power which we find (as it is confessed by all men) is the kingly power, which was both in this nation and in all other nations of the world long before any laws or any other kind of government was thought of. From whence we must necessarily infer that the common law itself, or common customs of this land, were originally the laws and commands of kings at first unwritten.

Nor must we think that the common customs (which are the principles of the common law, and are but few) to be such, or so many, as are able to give special rules to determine every particular cause. Diversity of cases are infinite, and impossible to be regulated by any law. And therefore we find even in the divine laws which were delivered by Moses, there be only certain principal laws which did not determine but only direct the high priest or magistrate, whose judgment in special cases did determine what the general law intended. It is so with the common law, for when there is no perfect rule judges do resort to those principles or common law axioms whereupon former judgments in cases somewhat like have been delivered by former judges, who all receive authority from the king, in his right and name, to give sentence according to the rules and precedents of ancient times. And where precedents have failed, the judges have resorted to the general law of reason, and accordingly given judgment without any common law to direct them. Nay, many times where there have been precedents to direct, they, upon better reason only, have changed the law both in

76   *Digest* I, 6.
77   Sir Thomas Egerton, *The Speech of the Lord Chancellor of England, in the Exchequer chamber, touching the Post-nati*, p. 35.

causes criminal and civil, and have not insisted so much on the examples of former judges as examined and corrected their reasons. Hence it is that some laws are now obsolete and out of use, and the practice quite contrary to what it was in former times, as the lord chancellor Egerton proves by several instances.

Nor is this spoken to derogate from the common law, for the case standeth so with the laws of all nations, although some of them have their laws and principles written and established. For witness to this, we have Aristotle his testimony in his *Ethics*, and in several places in his *Politics*. I will cite some of them:

> Every law (saith he) is in the general, but of some things there can be no general law ... When therefore the law speaks in general, and something falls out after beside the general rule, then it is fit that what the lawmaker hath omitted, or where he hath erred by speaking generally, it should be corrected or supplied, as if the lawmaker himself were present to ordain it.[78]
>
> The governor, whether he be one man or more, ought to be lord over all those things whereof it was impossible the law should exactly speak, because it is not easy to comprehend all things under general rules ... Whatsoever the law cannot determine, it leaves to the governors to give judgment therein, and permits them to rectify whatsoever upon trial they find to be better than the written laws.[79] [80]

<And the civil law agrees with Aristotle, for it saith: '*Jura constitui oportet (ut dixit Theophrastus) in his quae* ἔπι τὸ πλεῖστον *accidunt, non quae* ἐκ παραλόγου' ["it is proper (as Theophrastus says) that laws be established upon those things which usually happen, not upon exceptions"]. They are the words of Pomponius. Again: '*Ex his quae forte uno aliquo casu accidere possunt jura non constituuntur ... nam ad ea potius debet aptari jus quae et frequenter et facile, quam quae perraro eveniunt*' ["laws are not established from those things which by chance may happen in some one case ... for the law should be fitted to things which happen both often and readily, rather than very rarely"], saith Celsus. '*Quae semel aut bis accidunt praetereunt legislatores*' ["lawmakers disregard what happens once or twice"]. '*Neque*

---

78   Aristotle, *Nicomachean Ethics*, 1137ᵇ 13–14, 19–24.
79   Aristotle, *Politics*, 1282ᵇ 3–6.
80   Subsequent paragraph in angled brackets included from Cambridge manuscript.

leges ita scribi possunt, ut omnes casus qui quandoque inciderint compre-hendantur, sed sufficit et ea quae plerumque accidunt contineri' ["nor can laws be written to include all cases which might arise, but it suffices to comprise what happens for the most part"], saith Julianus. *'Cum in aliqua causa sententia eorum est manifesta, is qui jurisdictioni praeest, ad similia procedere atque ita jus dicere debet'* ["when a judgment is obvious in one case, the presiding should apply the law and proceed similarly in similar cases"].>

Besides, all laws are of themselves dumb, and some or other must be trusted with the application of them to particulars, by examining all cir-cumstances, to pronounce when they are broken or by whom. This work of right application of laws is not a thing easy or obvious for ordinary ca-pacities, but requires profound abilities of nature for the beating out of the truth. Witness the diversity and sometimes the contrariety of opinions of the learned judges in some difficult points.

(10) Since this is the common condition of laws, it is most reasonable that the lawmaker should be trusted with the application or interpretation of the laws. And for this cause anciently the kings of this land have sitten personally in courts of judicature, and are still representatively present in all courts. The judges are but substituted and called the king's justices, and their power ceaseth when the king is in place. To this purpose Bracton, that learned chief justice in the reign of Henry III, saith in express terms, 'In doubtful and obscure points the interpretation and will of our lord the king is to be expected, since it is his part to interpret who made the law'.[81] For, as he saith in another place, *'Rex et non alius debet judicare si solus ad id sufficere possit'*, etc:

> the king and nobody else ought to give judgment if he were able, since by virtue of his oath he is bound to it. Therefore the king ought to exercise power as the vicar or minister of God. But if our lord the king be not able to determine every cause, to ease part of his pains by distributing the burden to more persons, he ought to choose wise men, fearing God, etc., and make justices of them.[82]

Much to the same purpose are the words of King Edward I in the be-ginning of the book of laws written by his appointment by John Britton, bishop of Hereford. "'We will', saith the king, "that our own jurisdiction

---

81   Bracton, *De Legibus*, folio 34a; Egerton, *Speech*, p. 108.
82   Bracton, *De Legibus*, folio 107a.

be above all the jurisdictions of our realm, so as in all manner of felonies, trespasses, contracts, and in all other actions, personal or real, we have power to yield such judgments as do appertain, without other process, wheresoever we know the right truth as judges.'"[83] Neither may this be taken to be meant of an imaginary presence of the king's person in his courts, because he doth immediately after in the same place severally set forth by themselves the jurisdictions of his ordinary courts; but must necessarily be understood of a jurisdiction remaining in the king's royal person. 'And that this then was no new-made law, or first brought in by the Norman Conquest,'[84] appears by a Saxon law made by king Edgar in these words, as I find them in Mr. Lambarde: '*Nemo in lite regem appellato, nisi quidem domi justitiam consequi, aut impetrare non poterit, sin summo jure domi urgeatur, ad regem, ut is onus aliqua ex parte allevet, provocato*: Let no man in suit appeal to the king unless he may not get right at home. But if that right be too heavy for him, then let him go to the king to have it eased.'[85]

As the judicial power of kings was exercised before the Conquest, so in those settled times after the Conquest wherein parliaments were much in use, there was a high court following the king, which was the place of sovereign justice both for matter of law and conscience—as may appear by a parliament in King Edward I's time, taking order 'that the chancellor and the justices of the bench should follow the king, to the end that he might have always at hand able men' for his direction in suits that came before him. And this was after the time that the court of common pleas was made stationary, which is an evidence that the king reserved a sovereign power by which he did supply the want, or correct the rigour of the common law, because the positive law, being grounded upon that which happens for the most part, cannot foresee every particular which time and experience bring forth.

(11) Therefore, though the common law be generally good and just, yet in some special case it may need correction by reason of some considerable circumstance falling out which at the time of the lawmaking was not thought of. Also sundry things do fall out both in war and peace that require extraordinary help, and cannot wait for the usual care of common law, the which is not performed but altogether after one sort, and that not without delay of help and expense of time. So that, although all causes are and ought to be referred to the ordinary process of common law, yet rare

---

83   William Lambarde, *Archeion or, a Discourse upon the High Courts of Justice in England*, p. 57.
84   Lambarde, *Archeion*, p. 58.
85   Lambarde, *Archeion*, p. 58.

matters from time to time do grow up meet, for just reasons, to be referred to the aid of the absolute and indefinite authority of the prince. And the statute of Magna Carta hath been understood of the institution then made of the ordinary jurisdiction in common causes, and not for restraint of the absolute authority which serves in 'rare and singular cases'.[86] For though the subjects were put to great damage by false accusations and malicious suggestions made to the king and his council, especially during the time of King Edward III whilst he was absent in the wars in France, insomuch as in his reign divers statutes were made that provided none should be put to answer before the king and his council without due process, yet it is apparent the necessity of such proceedings was so great that both before Edward III's days, and in his time, and after his death, several statutes were made to help and order the proceedings of the king and his council.

As the parliament in 28 Edward 1, ch. 5, did provide 'that the chancellor and justices of the king's bench should follow the king so that he might have near unto him some that be learned in the laws, which be able to order all such matters as shall come unto the court at all times when need shall require'.[87] By the statute of 37 Edward III, ch. 18, taliation[88] was ordained in case the suggestion to the king proved untrue. Then 38 Edward III, ch. 9, takes away the taliation and appoints imprisonment till the king and party grieved be satisfied. In the statutes of 17 Richard II, ch. 6, and 15 Henry VI, ch. 4, damages and expenses are awarded in such cases. In all these statutes it is necessarily implied that complaints upon just causes might be moved before the king and his council.

At a parliament at Gloucester, 2 Richard II, when the Commons made petition that none might be forced by writ out of chancery or by privy seal to appear before the king and his council to answer touching free-hold, the king's answer was

> he thought it not reasonable that he should be constrained
> to send for his leiges upon causes reasonable. And albeit he
> did not purpose that such as were sent for should answer
> *finalment*, peremptorily, touching their freehold, but should
> be remanded for trial thereof as law required, 'Provided al-
> ways' (saith he) 'that at the suit of the party where the king

---

86   Lambarde, *Archeion*, p. 62.

87   *The Statutes at Large*, p. 51.

88   William Blackstone in his *Commentaries on the Laws of England Vol. 2* explains taliation in the same context as Filmer, with respect to 37 Edward III ch. 18: "to incur the same pain that the other should have had in case the suggestion was found to be untrue." See also, *lex talionis*.

and his council shall be credibly informed that because of maintenance, oppression, or other outrages, the common law cannot have duly her course, in such case the counsel may send for the party'.[89]

Also in the thirteenth year of his reign, when the Commons

did pray that, upon pain of forfeiture, the chancellor or council of the king should not after the end of the parliament make any ordinance against the common law, the king answered: 'Let it be used as it hath been used before this time, so as the regality of the king be saved; for the king will save his regalities as his progenitors have done'.[90]

Again, in the fourth year of Henry IV, when the Commons complained against subpoenas and other writs grounded upon false suggestions, the king answered:

'That he would give in charge to his officers that they should abstain more than before time they had to send for his subjects in that manner. But yet', saith he, 'it is not our intention that our officers shall so abstain that they may not send for our subjects in matters and causes necessary, as it hath been used in the time of our good progenitors'.[91]

Likewise, when for the same cause complaint was made by the Commons *anno* 3, Henry V, the king's answer was: '*Le roi s'advisera*: the king will be advised', which amounts to a denial for the present, by a phrase peculiar for the king's denying to pass any act that hath passed the Lords and Commons.

These complaints of the Commons, and the answers of the kings, discover that such moderation should be used that the course of the common law be ordinarily maintained lest subjects be convented before the king and his council without just cause, that the proceedings of the council table be not upon every slight suggestion, nor to determine finally concerning freehold of inheritance. And yet that, upon cause reasonable, 'upon credible information in matters of weight, the king's regality or prerogative in sending for his subjects be maintained, as of right it ought' and in for-

89   Lambarde, *Archeion*, p. 70.
90   Lambarde, *Archeion*, p. 71.
91   Lambarde, *Archeion*, p. 72.

mer times hath been constantly used.

King Edward I, finding 'that Bogo de Clare was discharged of an accusation brought against him in parliament, for that some formal imperfections were found in the complaint, commanded him nevertheless to appear before him and his council, 'ad faciendum et recipiendum quod per regem et ejus consilium fuerit faciendum'[92] ["to do and undergo what was decreed through the king and his council"], and so proceeded to an examination of the whole cause (anno 18 Edward I).

Edward III in the Star Chamber (which was the ancient council chamber at Westminster) upon the complaint of Elizabeth Audley, 'commanded James Audley to appear before him and his council, and determined a controversy between them touching lands contained in the covenants of her jointure. (Rotulo clauso de Anno ["in the close roll of the year"] 41 Edward III)'.[93]

Henry V,

> in a suit before him and his council for the titles of the manors of Serre and St. Lawrence in the isle of Thanet in Kent, took order for the sequestering of the profits till the right were tried, as well for avoiding the breach of the peace as for prevention of waste and spoil. (Rotulo patenti de Anno ["in the patent roll of the year"] 6 Henry V).[94]

Henry VI 'commanded the justices of the bench to stay the arraignment of one Verney of London till they had other commandment from him and his council. Because Verney, being indebted to the king and others, practised to be indicted of felony, wherein he might have his clergy, and make his purgation of intent to defraud his creditors. (34 Henry VI rotulo 37 in banco regis ["in the king's bench"])'.

Edward IV and his council in the Star Chamber

> heard the cause of the master and poor brethren of St. Leonards in York, complaining that Sir Hugh Hastings and others withdrew from them a great part of their living, which consisted chiefly upon the having of a thrave of corn of every plough-land within the counties of York, Westmorland, Cumberland, and Lancashire. (Rotulo patenti de Anno 8 Ed-

---

92 Lambarde, *Archeion*, p. 73.
93 Lambarde, *Archeion*, p. 73.
94 Lambarde, *Archeion*, p. 74.

ward IV, part 3, membrane 14).[95]

Henry VII and his council, in the Star Chamber,

> decreed that Margery and Florence Backet should sue no
> further in their cause against Alice Radley, widow, for lands
> in Woolwich and Plumstead in Kent, forasmuch as the mat-
> ter had been heard, first before the council of King Edward
> IV, after that before the president of the requests of that King
> Henry VII, and then lastly before the council of the said king
> (1 Henry VII).[96]

What is hitherto affirmed of the dependency and subjection of the common law to the sovereign prince, the same may be said as well of all statute
laws. For the king is the sole immediate author, corrector, and moderator
of them also. So that neither of these two kinds of laws are, or can be, any
diminution of that natural power which kings have over their people by
right of fatherhood, but rather are an argument to strengthen the truth
of it. For evidence whereof we may in some points consider the nature of
parliaments, because by them only all statutes are enacted.

(12) Though the name of 'parliament', as Mr. Camden saith, be 'of no great
antiquity', but brought in out of France, yet our ancestors the English Saxons had a meeting which they called the 'assembly of the wise'; termed
in Latin '*conventum magnatum*, or *praesentia regis, procerumque, praelatorum collectorum*; the meeting of the nobility, or the presence of the
king, prelates, and peers assembled';[97] or in general, *magnum concilium*, or
commune concilium ["great council" or "common council"]. And many of
our kings in elder times made use of such great assemblies for to consult
of important affairs of state, all which meetings in a general sense may be
termed parliaments.

  Great are the advantages which both the king and people may receive
by a well ordered parliament. There is nothing more expresseth the majesty and supreme power of a king than such an assembly, wherein all his
people acknowledge him for sovereign lord, and make all their addresses
to him by humble petition and supplication, and by their consent and approbation do strengthen all the laws which the king at their request and by
their advice and ministry, shall ordain. Thus they facilitate the government

95 Lambarde, *Archeion*, p. 75.
96 Lambarde, *Archeion*, p. 76.
97 William Camden, *Britain, or a Chorographicall Description of the most flourishing Kingdomes, England, Scotland, and Ireland*, p. 177.

of the king by making the laws unquestionable, either to the subordinate magistrates or refractory multitude. Then the benefit which accrues to the subject by parliaments is, that by their prayers and petitions kings are drawn many times to redress their just grievances, and are overcome by their importunity to grant many things which otherwise they would not yield unto—for the voice of a multitude is easilier heard. Many vexations of the people are without the knowledge of the king, who in parliament seeth and heareth his people himself, whereas at other times he commonly useth the eyes and ears of other men.

(13) Against the antiquity of parliaments we need not dispute, since the more ancient they be, the more they make for the honour of monarchy. Yet there be certain circumstances touching the forms of parliaments which are fit to be considered.

First, we are to remember, that until about the time of the Conquest there could be no parliaments assembled of the general states of the whole kingdom of England, because till those days we cannot find it was entirely united into one kingdom, but it was either divided into several kingdoms, or governed by several laws. When Julius Caesar landed he found 4 kings in Kent, and the British names of Danmonii, Durotriges, Belgae, Attrebatii, Trinobantes, Iceni, Silures, and the rest are plentiful testimonies of the several kingdoms of Britons when the Romans became our lords. As soon as ever the Romans left us, the Saxons divided us into seven kingdoms. When these Saxons were united into a monarchy, they had always the Danes their companions or masters in the empire till Edward the Confessor's days, since whose time the kingdom of England hath continued united as now it doth. But for a thousand years before we cannot find it was entirely settled during the time of any one king's reign. As for laws, we find the middle parts of the kingdom under the Mercian law; the West Saxons were confined to the Saxon laws; Essex, Norfolk, Suffolk, and some other places were vexed with the Danish laws. The Northumbrians also had their laws apart, and until Edward the Confessor's reign, who was the next but one before the Conqueror, the laws of the kingdom were so several and uncertain that he was forced to cull a few of the most indifferent and best of them, which were from him called St. Edward's laws. Yet some say that Edgar made those laws, and that the Confessor did but restore and amend them. Alfred also gathered out of Malmutius' laws such as he translated into the Saxon tongue. Thus during the time of the Saxons the laws were so variable that there is little or no likelihood to find any constant form of parliaments of the whole kingdom.

A second point considerable is whether in such parliaments as were in the Saxon's times the nobility and clergy only were of those assemblies, or whether the Commons were also called (Mr. Lambarde, *Archion*). Some are of opinion that though none of the Saxon laws do expressly mention the Commons, yet it may be gathered by the word '*witena*', 'wisemen', that the Commons are intended to be of those assemblies. And they bring (as they conceive) probable arguments to prove it from the antiquity of some boroughs that were decayed before the Conquest and yet send burgesses, and from the proscription of those in *ancient demesne* not to send any burgesses to parliament or pay knights' wages.

If it be true that the West Saxons had a custom to assemble burgesses out of some of their towns, yet it may be doubted whether other kingdoms had the same usage. But sure it is that during the Heptarchy the people could not elect any knights of the shire, because England was not then divided into shires.

On the contrary there be of our historians who do affirm that Henry I 'caused the Commons first to be assembled by knights and burgesses of their own appointment, for before his time only certain of the nobility and prelates of the realm were called to consultation about the most important affairs of state'[98] (Sir John Hayward in Henry I).[99]

<What the ancientest usage of the Normans was may best appear by such testimonies as Mr. Selden produceth in his *Titles of Honor*. King William the Conqueror in the fourth year of his reign by the consent of his barons had twelve men out of every county who showed what the customs of the kingdom were and by the assent of the barons those customs were confirmed for laws. Which appears also by the laws of King Henry I, where it is said 'I restore you the laws of King Edward with those amendments by which my father amended them by the counsel of his barons'.[100] It is probable, if there had been any custom in the Saxon times to have summoned knights and burgesses, that the Conqueror (who was so desirous to know and confirm the ancient customs) would rather have called such knights and burgesses than twelve men out of every county. Mr. Selden citeth proofs for other parliaments in King William I's reign, but in none of them any mention of any other but *comites et primates et principum conventus* ["earls and nobles and an assembly of leading men"], which was only earls and barons.

---

98   Sir John Hayward, *The Lives of the III Normans, Kings of England*, p. 283.
99   Subsequent seven paragraphs in angled brackets included from Cambridge manuscript, which has in its place the following sentence: "If this assertion be true it seems a mere matter of grace of this king, and proves not any natural right of the people to be admitted to choose their knights and burgesses of parliament."
100   John Selden, *Titles of Honor*, p. 701.

In the second year of King William II there was a parliament by *cunctis regni principibus* ["all the leading men of the kingdom"], and another which had *quosque regni proceres* ["each noble of the kingdom"]. 'At the coronation of King Henry I', all the people of the kingdom were called, and laws then made '*per commune consilium baronum*'[101] ["through the common council of the barons"]. 3 Henry I *proceres regni* ["the nobles of the kingdom"] were called, and another parliament at a while after *consensu comitum et baronum* ["with the agreement of the earls and barons"] and in his tenth year of *comites* and *proceres* ["the earls" and "nobles"]. In the eleventh year, at a parliament at Northampton, were summoned *omnes qui tenebant de rege in capite* ["all who held (land) from the king as vassals-in-chief"]. In the twenty-third year, *earls and barons*. The year following the same king held a parliament or great council with his *barons spiritual and temporal*.

In the fifth year of King John, '*Rex et magnates convenerunt* ["the king and magnates assembled"] and the roll of that year hath *commune consilium baronum meorum* ["the common council of my barons"] at Winchester'.[102] The grand charter made in the last year of King John mentions *maiores barones regni, et qui in capite tenent de nobis* ["the greater barons of the kingdom, and those who hold (land) from us as vassals-in-chief"]. King Henry III, *anno* 1225, called *omnes clericos et laicos totius regni* ["all the clergy and laity in the whole kingdom"]. King Edward I in his third year summoned the *communaltie* ["commonalty"] of the land. King Edward II in his fourteenth year had *tout le cominaltie de son royaume* ["all the commonalty of his kingdom"].

By these testimonies it appears that the ancientest and most usual summons was of earls and barons, and that kings did vary their summons at their pleasure. Which may be further confirmed out of Mr. Camden, who, speaking of barons, saith that

> King Henry III out of a great multitude which was seditious and turbulent called out the best of them by his writ to parliament. And the prudent King Edward I summoned always those barons of ancientest families that were most wise to his parliaments, but omitted their sons after their death if they were not answerable to their parents in understanding.[103]

King Henry III commanded '*duos milites gladio cinctos magis discretos et*

---

101   Selden, *Titles*, p. 702.
102   Selden, *Titles*, p. 707.
103   Camden, *Britain*, p. 169.

idoneos' ["two rather discreet and suitable soldiers armed with sword"] to be chosen to serve for knights of the shire. And it is the acknowledgement of Mr. Selden that the 'first writs we find accompanied with the other circumstances of a summons to parliament, as well for the Commons as Lords, is in the forty-ninth year of King Henry III'.[104] Amongst all those proofs which I can find produced for the antiquity of parliaments, I see nothing for the choosing of knights and burgesses by popular elections before the times of this King Henry III, although King Henry I were the first that summoned all the people.>

And it had been more for the honour of parliaments if a king whose title to the crown had been better than that of King Henry I had been author of the first calling the people to parliament, because he made use of it for his unjust ends. For thereby he secured himself against his competitor and elder brother, by taking the oaths of the nobility in parliament and getting the crown to be settled upon his children. And as the king made use of the people, so they, by colour of parliament, served their own turns. For after the establishment of parliaments by strong hand and by the sword, they drew from him the great charter, which he granted the rather to flatter the nobility and people, as Sir Walter Raleigh in his dialogue of parliaments doth affirm in these words:

> The great charter was not originally granted regally and free-ly, for Henry I did but usurp the kingdom, and therefore the better to assure himself against Robert his elder brother, he flattered the nobility and people with these charters. Yea, King John that confirmed them had the like respect, for Arthur Duke of Britain was the undoubted heir of the crown, upon whom King John usurped. And so, to conclude, these charters had their original from kings *de facto*, but not *de jure* ... The great charter had first an obscure birth by usurpation, and was secondly fostered and showed to the world by rebellion.[105]

(14) A third consideration must be that in the form of parliaments instituted and continued since King Henry I's and King Henry III's time is not to be found the usage of any natural liberty of the people. For all those liberties that are claimed in parliament are the liberties of grace from the king, and not the liberties of nature to the people. For if the liberty were natural it would give power to the multitude to assemble themselves *when*

104   Selden, *Titles*, p. 717.
105   Raleigh, *The Prerogative of Parliaments in England*, pp. 4, 6.

and *where* they please, to bestow sovereignty and by pactions to limit and direct the exercise of it, whereas the liberties of favour and grace which are claimed in parliaments are restrained both for time, place, persons, and other circumstances, to the sole pleasure of the king. The people cannot assemble themselves, but the king, by his writs, calls them to what place he pleases, and then again scatters them with his breath at an instant, without any other cause showed them than his will. Neither is the whole summoned, but only so many as the king's writs appoint. Nor have the whole people voices in the election of knights of the shire or burgesses, but only freeholders in the counties, and freemen in the cities and boroughs. Yet in the city of Westminster all the householders, though they be neither freemen nor freeholders, have voices in their election of burgesses.

Also, during the time of parliament those privileges of the House of Commons—of freedom of speech, power to punish their own members, to examine the proceedings and demeanour of courts of justice and officers, to have access to the king's person, and the like—are not due by any natural right, but are derived from the bounty or indulgence of the king, as appears by a solemn recognition of the House. For at the opening of the parliament, when the Speaker is presented to the king, he, in the behalf and name of the whole House of Commons, humbly craves of his majesty that he would be pleased to grant them their accustomed liberties of freedom of speech, of access to his person, and the rest. These privileges are granted with a condition implied that they keep themselves within the bounds and limits of loyalty and obedience, for else why do the House of Commons inflict punishment themselves upon their own members for transgressing in some of these points? And the king as head hath many times punished the members for the like offences. The power which the king giveth in all his courts to his judges or others to punish doth not exclude him from doing the like by way of prevention, concurrence, or evocation, even in the same point which he hath given in charge by a delegated power. For they who give authority by commission do always retain more than they grant. Neither of the two houses claim an infallibility of not erring, no more than a general council can. It is not impossible but that the greatest part may be in fault, or at least interested or engaged in the delinquency of one particular member. In such cases it is most proper for the head to correct, and not to expect the consent of the members, or for the parties peccant to be their own judges. Nor is it needful to confine the king in such cases within the circle of any one court of justice, who is supreme judge in all courts. And in rare and new cases rare and new remedies must be sought out, for it is a rule of the common law in '*novo casu, novum remedium est apponendum*' [in "a new case a new remedy must be applied"], and the statute of Westminster II, ch. 24, giveth power even to the clerks of the chancery to make new forms of writs in new cases, lest any man that came to the king's court of chancery for help should be sent away without remedy. A president cannot be found in every case, and of things that happen seldom and are not common there cannot be a common custom. Though crimes exorbitant do pose the king and council in finding a precedent for a condign punishment, yet they must not therefore pass unpunished.

I have not heard that the people by whose voices the knights and burgesses are chosen did ever call to an account those whom they had elected. They neither give them instructions or directions what to say or do in parliament, therefore they cannot punish them when they come home for doing amiss. If the people had any such power over their burgesses, then we might have some colour to call it the natural liberty of the people. But they are so far from punishing that they may be punished themselves for intermeddling with parliamentary business. They must only choose, and trust those whom they choose to do what they list, and that is as much liberty as many of us deserve for our irregular elections of burgesses.

(15) A fourth point to be considered is that in parliament all statutes or laws are made properly by the king alone at the rogation of the people, as his majesty King James, of happy memory, affirms in his *True Law of Free Monarchy*, and as Mr. Hooker teacheth us that 'Laws do not take their constraining force from the quality of such as devise them, but from the power that doth give them the strength of laws'.[106] '*Le roy le vault*: the king will have it so' is the interpretive phrase pronounced at the king's passing of every act of parliament. And it was the ancient custom for a long time, till the days of King Henry IV, that the kings, when any bill was brought unto them that had passed both houses, to take and pick out as much or as little thereof as they pleased and to leave out what they liked not, and so much as they chose was enacted for a law.[107] Which seems to prove that in ancient times the assent of the Commons was not always requisite, for though their assent may seem to ratify, yet it doth not follow that therefore their dissent must nullify an act of parliament. Those may have deliberative voices which have not always a negative.

Mr. Fuller, in his *Argument* against the proceedings of the High Commission court affirms that the statute of 2 Henry IV, ch. 15, which giveth power to ordinaries to imprison and set fines on subjects, was made without

---

106   Hooker, *Of the Laws*, x, 8.
107   The remainder of §15 is reproduced as per the Cambridge manuscript. Other manuscripts omit the final two sentences of the penultimate paragraph of §15 and place the final paragraph of that section at the end of §16.

the assent of the Commons because they are not mentioned in the act. If this argument be good we shall find very many ancient statutes of the same kind, for the assent of the Commons was seldom mentioned in the elder parliaments. The most usual title of parliaments in Edward III, Richard II, the three Henries IV, V, VI, in Edward IV, and Richard III's days was: 'The king in his parliament with the assent of the prelates, earls and barons, and at the petition, or at the special request or instance of the Commons, doth ordain'. The same Mr. Fuller saith that the statute made against Lollards was without the assent of the Commons, as appears by their petition in these words: 'The Commons beseech that whereas a statute was made in the last parliament etc., which was never assented to nor granted by the Commons, but that which was done therein was done without their assent'[108] (5 Richard II, ch. 5).

(16) The parliament is the king's court, for so all the oldest statutes call it, 'The king in his parliament'. But neither of the two houses are that supreme court, nor yet both of them together. They are only members and a part of the body, whereof the king is the head and ruler. The king's governing of this body of the parliament we may find most significantly proved, both by the statutes themselves, as also by such precedents as expressly show us how the king, sometimes by himself, sometimes by his council, and other times by his judges, hath overruled and directed the judgments of the Houses of parliament. For the king, we find that Magna Carta and the charter of forests and many other statutes about those times had only the form of the king's letters-patents, or grants under the great seal, testifying those great liberties to be the sole act and bounty of the king. The words of Magna Carta begin thus; Edward, by the grace of God, etc. To all our archbishops, etc., and to our faithful subjects, greeting. Know ye that we, of our *mere freewill* have granted to all freemen these liberties'.[109]

In the same style goeth the charter of forests and other statutes. *Statutum Hiberniae* ["the Statute of Ireland"], made at Westminster, February 9th, 14 Henry III, is but a letter of the king to Gerard son of Maurice, justiciar of Ireland. The statute *de anno bisextili* ["in the leap year"] begins thus: 'The king to his justices of the bench, greeting, etc'.[110] *Explanationes statuti Glocestriae* ["explanations of the statute of Gloucester"], made by the king and his justices only, were received always as statutes, and are still printed amongst them.

---

108   Nicholas Fuller, *The Argument of Master Nicholas Fuller, in the case of Thomas Lad, and Richard Maunsell his clients*, p. 8.
109   *Statutes*, p. 1.
110   *Statutes*, p. 25.

The statute made for correction of the twelfth chapter of the statute of Gloucester was signed under the great seal, and sent to the justices of the bench after the manner of a writ patent, with a certain writ closed, dated by the king's hand at Westminster, requiring that 'they should do and execute all and everything contained in it, although the same do not accord with the statute of Gloucester in all things'.[111]

The statute of Rutland is the king's letters to his treasurer and barons of his exchequer and to his chamberlain. The statute of *circumspecte agatis*[112] saith: 'The king to his judges sendeth greeting'.[113]

There are many other statutes of the same form, and some of them which run only in the majestic terms of 'The king commands', or 'The king wills', or 'Our Lord the king hath established', or 'our Lord the king hath ordained', or 'Of his special grace hath granted', without mention of consent of the Commons or people; insomuch that some statutes rather resemble proclamations than acts of parliament. And indeed some of them were no other than mere proclamations, as the provisions of Merton, made by the king at an assembly of the prelates and nobility for the coronation of the king and his queen Eleanor, which begins: '*Provisum est in curia domini regis apud Merton*'[114] ["it is provided in the court of the lord king at Merton"]. Also a provision was made, 19 Henry III, '*De assisa ultimae praesentationis*' ["concerning the assize of last presentation"] (20 Henry III), which 'was continued and allowed for law until Westminster II, *anno* 13 Edward I, ch. 5, which provides the contrary by express words'.[115] This provision begins: '*Provisum fuit coram domino rege, archiepiscopis, episcopis, et baronibus, quod*,'[116] ["it was provided in the presence of the lord king, the archbishops, bishops, and barons, that…"] etc. It seems originally the difference was not great between a proclamation and a statute. This latter the king made by common council of the kingdom. In the former he had but the advice only of his great council of the peers, or of his privy council only. For that the king had a great council besides his parliament appears by a record of 5 Henry IV about an exchange between the king and the Earl of Northumberland, whereby the king promiseth to deliver to the earl lands to the value, etc., by the advice of parliament, or otherwise by the advice of his grand council and other estates of the realm, which the king

---

111   *Statutes*, p. 26.
112   A statute passed 13 Edward I, intended to confine the jurisdiction of ecclesiastical courts to ecclesiastical cases, so named after its initial words.
113   *Statutes*, p. 43.
114   Egerton, *Speech*, p. 14.
115   Egerton, *Speech*, p. 15.
116   Egerton, *Speech*, p. 15.

will assemble in case the parliament do not meet.

We may find what judgment of later times parliaments have had of proclamations by the statute of 31 Henry VIII, ch. 8, in these words:

> Forasmuch as the king, by the advice of his council, hath
> set forth proclamations which obstinate persons have con-
> temned, not considering what a king by his royal power may
> do; considering that sudden causes and occasions fortune
> many times which do require speedy remedies, and that
> by abiding for a parliament in the meantime might happen
> great prejudice to ensue to the realm; and weighing also that
> his majesty, which by the kingly power and regal power giv-
> en him by God may do many things in such cases, should
> not be driven to extend the liberties and supremacy of his
> royal power and dignity by wilfulness of froward subjcts; it
> is therefore thought fit that the king with the advice of his
> honourable council should set forth proclamations for the
> good of the people and defence of his regal dignity, as neces-
> sity shall require.[117]

This opinion of a House of parliament was confirmed afterwards by a second parliament, and the statute made proclamations of as great validity
as if they had been made in parliament (34 Henry VIII, ch. 23). This law
continued until the government of the state came to be under a protector
during the minority of Edward VI, and in his first year it was repealed (1
Edward VI, ch. 12).

I find also that a parliament in the eleventh year of Henry VII did so great
reverence to the actions or ordinances of the king, that by statute they
provided a remedy or means to levy a benevolence granted to the king,
although by a statute made not long before, all benevolences were damned
and annulled for ever (I Richard III, ch. 2).[118]

But the custom of the later kings hath been so gracious as to allow always
of the entire bill as it hath passed both houses.

(17) How far the king's council hath directed and swayed in parliament
hath in part appeared by what hath been already produced. For further evidence we may add the statute of Westminster the first, which saith: 'These
be the acts of King Edward I, made at his first parliament general by his

---

117   *Statutes*, p. 640.
118   The final paragraph of §16 is reproduced as per the Cambridge manuscript.
Other manuscripts place this sentence at the end of the final paragraph of §15.

council, and by the assent of bishops, abbots, priors, earls, barons, and all the commonalty of the realm, etc.' The statute of bigamy saith: 'In the presence of certain reverend fathers, bishops of England, and others of the king's council, the constitutions underwritten were recited and after published before the king and his council. Forasmuch as all the king's council, as well justices as others, did agree that they should be put in writing and observed'[119] (4 Edward I).

The statute of Acton Burnell saith: 'The king, for himself and by his council, hath ordained and established'[120] (13 Edward I).

In *articuli super chartas*,[121] when the great charter was confirmed 'at the request of his prelates, earls and barons', we find these passages (28 Edward I): 1. 'Nevertheless the king and his council do not intend by reason of this statute to diminish the king's right,'[122] etc. (ch. 2). 2.' And notwithstanding all these things before mentioned or any part of them, both the king and his council and all they that were present at the making of this ordinance, will and intend that the right and prerogatives of his crown shall be saved to him in all things'[123] (ch. 20). Here we may see in the same parliament the charter of the liberties of the subjects confirmed, and a saving of the king's prerogative. Those times neither stumbled at the name, nor conceived any such antipathy between the terms as should make them incompatible.

The statute of escheators hath this title: 'At the parliament of our sovereign lord the king, by his council it was agreed, and also by the king himself commanded'[124] (29 Edward I).

And the ordinance of inquest goeth thus: 'It is agreed and ordained by the king and all his council'[125] (33 Edward I).

The statute made at York 9 Edward III saith:

> Whereas the knights, citizens, and burgesses desired our sovereign lord the king in his parliament by their petition, that for his profit and the commodity of his prelates, earls, barons, and commons, it may please him to provide remedy; our sovereign lord the king desiring the profit of his people by the assent of his prelates, earls, barons, and other nobles

119   *Statutes*, p. 23.
120   *Statutes*, p. 27.
121   "Articles upon the charters", a statute passed in 28 Edward I expanding upon many particulars in the Magna Carta and charter of forests.
122   *Statutes*, p. 50.
123   *Statutes*, p. 52.
124   *Statutes*, p. 52.
125   *Statutes*, p. 54.

of his realm, summoned at his parliament, and by the advice of his council being there, hath ordained (9 Edward III).[126]

In the parliament 2 Edward III, where Magna Carta was confirmed, I find this preamble: 'At the request of the commonalty by their petition made before the king and his council in parliament, by the assent of the prelates, earls, barons, and other great men assembled, it was granted'.[127]

The Commons presenting a petition unto the king which the king's council did mislike, were content thereupon to amend and explain their petition; the form of which petition is in these words:

> To their most redoubted sovereign lord the king, praying the said Commons, that whereas they have prayed him to be discharged of all manner of articles of the eyre, etc; which petition seemeth to his council to be prejudicial unto him, and in disinherison of his crown, if it were so generally granted; his said Commons, not willing nor desiring to demand things of him which should fall in disinherison of him or his crown perpetually, as of escheats, etc., but of trespasses, misprisions, negligences, and ignorances, etc. ...[128]
> (27 Edward III)

In the time of Henry III an order or provision was made by the king's council, and it was pleaded at the common law in bar to a writ of dower (4 Henry III). 'The plaintiff's attorney could not deny it and thereupon the judgment was *ideo sine die* ["for that reason (postponed) indefinitely"] (Fitzherbert *Dower* 179)'.[129] It seems in those days an order of the council board was either parcel of the common law or above it.

'The reverend judges have had regard in their proceedings that before they would resolve or give judgment in new cases they consulted with the king's privy council'.[130] In the case of Adam Brabson, who was assaulted by R.W. in the presence of the justices of assize at Winchester, the judges would have 'the advice of the king's council, for in a like case, because R.C. did strike a juror at Westminster, which passed in an inquest against one of his friends, it was adjudged by all the council that his right hand should

---

126 *Statutes*, p. 74.
127 *Statutes*, p. 67.
128 *Statutes*, p. 119–20.
129 Egerton, *Speech*, p. 13.
130 Egerton, *Speech*, p. 50.

be cut off and his lands and goods forfeited to the king.'[131]

'Green and Thorpe were sent by the judges of the bench to the king's council to demand of them whether by the statute of 14 Edward III, ch. 16, a word may be amended in a writ. And it was answered that a word may well be amended, although the statute speak but of a letter or syllable.'[132]

In the case of Sir Thomas Ughtred, knight, who

> brought a formedon against a poor man and his wife, they came and yielded to the demandant, which seemed suspicious to the court, whereupon judgment was stayed (39 Edward III). And Thorpe said that in the like case of Giles Blacket it was spoken of in parliament, and we were commanded that when any like case should come we should not go to judgment without good advice.[133]

Therefore the judges' conclusion was: '*Sues au counseil et comment ils voillet que nous devumus faire, nous volumus faire, et auterment nient en cest case*: Sue to the Council, and as they will have us to do, we will; and otherwise not in this case'.

(18) In the last place we may consider how much hath been attributed to the opinions of the king's judges by parliaments, and so find that the king's council hath guided and ruled the judges, and the judges guided the parliament.

> In the parliament of 28 Henry VI, the Commons made suit that William de la Pole, Duke of Suffolk, should be committed to prison for many treasons and other crimes. The lords of the higher house were doubtful what answer to give. The opinion of the judges was demanded. Their opinion was that he ought not to be committed, for that the Commons did not charge him with any particular offence, but with general reports and slanders. This opinion was allowed.[134]

In another parliament (which was prorogued) (31 Henry VI) in the vacation the Speaker of the House of Commons

> was condemned in a thousand pounds damages in an action

---

131   Egerton, *Speech*, p. 51.
132   Egerton, *Speech*, p. 52.
133   Egerton, *Speech*, p. 52.
134   Egerton, *Speech*, p. 19.

of trespass, and was committed to prison in execution for the same. When the parliament was reassembled the Commons made suit to the king and Lords to have their Speaker delivered. The Lords demanded the opinions of the judges whether he might be delivered out of prison by privilege of parliament.[135]

Upon the judges' answer it was concluded that the Speaker

should still remain in prison according to the law, notwithstanding the privilege of parliaments and that he was the Speaker. Which resolution was declared to the Commons by Moyle, the king's serjeant at law, and the Commons were commanded in the king's name by the bishop of Lincoln (in the absence of the archbishop of Canterbury, then chancellor) to choose another Speaker.[136]

In 7 Henry VIII

a question was moved in parliament, whether spiritual persons might be convented before temporal judges for criminal cases? There Sir John Fineux and the other judges delivered their opinion that they might and ought to be. And their opinion was allowed and maintained by the king and Lords. And Dr. Standish, who before had holden the same opinion, was delivered from the bishops.[137]

If a writ of error be sued in parliament upon a judgment given in the king's bench, the lords of the higher house alone (without the Commons) are to examine the errors. The Lords are to proceed according to law, and for their judgment therein they are to be informed by the advice and counsel of the judges, who are to inform them what the law is, and so to direct them in their judgment. For the lords are not to follow their own opinions or discretions otherwise. [138]

'So it was in a writ of error brought in parliament by the Dean and chapter of Lichfield against the Prior and convent of Newtonpanell, as appeareth

---

135   Egerton, *Speech*, p. 20.
136   Egerton, *Speech*, p. 21.
137   Egerton, *Speech*, p. 22.
138   Egerton, *Speech*, p. 22.

by the record (17 Richard II)'.[139] See Flower Dew's case, pg. 1. Henry VII, fol. 19.

139 Egerton, *Speech*, p. 23.

OBSERVATIONS UPON
Mr. HUNTON'S
Treatise of Monarchy:

OR, THE ANARCHY
Of a Limited or Mixed Monarchy.

These observations on the treatise of monarchy written by Mr. Hunton, being of like argument with the former, are here annexed with this advertisement, that the treatise itself consists of two parts: the first concerning monarchy in general, the latter concerning this particular monarchy, and is seconded with a vindication which alledgeth new matter about the nature, kinds, causes, and means of limitation in government, intimating a mistrust that the treatise had not fully or sufficiently discovered these points.

These observations reach only to the first part of the treatise concerning monarchy in general, whether it can possibly be limited or mixed. If this be not made good, it is but vain labour to trouble the reader with the dispute about the nature, kinds, and causes of that which is not nor cannot at all be, or to handle the hypothesis about this particular monarchy, for which the prime and chief arguments are of no greater antiquity than some concessions since these present troubles.

The ancient doctrine of government in these later days hath been strangely refined by the Romanists and wonderfully improved since the Reformation, especially in point of monarchy, by an opinion that the people have originally a power to create several sorts of monarchy and to limit and compound them at their pleasure. The consideration hereof caused me to scruple the modern piece of politics touching limited and mixed monarchy. And finding it only presented us by this author, I have drawn these few observations upon the most considerable part of his treatise, desiring to receive satisfaction from the author, or any other for him.

The novelty of this point challengeth a modest debate; the rather, for that the treatise acknowledgeth that not only monarchy, but also aristocracy and democracy may be either simple, or mixed of two or all three together, though it do not determine whether they can be absolute or limited.

THE PREFACE

We do but flatter ourselves, if we hope ever to be governed without an arbitrary power. No, we mistake. The question is not whether there shall be an arbitrary power, but the only point is who shall have that arbitrary power, whether one man or many? There never was, nor ever can be any people governed without a power of making laws, and every power of making laws must be arbitrary. For to make a law according to law is *contradictio in adjecto*.[1] It is generally confessed that in a democracy the supreme or arbitrary power of making laws is in a multitude, and so in an aristocracy the like legislative or arbitrary power is in a few, or in the nobility. And therefore by a necessary consequence, in a monarchy the same legislative power must be in one according to the rule of Aristotle, who saith 'government is in one, or in a few, or in many'.[2]

This ancient doctrine of government in these latter days hath been strangely refined by the Romanists, and wonderfully improved since the Reformation, especially in point of monarchy, by an opinion that the people have originally a power to create several sorts of monarchy, to limit and compound them with other forms of government at their pleasure.

As for this natural power of the people, they find neither scripture, reason, nor practice to justify it. For though several kingdoms have several and distinct laws one from another, yet that doth not make several sorts of monarchy, nor doth the difference of obtaining the supreme power—whether by conquest, election, succession, or by any other way—make different sorts of government. It is the difference only of the authors of the laws, and not of the laws themselves, that alters the form of government—that is, whether one man, or more than one, make the laws.

Since the growth of this new doctrine of the limitation and mixture of monarchy, it is most apparent that monarchy hath been crucified (as it were) between two thieves, the pope and the people. For what principles the papists make use of for the power of the pope above kings, the very same (by blotting out the word pope, and putting in the word people) the plebists take up to use against their sovereigns.

If we would truly know what popery is, we shall find by the laws and

---

1 "Contradiction in adjective". A logical inconsistency between a noun and its modifying adjective, distinct from a contradiction in terms.
2 Aristotle, *Politics*, 1279ᵃ 27–8.

statutes of the realm that the main, and indeed the only point of popery is the alienating and withdrawing of subjects from their obedience to their prince, to raise sedition and rebellion. If popery and popularity agree in this point, the kings of Christendom that have shaken off the power of the pope have made no great bargain of it, if in place of one lord abroad, they get many lords at home within their own kingdoms.

I cannot but reverence that form of government which was allowed and made use of for God's own people, and for all other nations. It were impiety to think that God, who was careful to appoint judicial laws for his chosen people, would not furnish them with the best form of government, or to imagine that the rules given in divers places in the gospel by our blessed Saviour and his apostles for obedience to kings should now, like almanacs out of date, be of no use to us, because it is pretended we have a form of government now not once thought of in those days. It is a shame and scandal for us Christians to seek the original of government from the inventions or fictions of poets, orators, philosophers, and heathen historians, who all lived thousands of years after the creation, and were (in a manner) ignorant of it; and to neglect the Scriptures, which have with more authority most particularly given us the true grounds and principles of government.

These considerations caused me to scruple this modern piece of politics touching limited and mixed monarchy, and finding no other that presented us with the nature and means of limitation and mixture but an anonymous author, I have drawn a few brief observations upon the most considerable part of his *Treatise*, in which I desire to receive satisfaction from the author himself, if it may be, according to his promise in his preface; or if not from him, from any other for him.

THE ANARCHY Of a Limited or Mixed MONARCHY.

There is scarce the meanest man of the multitude but can now in these days tell us that the government of the kingdom of England is a limited and mixed monarchy, and it is no marvel, since all the disputes and arguments of these distracted times both from the pulpit and press do tend and end in this conclusion.

The author[3] of the *Treatise of Monarchy* hath copiously handled the nature and manner of limited and mixed monarchy and is the first and only man (that I know) hath undertaken the task of describing it. Others only mention it, as taking it for granted.

3   Philip Hunton.

Doctor Ferne gives the author of this *Treatise of Monarchy* this testimony, that 'the mixture of government is more accurately delivered and urged by this treatise' than by the author[4] of the *Fuller Answer* (p. 3). And in another place Doctor Ferne saith he allows his 'distinction of monarchy into limited and mixed'.[5] (p. 13).

I have with some diligence looked over this *Treatise*, but cannot approve of these distinctions which he propounds. I submit the reasons of my dislike to others' judgments. I am somewhat confident that his doctrine of limited and mixed monarchy is an opinion but of yesterday, and of no antiquity, a mere innovation in policy, not so old as New England, though calculated properly for that meridian. For in his first part of the treatise which concerns monarchy in general, there is not one proof, text, or example in Scripture that he hath produced to justify his conceit of limited and mixed monarchy. Neither doth he afford us so much as one passage or reason out of Aristotle, whose books of *Politics* and whose natural reasons are of greatest authority and credit with all rational men, next to the sacred Scripture. Nay, I hope I may affirm and be able to prove that Aristotle doth confute both limited and mixed monarchy, howsoever Doctor Ferne think these new opinions to be raised upon Aristotle's principles (p. 6). As for other politicians or historians either divine or human, ancient or modern, our author brings not one to confirm his opinions. Nor doth he, nor can he, show that ever any nation or people were governed by a limited or mixed monarchy.

Machiavelli is the first in Christendom that I can find that wrote of a mixed government, but not one syllable of a mixed monarchy. He, in his discourses or disputations upon the decades of Livy, falls so enamoured with the Roman commonwealth that he thought he could never sufficiently grace that popular government unless he said there was something of monarchy in it. Yet he was never so impudent as to say it was a mixed monarchy. And what Machiavelli hath said for Rome, the like hath Contareni for Venice. But Bodin hath laid open the errors of both these, as also of Polybius and some few others that held the like opinions. As for the kingdom of England, if it hath found out a form of government (as the *Treatise* layeth it down) of such perfection as never any other people could, it is both a glory to the nation and also to this author who hath first deciphered it.

I now make my approach to the book itself. The title is *A Treatise of Mon-*

---

4 Charles Herle.
5 Henry Ferne, *A Reply unto Severall Treatises pleading for the Armes now taken up by Subjects*.

archy. The first part of it is of 'Monarchy in general', where first I charge the author that he hath not given us any definition or description of monarchy in general. For by the rules of method he should have first defined, and then divided. For if there be several sorts of monarchy then in something they must agree, which makes them to be monarchies; and in something they must disagree and differ, which makes them to be several sorts of monarchies. In the first place he should have showed us in what they all agreed, which must have been a definition of monarchy in general, which is the foundation of the treatise—and except that be agreed upon, we shall argue upon we know not what. I press not this main omission of our author out of any humour of wrangling, but because I am confident that had he pitched upon any definition of monarchy in general, his own definition would have confuted his whole treatise. Besides, I find him pleased to give us a handsome definition of absolute monarchy, from whence I may infer that he knew no other definition that would have fitted all his other sorts of monarchy; it concerned him to have produced it, lest it might be thought there could be no monarchy but absolute.

What our author hath omitted I shall attempt to supply, and leave to the scanning. And it shall be a real as well as nominal definition of monarchy. A monarchy is the government of one alone. For the better credit of this definition, though it be able to maintain itself, yet I shall deduce it from the principles of our author of the *Treatise of Monarchy*.

We all know that this word monarch is compounded of two Greek words, μόνος and ἀρχεῖν. Ἀρχεῖν is *imperare*, to govern and rule; μόνος signifies one alone. The understanding of these two words may be picked out of our author. First, for government he teacheth us it is '*potestatis exercitium*, the exercise of a moral power'[6] (p. 1); next he grants us that every monarch (even his limited monarch) must 'have the supreme power of the state in him, so that his power must no way be limited by any power above his; for then he were not a monarch, but a subordinate magistrate' (p. 12). Here we have a fair confession of a supreme unlimited power in his limited monarch. If you will know what he means by these words 'supreme power', turn to his 26th page, there you will find 'Supreme power' is 'either legislative, or gubernative' and that the 'legislative power is the chief of the two'.[7] He makes both supreme, and yet one chief. The like distinction he hath before, where he saith the power of magistracy 'in respect of its degrees, is *nomothetical* or *architectonical*; and *gubernative* or *executive*'. (p.

---

6   Philip Hunton, *A Treatise of Monarchie*. Any page numbers in this chapter not otherwise footnoted refer to Hunton's *Treatise*.
7   Hunton, *Treatise*, p. 26.

5) By these words of legislative, nomothetical, and architectonical power, in plain English, he understands a power of making laws. And by gubernative and executive, a power of putting those laws in execution by judging and punishing offenders.

The result we have from hence is that by the author's acknowledgment every monarch must have the supreme power, and that supreme power is a power to make laws. And howsoever the author makes the gubernative and executive power a part of the supreme power, yet he confesseth the legislative to be chief, or the highest degree of power, for he doth acknowledge degrees of supreme power. Nay, he afterwards teacheth us that 'the legislative power is the height of power, to which the other parts are subsequent and subservient' (p. 40). If gubernative be subservient to legislative, how can gubernative power be supreme?

Now let us examine the author's limited monarch by these his own rules. He tells us that in a moderated, limited, stinted, conditionate, legal or allayed monarchy (for all these terms he hath for it) the 'supreme power must be restrained by some law according to which this power was given and by direction of which this power must act' (p. 12); when in a line before he said that 'the monarch's power must not be limited by any power above his'. Yet here he will have his supreme power restrained—not limited, and yet restrained. Is not a restraint a limitation? And if restrained, how is it supreme? And if restrained by some law, is not the power of that law, and of them that made that law, above his supreme power? And if by the direction of such law only he must govern, where is the legislative power, which is the chief of supreme power? When the law must rule and govern the monarch, and not the monarch the law, he hath at the most but a gubernative or executive power. If his authority 'transcends its bounds if it command beyond the law, the subject is not bound legally to subjection in such cases' (p. 14), and if 'the utmost extent of the law of the land'[8] be the measure of the limited monarch's power, and subject's duty (p. 16), where shall we find the supreme power, that *culmen* or *apex potestatis* ["acme" or "summit of power"], that prime ἀρχὺ, which our author saith must be in every monarch? The word ἀρχὺ, which signifies principality and power, doth also signify *principium*, beginning—which doth teach us that by the word prince or principality the *principium* or beginning of government is meant. This, if it be given to the law, it robs the monarch, and makes the law the *primum mobile*[9]—and so that which is but the instrument or servant to the monarch becomes the master. Thus much of the word ἀρχεῖν.

---

8   Hunton, *Treatise*.
9   Literally "first moved", but more generally "prime mover".

The other word is μόνος, *solus*, one alone: the monarch must not only have the supreme power unlimited, but he must have it alone—without any companions. Our author teacheth us he is 'no monarch, if the supreme power be not in one'.[10] And again he saith, if 'you put the *apex potestatis*', or supreme power 'in the whole body, or a part of it', you 'destroy the being of monarchy' (p. 17).

Now let us see if his mixed monarchy be framed according to these his own principles. First, he saith, in a mixed monarchy 'the sovereign power must be originally in all three' estates (p. 25). And again his words are, 'the three estates are all sharers in the supreme power; the primity[11] of share in the supreme power is in one' (p. 25). Here we find that he that told us the supreme power must be in one will now allow his mixed monarch but one share only of the supreme power, and gives other shares to the estates. Thus he destroys the being of monarchy, by putting the supreme power, or *culmen potestatis*, or a part of it, in the whole body or a part thereof. And yet formerly he confesseth that 'the power of magistracy cannot well be divided, for it is one simple thing or indivisible beam of divine perfection' (p. 5). But he can make this indivisible beam to be divisible into three shares. I have done with the word μόνος, *solus*, alone.

I have dwelt the longer upon this definition of monarchy because the apprehending of it out of the author's own grounds quite overthrows both his monarch limited by law and his monarch mixed with the states. For to govern is to give a law to others, and not to have a law given to govern and limit him that governs. And to govern alone is not to have sharers or companions mixed with the governor. Thus the two words of which monarchy is compounded contradict the two sorts of monarchy which he pleads for, and by consequence his whole treatise. For these two sorts of limited and mixed monarchy take up (in a manner) his whole book.

I will now touch some few particular passages in the *Treatise*.

Our author first confesseth, 'It is God's express ordinance there should be government' (p. 2), and he proves it by Genesis 3:16, where God ordained Adam to rule over his wife, and her desires were to be subject to his; and as hers, so all theirs that should come of her. Here we have the original grant of government and the fountain of all power placed in the father of all mankind. Accordingly we find the law for obedience to government given in the terms of 'honour thy father'. Not only the constitution of power in general, but the limitation of it to one kind (that is, to monarchy,

---

10   Hunton, *Treatise*.
11   *Webster's Revised Unabridged Dictionary* defines as "Quality of being first; primitiveness."

or the government of one alone) and the determination of it to the individual person and line of Adam, are all three ordinances of God. Neither Eve nor her children could either limit Adam's power or join others with him in the government. And what was given unto Adam was given in his person to his posterity. This paternal power continued monarchical to the Flood, and after the Flood to the confusion of Babel. When kingdoms were first erected, planted, or scattered over the face of the world, we find Genesis 10:11, it was done by colonies of whole families, over which the prime fathers had supreme power and were kings, who were all the sons or grandchildren of Noah, from whom they derived a fatherly and regal power over their families. Now if this supreme power was settled and founded by God himself in the fatherhood, how is it possible for the people to have any right or title to alter and dispose of it otherwise? What commission can they show that gives them power either of limitation or mixture? It was God's ordinance that supremacy should be unlimited in Adam, and as large as all the acts of his will; and as in him, so in all others that have supreme power, as appears by the judgment and speech of the people to Joshua when he was supreme governor. These are their words to him: 'All that thou commandest us we will do; whosoever he be that doth rebel against thy commandment and will not hearken unto thy words in all that thou commandest him, he shall be put to death'.[12] We may not say that these were evil councillors or flattering courtiers of Joshua, or that he himself was a tyrant for having such arbitrary power. Our author, and all those who affirm that power is conveyed to persons by public consent, are forced to confess that it is the fatherly power that first enables a people to make such conveyance. So that admitting (as they hold) that our ancestors did at first convey power, yet the reason why we now living do submit to such power is for that our forefathers everyone for himself, his family, and posterity, had a power of resigning up themselves and us to a supreme power. As the Scripture teacheth us that supreme power was originally in the fatherhood without any limitation, so likewise reason doth evince it, that if God ordained that supremacy should be, that then supremacy must of necessity be unlimited. For the power that limits must be above that power which is limited. If it be limited it cannot be supreme. So that if our author will grant supreme power to be the ordinance of God, the supreme power will prove itself to be unlimited by the same ordinance— because a supreme limited power is a contradiction.

The monarchical power of Adam, the father of all flesh, being by a general binding ordinance settled by God in him and his posterity by right of

---

12   Joshua 1:16–18.

fatherhood, the form of monarchy must be preferred above other forms, except the like ordinance for other forms can be showed. Neither may men according to their relations to the form they live under, to their affections and judgments in divers respects, prefer or compare any other form with monarchy. The point that most perplexeth our author and many others is that if monarchy be allowed to be the ordinance of God, an absurdity would follow, that we should uncharitably condemn all the communities which have not that form for violation of God's ordinance, and pronounce those other powers unlawful. If those who live under a monarchy can justify the form they live under to be God's ordinance, they are not bound to forbear their own justification because others cannot do the like for the form they live under. Let others look to the defence of their own government. If it cannot be proved or showed that any other form of government had ever any lawful beginning, but was brought in or erected by rebellion, must therefore the lawful and just obedience to monarchy be denied to be the ordinance of God?

To proceed with our author, in the third page he saith 'The higher power is God's ordinance: that it resideth in one or more; in such or such a way is from human designment': God by 'no word' binds any people to this or that form till they by their own act bind themselves. Because the power and consent of the people in government is the burden of the whole book, and our author expects it should be admitted as a magisterial postulation without any other proof than a naked supposition; and since others also maintain that originally power was or now is in the people, and that the first kings were chosen by the people, they may not be offended if they be asked in what sense they understand the word 'people', because this—as many other words—hath different acceptions,[13] being sometimes taken in a larger, other whiles in a stricter sense. Literally, and in the largest sense, the word people signifies the whole multitude of mankind. But figuratively and synecdochically[14] it notes many times the major part of a multitude, or sometimes the better, or the richer, or the wiser, or some other part. And oftentimes a very small part of the people, if there be no other apparent opposite party, hath the name of the people by presumption.

If they understand that the entire multitude or whole people have originally by nature power to choose a king, they must remember that by their own principles and rules, by nature all mankind in the world makes but one people, who they suppose to be born alike to an equal freedom from subjection—and where such freedom is, there all things must of necessity

---

13   "Acceptations".
14   In which a part is used for the whole, in the manner of a synechdoche.

be common. And therefore without a joint consent of the whole people of the world, no one thing can be made proper to any one man, but it will be an injury and an usurpation upon the common right of all others. From whence it follows that natural freedom being once granted, there cannot be any one man chosen a king without the universal consent of all the people of the world at one instant, *nemine contradicente*.[15] Nay, if it be true that nature hath made all men free, though all mankind should concur in one vote, yet it cannot seem reasonable that they should have power to alter the law of nature. For if no man have power to take away his own life without the guilt of being a murderer of himself, how can any people confer such a power as they have not themselves upon any one man, without being accessories to their own deaths, and every particular man become guilty of being *felo de se* ["his own killer"]?

If this general signification of the word people be disavowed and men will suppose that the people of particular regions or countries have power and freedom to choose unto themselves kings, then let them but observe the consequence. Since nature hath not distinguished the habitable world into kingdoms, nor determined what part of a people shall belong to one kingdom and what to another, it follows that the original freedom of mankind being supposed, every man is at liberty to be of what kingdom he please. And so every petty company hath a right to make a kingdom by itself; and not only every city, but every village, and every family, nay and every particular man, a liberty to choose himself to be his own king if he please. And he were a madman that being by nature free, would choose any man but himself to be his own governor. Thus to avoid the having but of one king of the whole world, we shall run into a liberty of having as many kings as there be men in the world, which upon the matter, is to have no king at all, but to leave all men to their natural liberty—which is the mischief the pleaders for natural liberty do pretend they would most avoid.

But if neither the whole people of the world nor the whole people of any part of the world be meant, but only the major part, or some other part of a part of the world, yet still the objection will be the stronger. For besides that nature hath made no partition of the world or of the people into distinct kingdoms, and that without an universal consent at one and the same instant no partition can be made, yet if it were lawful for particular parts of the world by consent to choose their kings, nevertheless their elections would bind none to subjection but only such as consented. For the major part never binds but where men at first either agree to be so bound, or where a higher power so commands. Now, there being no higher power than nature but God himself, where neither nature nor God appoints the major part to bind, their consent is not binding to any but only to themselves who consent.

Yet, for the present to gratify them so far as to admit that either by nature or by a general consent of all mankind the world at first was divided into particular kingdoms, and the major part of the people of each kingdom assembled, allowed to choose their king: yet it cannot truly be said that ever the whole people, or the major part, or indeed any considerable part of the whole people of any nation ever assembled to any such purpose. For except by some secret miraculous instinct they should all meet at one time and place, what one man or company of men less than the whole people hath power to appoint either time or place of elections, where all be alike free by nature? And without a lawful summons it is most unjust to bind those that be absent. The whole people cannot summon itself; one man is sick, another is lame, a third is aged, and a fourth is under age of discretion. All these at some time or other, or at some place or other, might be able to meet if they might choose their own time and place, as men naturally free should.

In assemblies that are by human politic constitution, the superior power that ordains such assemblies can regulate and confine them, both for time, place, persons, and other circumstances. But where there is an equality by nature, there can be no superior power. There every infant at the hour it is born in hath a like interest with the greatest and wisest man in the world. Mankind is like the sea, ever ebbing or flowing, every minute one is born, another dies; those that are the people this minute are not the people the next minute. In every instant and point of time there is a variation. No one time can be indifferent for all mankind to assemble. It cannot but be mischievous always at the least to all infants and others under age of discretion—not to speak of women, especially virgins, who by birth have as much natural freedom as any other and therefore ought not to lose their liberty without their own consent.

But in part to salve this, it will be said that infants and children may be concluded by the votes of their parents. This remedy may cure some part of the mischief, but it destroys the whole cause and at last stumbles upon the true original of government. For if it be allowed that the acts of parents bind the children, then farewell the doctrine of the natural freedom of mankind. Where subjection of children to parents is natural, there can be no natural freedom. If any reply that not all children shall be bound by their parents' consent but only those that are under age, it must be considered that in nature there is no nonage. If a man be not born free, she doth not assign him any other time when he shall attain his freedom, or if she did, then children attaining that age should be discharged of their parents' contract. So that in conclusion, if it be imagined that the people were ever but once free from subjection by nature, it will prove a mere impossibility ever lawfully to introduce any kind of government whatsoever without apparent wrong to a multitude of people.

It is further observable that ordinarily children and servants are far a greater number than parents and masters, and for the major part of these to be able to vote and appoint what government or governors their fathers and masters shall be subject unto is most unnatural, and in effect to give the children the government over their parents.

To all this it may be opposed: what need dispute how a people can choose a king since there be multitude of examples that kings have been, and are nowadays chosen by their people? The answer is:

1. The question is not of the fact, but of the right—whether it have been done by a natural or by an usurped right.

2. Many kings are and have been chosen by some small part of a people. But by the whole or major part of a kingdom not any at all. Most have been elected by the nobility, great men, and princes of the blood, as in Poland, Denmark, and in Sweden—not by any collective or representative body of any nation. Sometimes a factious or seditious city, or a mutinous army hath set up a king, but none of all those could ever prove they had right or just title either by nature or any otherwise for such elections. We may resolve upon these two propositions:

1. That the people have no power or right of themselves to choose kings.

2. If they had any such right, it is not possible for them any way lawfully to exercise it.

You will say 'there must necessarily be a right in somebody to elect, in case a king die without an heir'. I answer, no king can die without an heir as long as there is any one man living in the world. It may be the heir may be unknown to the people, but that is no fault in nature, but the negligence or ignorance of those whom it concerns. But if a king could die without an heir, yet the kingly power in that case shall not escheat to the whole people, but to the supreme heads and fathers of families. Not as they are the people, but *quatenus* ["to the extent that"] they are fathers of people, over whom they have a supreme power devolved unto them after the death of their sovereign ancestor. And if any can have a right to choose a king, it must be these fathers, by conferring their distinct fatherly powers upon one man alone. Chief fathers in Scripture are accounted as all the people, as 'all the children of Israel', as 'all the congregation', as the text plainly expounds itself (2 Chronicles 1:2) where Solomon speaks to 'all Israel', that is, 'to the captains, the judges, and to every governor, the chief of the fathers', and so the elders of Israel are expounded to be the chief of the fathers of the children of Israel, 1 Kings 8:1, and the 2 Chronicles 5:2.

If it be objected that kings are not now (as they were at the first planting or peopling of the world) the fathers of their people or kingdoms and that the fatherhood hath lost the right of governing, an answer is that all kings that now are or ever were, are, or were either fathers of their people, or the heirs of such fathers, or usurpers of the right of such fathers. It is a truth undeniable that there cannot be any multitude of men whatsoever, either great or small, though gathered together from the several corners and remotest regions of the world, but that in the same multitude considered by itself, there is one man amongst them that in nature hath a right to be the king of all the rest, as being the next heir to Adam, and all the other subject unto him. Every man by nature is a king, or a subject. The obedience which all subjects yield to kings is but the paying of that duty which is due to the supreme fatherhood. Many times by the act either of an usurper himself or of those that set him up, the true heir of a crown is dispossessed, God using the ministry of the wickedest men for the removing and setting up of kings. In such cases the subjects' obedience to the fatherly power must go along and wait upon God's providence, who only hath right to give and take away kingdoms, and thereby to adopt subjects into the obedience of another fatherly power, according to that of Aristotle ʽπατρικὴ γὰρ ἀρχὴ βούλεται ἡ βασιλεία εἶναι: A monarchy or kingdom will be a fatherly government'.[16] (Ethics book 8, ch. 12).

However the natural freedom of the people be cried us as the sole means to determine the kind of government and the governors, yet in the close, all the favourers of this opinion are constrained to grant that the obedience which is due to the fatherly power is the true and only cause of the subjection which we that are now living give to kings—since none of us gave consent to government, but only our forefathers' act and consent hath concluded us.

Whereas many confess that government only in the *abstract* is the ordinance of God, they are not able to prove any such ordinance in the Scripture, but only in the fatherly power; and therefore we find the commandment that enjoins obedience to superiors given in the terms of 'honour thy father'. So that not only the power or right of government, but the form of the power of governing, and the person having that power, are all the ordinance of God. The first father had not only simply power, but power monarchical, as he was a father, immediately from God. For by the

16   Aristotle, *Nicomachean Ethics*, 1160ᵇ 26–7.

appointment of God, as soon as Adam was created he was monarch of the world, though he had no subjects. For though there could not be actual government until there were subjects, yet by the right of nature it was due to Adam to be governor of his posterity. Though not in *act*, yet at least in *habit* Adam was a king from his creation, and in the state of innocency he had been governor of his children. For the integrity or excellency of the subjects doth not take away the order or eminency of the governor. Eve was subject to Adam before he sinned; the angels, who are of a pure nature, are subject to God—which confutes their saying who, in disgrace of civil government or power, say it was brought in by sin. Government as to *coactive* power was after sin, because coaction supposeth some disorder, which was not in the state of innocency: but as for *directive* power, the condition of human nature requires it, since civil society cannot be imagined without power of government. For although as long as men continued in the state of innocency they might not need the direction of Adam in those things which were necessarily and morally to be done, yet things indifferent[17]—that depended merely on their free will—might be directed by the power of Adam's command.

If we consider the first plantations of the world (which were after the building of Babel when the confusion of tongues was), we may find the division of the earth into distinct kingdoms and countries by several families, whereof the sons or grandchildren of Noah were the kings or governors by a fatherly right. And for the preservation of this power and right in the fathers, God was pleased upon several families to bestow a language on each by itself, the better to unite it into a nation or kingdom. As appears by the words of the text, Genesis 10, 'These are the families of the sons of Noah, after their generations in their nations, and by these were the nations divided in the earth after the Flood, everyone after his tongue, after their families in their nations'.[18]

The kings of England have been graciously pleased to admit and accept the Commons in parliament as the representees of the kingdom, yet really and truly they are not the representative body of the whole kingdom.

The Commons in parliament are not the representative body of the whole kingdom. They do not represent the king, who is the head and principal member of the kingdom. Nor do they represent the lords, who are the nobler and higher part of the body of the realm, and are personally present in parliament, and therefore need no representation. The Commons only represent a part of the lower or inferior part of the body of the

---

17   i.e. not concerning God's command.
18   Genesis 10:31–2.

people, which are the freeholders worth forty shillings by the year, and the commons or freemen of cities and boroughs, or the major part of them. All which are not one quarter, nay, not a tenth part of the commons of the kingdom. For in every parish, for one freeholder there may be found ten that are no freeholders, and anciently—before rents were improved—there were nothing near so many free-holders of forty shillings by the year as now are to be found.

The scope and conclusion of this discourse and argument is that the people taken in what notion or sense soever—either diffusively, collectively, or representatively—have not, nor cannot exercise any right or power of their own by nature, either in choosing or in regulating kings. But whatsoever power any people doth lawfully exercise, it must receive it from a supreme power on earth, and practise it with such limitations as that superior power shall appoint. To return to our author.

He divides Monarchy into $\begin{cases} \text{absolute,} \\ \\ \text{limited.} \end{cases}$

'Absolute monarchy', saith he, 'is when the sovereignty is so fully in one, that it hath no limits or bounds under God but his own will' (p. 6). This definition of his I embrace. And as before I charged our author for not giving us a definition of monarchy in general, so I now note him for not affording us any definition of any other particular kind of monarchy but only of absolute. It may peradventure make some doubt that there is no other sort but only that which he calls absolute.

Concerning absolute monarchy, he grants that 'such were the ancient eastern monarchies, and that of the Turk and Persian at this day'. Herein he saith very true. And we must remember him, though he do not mention them, that the monarchs of Judah and Israel must be comprehended under the number of those he calls the eastern monarchies. And truly, if he had said that all the ancient monarchies of the world had been absolute, I should not have quarrelled at him, nor do I know who could have disproved him.

Next it follows that absolute monarchy is 'when a people are absolutely resigned or resign up themselves to be governed by the will of one man ... Where men put themselves into this utmost degree of subjection by oath and contract, or are born and brought unto it by God's providence' (p. 6). In both these places he acknowledgeth there may be other means of obtaining a monarchy besides the contract of a nation or people's resigning up themselves to be governed—which is contrary to what he after says, that 'the sole mean or root of all sovereignty is the consent and fundamental contract of a nation of men' (p. 12).

Moreover, the author determines that 'absolute monarchy is a lawful government' and that men may be 'borne and brought unto it by God's providence, it binds them and they must abide it, because an oath to a lawful thing is obligatory'.[19] This position of his I approve, but his reason doth not satisfy. For men are bound to obey a lawful governor though neither they nor their ancestors ever took oath.

Then he proceeds, and confesseth that in Romans 13 'the power which then was, was absolute. Yet the apostle not excluding it, calls it *God's ordinance*, and commands subjection to it. So Christ commands tribute to be paid, and pays it himself. Yet it was an arbitrary tax, the production of an absolute power' (p. 7). These are the loyal expressions of our author touching absolute or arbitrary monarchy. I do the rather mention these passages of our author because very many in these days do not stick to maintain that an arbitrary or absolute monarch not limited by law is all one with a tyrant; and to be governed by one man's will is to be made a slave. It is a question whether our author be not of that mind when he saith, 'absolute subjection' is 'servitude'.[20] And thereupon a late friend to limited monarchy affirms in *A Discourse upon the Questions in Debate Between the King and Parliament*,[21] 'That to make a king by the standard of God's word, is to make the subjects slaves for conscience sake'[22] (p. 54)—a hard saying, and I doubt whether he that gives this censure can be excused from blasphemy. It is a bold speech to condemn all the kings of Judah for tyrants, or to say all their subjects were slaves. But certainly the man doth not know either what a tyrant is, or what a slave is. Indeed the words are frequent enough in every man's mouth, and our old English translation of the Bible useth sometimes the word tyrant. But the authors of our new translation have been so careful as not once to use the word, but only for the proper name of a man—Acts 19:9—because they find no Hebrew word in the Scripture to signify a tyrant or a slave. Neither Aristotle, Bodin, nor Sir Walter Raleigh (who were all men of deep judgment) can agree in a definition or description of tyranny, though they have all three laboured in the point. And I make some question whether any man can possibly describe what a tyrant is, and then tell me any one man that ever was in the world that was a tyrant according to that description.

19 Hunton, *Treatise*.
20 Hunton, *Treatise*.
21 London, 1642.
22 *A Discourse upon the Questions in debate between the King and Parliament*, p. 3.

I return again to our *Treatise of Monarchy*, where I find 'three degrees' of absolute monarchy:

1. Where 'the monarch, whose will is the law, doth set himself no law to rule by, but by commands of his own judgment as he thinks fit.'[23]

2. 'When he sets a law by which he will ordinarily govern, reserving to himself a liberty to vary from it as oft as in his discretion he thinks fit; and in this the sovereign is as free as the former.'[24]

3. Where 'he not only sets a rule but promiseth in many cases not to alter it. But this promise or engagement is an after-condescent or act of grace, not dissolving the absolute oath of subjection which went before it.'[25]

For the first of these three there is no question but it is a pure absolute monarchy. But as for the other two, though he say they be absolute, yet in regard they set themselves limits or laws to govern by, if it please our author to term them limited monarchs, I will not oppose him. Yet I must tell him that his third degree of absolute monarchy is such a kind as I believe never hath been nor ever can be in the world. For a monarch to promise and engage in many cases not to alter a law, it is most necessary that those many cases should be particularly expressed at the bargain-making. Now he that understands the nature and condition of all human laws knows that particular cases are infinite and not comprehensible within any rules or laws. And if many cases should be comprehended, and many omitted, yet even those that were comprehended would admit of variety of interpretations and disputations. Therefore our author doth not, nor can tell us of any such reserved cases promised by any monarch.

Again, where he saith 'an after condescent or act of grace' doth not dissolve 'the absolute oath of subjection which went before it', though in this he speak true, yet still he seems to insinuate that an oath only binds to subjection—which oath, as he would have us believe, was at first arbitrary. Whereas subjects are bound to obey monarchs though they never take oath of subjection, as well as children are bound to obey their parents though they never swear to do it.

Next, his distinction between the 'rule of power' and the 'exercise of it' (p. 7), is vain. For to rule is to exercise power—for himself saith 'that government is *potestatis exercitium*, the exercise of a moral power' (p. 1).

Lastly, whereas our author saith a monarch 'cannot break' his promise 'without sin',[26] let me add that if the safety of the people—*salus populi*—

---

23   Hunton, *Treatise*, p. 7.
24   Hunton, *Treatise*, p. 7.
25   Hunton, *Treatise*, p. 7.
26   Hunton, *Treatise*, p. 7.

require a breach of the monarch's promise, then the sin, if there be any, is rather in the making than breaking of the promise. The safety of the people is an exception implied in every monarchical promise.

But it seems these three degrees of monarchy do not satisfy our author. He is not content to have a monarch have a law or rule to govern by, but he must have this limitation or law to be '*ab externo*', from somebody else, and not from 'the determination' of the monarch's 'own will' (p. 12). And therefore he saith 'by original constitution the society public confers on one man a power by limited contract, resigning themselves to be governed by such a law' (p. 13). Also, before, he told us 'the sole means' of sovereignty is 'the consent and fundamental contract, which consent puts them in their power—which can be no more nor other than is conveyed to them by such contract of subjection'.[27] If the sole means of a limited monarchy be the consent and fundamental contract of a nation, how is it that he saith a monarch may be limited 'by after condescent'?[28] Is an after condescent all one with a fundamental contract, with original and radical constitution? Why yea: he tells us 'it is a secondary original constitution'.[29] A secondary original, that is, a second first. And if that condescent be an act of grace, doth not this condescent to a limitation come from the free determination of the monarch's will if he either 'formally or virtually' (as our author supposeth) desert his absolute or arbitrary power which he hath 'by conquest, or other right'?[30]

And if it be from the free will of the monarch, why doth he say the limitation must be *ab externo*? He told us before that subjection cannot be 'dissolved or lessened by an act of grace coming afterwards' (p. 8). But he hath better bethought himself, and now he will have acts of grace to be of two kinds, and the latter kind may 'amount', as he saith, 'to a resignation' of absolute monarchy. But can any man believe that a monarch who by conquest or other right hath an absolute arbitrary power, will voluntarily resign that absoluteness and accept so much power only as the people shall please to give him, and such laws to govern by as they shall make choice of? Can he show that ever any monarch was so gracious or kind-hearted as to lay down his lawful power freely at his subjects' feet? Is it not sufficient grace if such an absolute monarch be content to set down a law to himself by which he will ordinarily govern, but he must needs relinquish his old independent commission and take a new one from his subjects, clogged

27   Hunton, *Treatise*.
28   Hunton, *Treatise*.
29   Hunton, *Treatise*.
30   Hunton, *Treatise*, p. 13.

with limitations?

Finally, I observe that howsoever our author speak big of the radical, fundamental, and original power of the people as the root of all sovereignty, yet in a better mood he will take up and be contented with a monarchy limited by an after condescent and act of grace from the monarch himself.

Thus I have briefly touched his grounds of limited monarchy. If now we shall ask what proof or examples he hath to justify his doctrine, he is as mute as a fish: only Pythagoras hath said it, and we must believe him. For though our author would have monarchy to be limited, yet he could be content his opinion should be absolute, and not limited to any rule or example.

The main charge I have against our author now remains to be discussed, and it is this—that instead of a treatise of *monarchy*, he hath brought forth a treatise of *anarchy*. And that by his own confessions shall be made good.

First, he holds a limited monarch 'transcends his bounds if he commands beyond the law, and the subject legally is not bound to subjection in such cases.'[31]

Now if you ask the author who shall be judge whether the monarch transcend his bounds, and of the excesses of the sovereign power; his answer is: 'there is an impossibility of constituting a judge to determine this last controversy (p. 16) ... I conceive in a limited legal monarchy there can be no stated internal judge of the monarch's actions, if there grow a fundamental variance between him and the community ... There can be no judge legal and constituted within that form of government' (p. 17). In these answers it appears there is no judge to determine the sovereign's or the monarch's transgressing his fundamental limits. Yet our author is very cautelous[32] and supposeth only a fundamental variance betwixt the monarch and the community. He is ashamed to put the question home. I demand of him if there be a variance betwixt the monarch and any of the meanest persons of the community, who shall be the judge? For instance, the king commands me, or gives judgment against me; I reply, his commands are illegal, and his judgment not according to law. Who must judge? If the monarch himself judge, then you destroy the frame of the state, and make it absolute, saith our author; and he gives his reason: for, to confine a monarch to a law, and then to make him judge of his own deviations from that law, is to absolve him from all law. On the other side, if any, or all the people may judge, then you put the sovereignty in the whole body, or part of it, and destroy the being of monarchy. Thus our author hath caught himself in a

---

31 Hunton, *Treatise*, p. 14.
32 Merriam-Webster defines as "crafty, cunning".

plain dilemma: if the king be judge, then he is no limited monarch; if the people be judge, then he is no monarch at all. So farewell limited monarchy. Nay farewell all government, if there be no judge.

Would you know what help our author hath found out for this mischief? First, he saith that 'a subject is bound to yield to a magistrate when he cannot *de jure* challenge obedience if it be in a thing in which he can possibly without subversion, and in which his act may not be made a leading case, and so bring on a prescription against public liberty' (p. 14). Again he saith, 'if the act in which the exorbitance or transgression of the monarch is supposed to be, be of lesser moment, and not striking at the very being of that government, it ought to be born by public patience, rather than to endanger the being of the state' (p. 17). The like words he uses in another place, saying, 'if the will of the monarch exceed the limits of the law, it ought to be submitted to, so it be not contrary to God's law, nor bring with it such an evil to ourselves or the public that we cannot be accessory to it by obeying' (p. 49). These are but fig-leaves to cover the nakedness of our author's limited monarch, formed upon weak supposals in cases of lesser moment. For if the monarch be to govern only according to law, no transgression of his can be of so small moment, if he break the bounds of law, but it is a subversion of the government itself, and may be made a leading case, and so bring on a prescription against public liberty. It strikes at the very being of the government, and brings with it such an evil as the party that suffers, or the public cannot be accessory to. Let the case be never so small, yet if there be illegality in the act, it strikes at the very being of limited monarchy, which is to be legal. Unless our author will say, as in effect he doth, that his limited monarch must govern according to law in great and public matters only, and that in smaller matters which concern private men, or poor persons, he may rule according to his own will.

Secondly, our author tells us, if the monarch's act of exorbitancy or transgression

> be mortal, and such as suffered dissolves the frame of government and public liberty, then the illegality is to be set open, and redressment sought by petition; which if failing, prevention by resistance ought to be; and if it be apparent, and appeal be made to the consciences of mankind, then the fundamental laws of that monarchy must judge and pronounce the sentence in every man's conscience, and every man (so far as concerns him) must follow the evidence of truth in his own soul to oppose or not to oppose, according

as he can in conscience acquit or condemn the act of the
governor or monarch (p. 17).

Whereas my author requires that the destructive nature of illegal commands shall be set open, surely his mind is that each private man in his
particular case should make a public remonstrance to the world of the
illegal act of the monarch; and then if upon his petition he cannot be re-
lieved according to his desire, he ought, or it is his duty to make resistance.
Here I would know, who can be the judge whether the illegality be made
apparent? It is a main point, since every man is prone to flatter himself in
his own cause and to think it good, and that the wrong or injustice he suffers is apparent, when other moderate and indifferent men can discover no
such thing. And in this case the judgment of the common people cannot
be gathered or known by any possible means, or if it could, it were like to
be various and erroneous.

Yet our author will have an appeal made to the conscience of all mankind, and that being made, he concludes 'the fundamental laws must judge
and pronounce sentence in every man's conscience' (p. 18). Whereas he
saith 'the fundamental laws must judge'; I would very gladly learn of him,
or of any other for him, what a fundamental law is, or else have but any
one law named me that any man can say is a fundamental law of the monarchy. I confess he tells us that the common laws are the foundation, and
the statute laws are 'superstructive' (p. 38). Yet I think he dares not say
that there is any one branch or part of the common law but that it may be
taken away by an act of parliament. For many points of the common law
de facto have; and *de jure* any point may be taken away. How can that be
called fundamental which hath and may be removed, and yet the statute
laws stand firm and stable? It is contrary to the nature of fundamental for
the building to stand when the foundation is taken away.

Besides, the common law is generally acknowledged to be nothing else
but common usage or custom, which by length of time only obtains authority. So that it follows in time after government, but cannot go before
it and be the rule to government by any original or radical constitution.

Also the common law being unwritten, doubtful, and difficult, cannot
but be an uncertain rule to govern by, which is against the nature of a
rule—which is and ought to be certain.

Lastly, by making the common law only to be the foundation, Magna
Carta is excluded from being a fundamental law, and also all other statutes
from being limitations to monarchy, since the fundamental laws only are
to be judge.

Truly the conscience of all mankind is a pretty large tribunal for the fundamental laws to pronounce sentence in. It is very much that laws—which in their own nature are dumb and always need a judge to pronounce sentence—should now be able to speak and pronounce sentence themselves. Such a sentence surely must be upon the hearing of one party only, for it is impossible for a monarch to make his defence and answer, and produce his witnesses in every man's conscience, in each man's cause, who will but question the legality of the monarch's government. Certainly the sentence cannot but be unjust, where but one man's tale is heard. For all this, the conclusion is, every man must oppose or not oppose the monarch according to his own conscience. Thus at the last, every man is brought by this doctrine of our author's to be his own judge. And I also appeal to the consciences of all mankind, whether the end of this be not utter confusion, and anarchy.

Yet after all this, the author saith this power of every man's judging the illegal acts of the monarch 'argues not a superiority of those who judge over him who is judged' (p. 18). And he gives a profound reason for it: his words are 'it is not authoritative and civil, but moral, residing in reasonable creatures, and lawful for them to execute'.[33] What our author means by these words, 'not authoritative and civil, but moral' perhaps I understand not, though I think I do. Yet it serves my turn that he saith that 'resistance ought to be made, and every man must oppose or not oppose, according as in conscience he can acquit or condemn the acts of his governor'.[34] For if it enable a man to resist and oppose his governor, without question it *is* authoritative and civil. Whereas he adds that 'moral judgment is residing in reasonable creatures, and lawful for them to execute', he seems to imply that authoritative and civil judgment doth not reside in reasonable creatures, nor can be lawfully executed. Such a conclusion fits well with anarchy, for he that takes away all government and leaves every man to his own conscience, and so makes him an independent in state, may well teach that authority resides not in reasonable creatures, nor can be lawfully executed.

I pass from his absolute and limited monarchy to his division or partition (for he allows no division) of monarchy into simple and mixed, viz. of a monarch, the nobility, and community.

Where first, observe a doubt of our author's whether a 'firm union can be in a mixture of equality'. He rather thinks there must be a 'priority of order in one of the three or else there can be no unity' (p. 25). He must know that priority of order doth not hinder but that there may be an equality of mixture if the shares be equal, for he that hath the first share may have no

33 Hunton, *Treatise.*
34 Hunton, *Treatise.*

more than the others. So that if he will have an inequality of mixture, a primity of share will not serve the turn. The first share must be greater or better than the others, or else they will be equal, and then he cannot call it a mixed monarchy, where only a primity of share in the supreme power is in one. But by his own confession he may better call it a mixed aristocracy or mixed democracy than a mixed monarchy, since he tells us the Houses of parliament 'sure have two parts of the greatest legislative authority' (p. 56); and if the king have but a third part, sure their shares are equal.

The first step our author makes is this: 'the sovereign power must be originally in all three'. Next he finds that if there be an equality of shares in three estates, there can be no ground to denominate a monarch, and then his mixed monarch might be thought but an empty title. Therefore in the third place he resolves us that to salve all 'a power must be sought out wherewith the monarch must be invested, which is not so great as to destroy the mixture, nor so titular as to destroy the monarchy' (p. 25). And therefore he conceives it may be in these particulars:

1. First, a monarch in a mixed monarchy may be said to be a monarch, as he conceives, 'if he be the head and fountain of the power which governs and executes the established laws' (p. 26). That is, a man may be a monarch though he do but give power to others to govern and execute the established laws. Thus he brings his monarch one step or peg lower still than he was before. At first he made us believe his monarch should have the supreme power, which is the legislative. Then he falls from that, and tells us a limited monarch must govern according to law only. Thus he is brought from the legislative to the gubernative or executive power only. Nor doth he stay here, but is taken a hole lower, for now he must not govern but he must constitute officers to govern by laws. If choosing officers to govern be governing, then our author will allow his monarch to be a governor, not else. And therefore he that divided supreme power into legislative and gubernative, doth now divide it into legislative, and power of constituting officers for governing by laws—and this, he saith, is left to the monarch. Indeed you have left him a fair portion of power. But are we sure he may enjoy this? It seems our author is not confident in this neither, and some others do deny it him. Our author speaking of the government of this kingdom saith the choice of the officers is entrusted to the judgment of the monarch 'for ought I know' (p. 38). He is not resolute in the point, but for ought he knows, and for ought I know, his monarch is but titular—an empty title, certain of no power at all.

The power of choosing officers only is the basest of all powers. Aristotle, as I remember, saith the common people are fit for nothing but 'to choose officers and to take accounts'.[35] And indeed, in all popular governments the multitude perform this work, and this work in a king puts him below all his subjects and makes him the only subject in a kingdom, or the only man that cannot govern. There is not the poorest man of the multitude but is capable of some office or other, and by that means may some time or other perhaps govern according to the laws. Only the king can be no officer, but to choose officers; his subjects may all govern, but he may not.

Next, I cannot see how in true sense our author can say his monarch is 'the head and fountain of power',[36] since his doctrine is that in a limited monarchy 'the public society by original constitution confer on one man power'.[37] Is not then the public society the head and fountain of power, and not the king?

Again, when he tells us of his monarch that 'both the other states, as well *conjunctim* ["jointly"] as *divisim* ["separately"] be his sworn subjects and owe obedience to his commands',[38] he doth but flout his poor monarch. For why are they called his subjects and his commons? He (without any complement) is their subject. For they, as officers, may govern and command according to law, but he may not, for he must judge by his judges in courts of justice only—that is, he may not judge or govern at all.

2. As for the second particular, the 'sole or chief power in capacitating persons'[39] for the supreme power, and

3. As to this third particular, the power of 'convocating' such persons, they are both so far from making a monarch that they are the only way to make him none, by choosing and calling others to share in the supreme power.

4. Lastly, concerning his authority being 'the last and greatest' in the establishing every act, it makes him no monarch, except he be sole that hath that authority. Neither his primity of share in the supreme power, nor his authority being last, no, nor his having the greatest authority, doth make him a monarch unless he have that authority *alone*.

Besides, how can he show that in his mixed monarchy the monarch's power is the greatest? The greatest share that our author allows him in the legislative power is a negative voice, and the like is allowed to the nobility and commons. And truly, a negative voice is but a base term to express a legislative power. A negative voice is but a privative power, or indeed, no

---

35 Aristotle, *Politics*, 1281^b 32–3.
36 Hunton, *Treatise*, p. 26.
37 Hunton, *Treatise*, p. 13.
38 Hunton, *Treatise*, p. 26.
39 Hunton, *Treatise*, p. 26.

power at all to do anything, only a power to hinder an act from being done.

Wherefore, I conclude, not any of his four nor all of them put into one person makes the state monarchical (p. 26).

This mixed monarchy, just like the limited, ends in confusion and destruction of all government. You shall hear the author's confession

> That one inconvenience must necessarily be in all mixed governments, which I showed to be in limited governments: there can be no constituted legal authoritative judge of the fundamental controversies arising between the three estates. If such do rise, it is the fatal disease of those governments, for which no salve can be applied. It is a case beyond the possible provision of such a government; of this question there is no legal judge. The accusing side must make it evident to every man's conscience … The appeal must be to the community, as if there were no government; and as by evidence consciences are convinced, they are bound to give their assistance (p. 28).

The wit of man cannot say more for anarchy.

Thus have I picked out the flowers out of his doctrine about limited monarchy, and presented them with some brief annotations. It were a tedious work to collect all the learned contradictions, and ambiguous expressions that occur in every page of his platonic monarchy. The book hath so much of fancy that it is a better piece of poetry than policy.

Because many may think that the main doctrine of limited and mixed monarchy may in itself be most authentical, and grounded upon strong and evident reason, although our author perhaps have failed in some of his expressions and be liable to exceptions, therefore I will be bold to inquire whether Aristotle could find either reason or example of a limited or mixed monarchy—and the rather because I find our author altogether insists upon a rational way of justifying his opinion. No man I think will deny but that Aristotle was sufficiently curious in searching out the several forms of commonwealths and kingdoms. Yet I do not find that he ever so much as dreamed of either a limited or mixed monarchy. Several other sorts of monarchies he reckons up. In the third book of his *Politics* he spends three whole chapters together upon the several kinds of monarchy.

First, in his fourteenth chapter he mentions four kinds of monarchy:

The Laconic or Lacedaemonian

The barbaric

The Aesymnetical

The heroic

The Laconic or Lacedemonian king, saith he, had only supreme power when he was out of the bounds of the Lacedemonian territories. Then he had absolute power, his kingdom was like to a perpetual lord general of an army.

> The barbaric king (saith Aristotle) had a power very near to tyranny. Yet they were lawful and paternal, because the barbarians are of a more servile nature than the Grecians, and the Asiatics than the Europeans. They do willingly, without repining, live under a masterly government. Yet their government is stable and safe because they are paternal and lawful kingdoms, and their guards are royal and not tyrannical. For kings are guarded by their own subjects, and tyrants are guarded by strangers.[40]

'The Aesymnetical king', saith Aristotle, 'in old time in Greece was an elective tyrant, and differed only from the barbarian kings in that he was elective and not paternal'. 'These sorts of kings, because they were tyrannical, were masterly. But because they were over such as voluntarily elected them, they were regal'.

> The heroic were those (saith Aristotle) which flourished in the heroical times, to whom the people did willingly obey; and they were paternal and lawful because these kings did deserve well of the multitude, either by teaching them arts, or by warring for them, or by gathering them together when they were dispersed, or by dividing lands amongst them. These kings had supreme power in war, in sacrifices, in judicature.[41]

These four sorts of monarchy hath Aristotle thus distinguished, and after sums them up together, and concludes his chapter as if he had forgot him-

---

40   Aristotle, *Politics*, 1285ᵃ 18–27.
41   Aristotle, *Politics*, 1285ᵃ 4–11.

self, and reckons up a fifth kind of monarchy—which is, saith he, 'when one alone hath supreme power of all the rest; for as there is a domestical kingdom of one house, so the kingdom of a city, or of one or many nations, is a family'.[42]

These are all the sorts of monarchy that Aristotle hath found out, and he hath strained hard to make them so many. First, for his Lacedemonian king, himself confesseth that he was but a kind of military commander in war, and so in effect no more a king than all generals of armies; and yet this no-king of his was not limited by any law nor mixed with any companions of his government. When he was in the wars out of the confines of Lacedaemon, he was, as Aristotle styles him, Ἀυτοκράτωρ—'of full and absolute command',[43] no law, no companion to govern his army but his own will.

Next, for Aristotle's Aesymnetical king, it appears he was out of date in Aristotle's time. For he saith he was 'amongst the ancient Greeks',[44] ἐν τοῖς ἀρχαίοις Ἕλλησιν. Aristotle might well have spared the naming him (if he had not wanted other sorts) for the honour of his own nation. For he that but now told us the barbarians were of a more servile nature than the Grecians, comes here and tells us that these old Greek kings were elective tyrants. The barbarians did but suffer tyrants in show, but the old Grecians chose tyrants indeed; which then must we think were the greater slaves, the Greeks or the barbarians? Now if these sorts of kings were tyrants, we cannot suppose they were limited either by law, or joined with companions. Indeed, Aristotle saith some of these tyrants were limited to certain times and actions, for they had not all their power for term of life, nor could meddle but in certain businesses. Yet during the time they were tyrants, and in the actions whereto they were limited, they had absolute power to do what they list according to their own will, or else they could not have been said to be tyrants.

As for Aristotle's heroic king, he gives the like note upon him that he did upon the Aesymnet, that he was in old time: κατὰ τοὺς ἡρωικοὺς χρόνους, 'in the heroic times'.[45] The thing that made these heroical kingdoms differ from other sorts of kingdoms was only the means by which the first kings obtained their kingdoms, and not the manner of government. For in that they were as absolute as other kings were, without either limitation by law, or mixture of companions.

42   Aristotle, *Politics*, 1285ª 29–33.

43   Aristotle, *Politics*, 1285ª 7.

44   Aristotle, *Politics*, 1285ª 30.

45   Aristotle, *Politics*, 1285ᵇ 4–5.

Lastly, as for Aristotle's barbaric sort of kings, since he reckoned all the world barbarians except the Grecians, his barbaric king must extend to all other sorts of kings in the world besides those of Greece, and so may go under Aristotle's fifth sort of kings, which in general comprehends all other sorts, and is no special form of monarchy.

Thus upon a true account it is evident that the five several sorts of kings mentioned by Aristotle are at the most but different and accidental means of the first obtaining or holding of monarchies, and not real or essential differences of the manner of government, which was always absolute, without either limitation or mixture.

I may be thought perhaps to mistake or wrong Aristotle in questioning his diversities of kings. But it seems Aristotle himself was partly of the same mind. For in the very next chapter, when he had better considered of the point, he confessed that, to speak the truth, 'there were almost but two sorts of monarchies worth the considering',[46] that is, his first or Laconic sort, and his fifth or last sort, where one alone hath supreme power over all the rest. Thus he hath brought his five sorts to two. Now for the first of these two, his Lacedemonian king, he hath confessed before that 'he was no more than a generalissimo'[47] of an army, and so upon the matter no king at all; and then there remains only his last sort of kings, 'where one alone hath the supreme power'.[48] And this in substance is the final resolution of Aristotle himself. For in his sixteenth chapter, where he delivers his last thoughts touching the kinds of monarchy, he first dischargeth his Laconic king from being any sort of monarch, and then gives us two exact rules about monarchy, and both these are point blank against limited and mixed monarchy. Therefore I shall propose them to be considered of, as concluding all monarchy to be absolute and arbitrary:

1. The one rule is that 'he that is said to be a king according to law is no sort of government or kingdom at all'[49] (Aristotle, *Politics*, book 3, ch. 16).

2. The second rule is that a true king 'is he that ruled all according to his own will'.[50]

This latter frees a monarch from the mixture of partners or sharers in government, as the former rule doth from limitation by laws.

Thus in brief I have traced Aristotle in his crabbed and broken passages touching diversities of kings. Where he first finds but four sorts, and then

46 Aristotle, *Politics*, 1285ᵇ 34–5.
47 Aristotle, *Politics*, 1285ᵃ 7.
48 Aristotle, *Politics*, 1285ᵇ 29–30.
49 Aristotle, *Politics*, 1287ᵃ 3–4. ὁ μὲν γὰρ κατὰ νόμον λεγόμενος βασιλεὺς οὐκ ἔστιν εἶδος, καθάπερ εἴπομεν, πολιτείας.
50 Aristotle, *Politics*, 1287ᵃ 1. κατὰ τὴν ἑαυτοῦ βούλησιν.

he stumbles upon a fifth, and in the next chapter contents himself only with two sorts of kings, but in the chapter following concludes with one— which is the true perfect monarch who rules all by his own will. In all this we find nothing for a regulated or mixed monarchy, but against it.

Moreover, whereas the author of the *Treatise of Monarchy* affirms it as a prime principle, that all monarchies (except that of the Jews) depend upon human designment, when the consent of a society of men, and a fundamental contract of a nation, by original or radical constitution confers power, he must know that Aristotle—searching into the original of government—shows himself in this point a better divine than our author, and as if he had studied the book of Genesis, teacheth that monarchies fetch their pedigree from the right of fathers and not from the gift or contract of people. His words may thus be Englished: 'At the first, cities were governed by kings, and so even to this day are nations also. For such as were under kingly government did come together, for every house is governed by a king, who is the eldest; and so also colonies are governed for kindred sake'. And immediately before, he tells us that the 'first society made of many houses is a village, which naturally seems to be a colony of a house, which some call foster-brethren, or children, and children's children'.[51]

So in conclusion we have gained Aristotle's judgment in three main and essential points:

1. A king according to law makes no kind of government.

2. A king must rule according to his own will.

3. The original of kings is from the right of fatherhood.

What Aristotle's judgment was two thousand years since is agreeable to the doctrine of the great modern politician Bodin. Hear him touching limited monarchy:

> Unto majesty or sovereignty (saith he) belongeth an absolute power, not subject to any law ... chief power given unto a prince with condition is not properly sovereignty, or power absolute, except such conditions annexed to the sovereignty be directly comprehended within the laws of God and nature ... Albeit by the sufferance of the king of England controversies between the king and his people are sometimes determined by the high court of parliament, and sometimes by the lord chief justice of England; yet all the estates re-

51   Aristotle, *Politics*, 1252^b 15–21.

main in full subjection to the king, who is no ways bound to follow their advice, neither to consent to their requests … It is certain that the laws, privileges, and grants of princes have no force but during their life, if they be not ratified by the express consent, or by sufferance of the prince following, especially privileges … Much less should a prince be bound unto the laws he maketh himself; for a man may well receive a law from another man, but impossible it is in nature for to give a law unto himself, no more than it is to command a man's self in a matter depending of his own will. The law saith, '*Nulla obligatio consistere potest, quae a voluntate promittentis statum capit*' ["there can be no obligation which depends on the will of the one promising"]. The sovereign prince may derogate unto the laws that he hath promised and sworn to keep, if the equity thereof be ceased; and that of himself, without the consent of his subjects … The majesty of a true sovereign prince is to be known when the estates of all the people assembled, in all humility present their requests and supplications to their prince, without having power in anything to command, determine, or give voice, but that that which it pleaseth the king to like or dislike, to command or bid,[52] is holden for law; wherein they which have written of the duty of magistrates have deceived themselves in maintaining that the power of the people is greater than the prince; a thing which causeth oft true subjects to revolt from their obedience to their prince, and ministereth matter of great troubles in commonwealths; of which their opinion there is neither reason nor ground. For if the king be subject unto the assemblies and decrees of the people, he should neither be king nor sovereign, and the commonwealth neither realm nor monarchy, but a mere aristocracy … So we see the principal point of sovereign majesty and absolute power to consist principally in giving laws unto the subjects in general without their consent. (Bodin, *De Republica*, book 1, ch. 8)

To confound the state of monarchy with the popular or aristocratical estate is a thing impossible, and in effect incompatible, and such as cannot be imagined. For sovereignty being of itself indivisible, how can it at one and the same

---

52   Bodin's Latin has *prohibendi*, a gerund of "forbid".

time be divided betwixt one prince, the nobility, and the people in common? The first mark of sovereign majesty is to be of power to give laws, and to command over them unto the subjects; and who should those subjects be that should yield their obedience to the law, if they should have also power to make the laws? Who should he be that could give the law, being himself constrained to receive it of them unto whom himself gave it? So that of necessity we must conclude that as no one in particular hath the power to make the law in such a state, that then the state must needs be a state popular ... Never any commonwealth hath been made of an aristocracy and popular estate, much less of the three estates of a commonweal ... Such states wherein the rights of sovereignty are divided are not rightly to be called commonweals, but rather the corruption of commonweals, as Herodotus has most briefly but truly written ... Commonweals which change their state, the sovereign right and power of them being divided, find no rest from civil wars and broils till they again recover some one of the three forms, and the sovereignty be wholly in one of the states or other.[53]

'Where the rights of the sovereignty are divided betwixt the prince and his subjects, in that confusion of state there is still endless stirs and quarrels for the superiority, until that some one, some few, or all together, have got the sovereignty'. *idem*, book 2, ch 1.

This judgment of Bodin's touching limited and mixed monarchy is not according to the mind of our author, nor yet of the Observator,[54] who useth the strength of his wit to overthrow absolute and arbitrary government in this kingdom, and yet in the main body of his discourse lets fall such truths from his pen as give a deadly wound to the cause he pleads for, if they be indifferently weighed and considered. I will not pick a line or two here and there to wrest against him, but will present a whole page of his book, or more together, that so we may have an entire prospect upon the Observator's mind:

Without society (saith the Observator) men could not live, without laws men could not be sociable, and without au-

53   Jean Bodin, *The Six Bookes of a Commonweale*, tr. Richard Knolles, book 2, ch. 1.
54   Henry Parker, parliamentarian propagandist and author of *Observations Upon Some of His Majesties Late Answers and Expresses*.

thority somewhere to judge according to law, law was vain. It was soon therefore provided that laws according to the dictate of reason should be ratified by common consent. When it afterward appeared that man was yet subject to unnatural destruction by the tyranny of entrusted magistrates—a mischief almost as fatal as to be without all magistracy—how to provide a wholesome remedy therefore, was not so easy to be invented. It was not difficult to invent laws for the limiting of supreme governors. But to invent how those laws should be executed, or by whom interpreted, was almost impossible, *'nam quis custodiet ipsos custodes?'* ["for who may guard the guardians themselves?"] To place a superior above a supreme was held unnatural. Yet what a lifeless thing would law be without any judge to determine and force it? If it be agreed upon, that limits should be prefixed to princes, and judges to decree according to those limits, yet another inconvenience will presently affront us. For we cannot restrain princes too far, but we shall disable them from some good ... Long it was ere the world could extricate itself out of all these extremities, or find out an orderly means whereby to avoid the danger of unbounded prerogative on this hand, and of excessive liberty on the other, and scarce has long experience yet fully satisfied the minds of all men in it. In the infancy of the world, when man was not so artificial and obdurate in cruelty and oppression as now, and policy most rude, most nations did choose rather to subject themselves to the mere discretion of their lords than rely upon any limits; and to be ruled by arbitrary edicts, than written statutes. But since tyranny being more exquisite, and policy more perfect, especially where learning and religion flourish, few nations will endure the thraldom which usually accompanies unbounded and unconditionate royalty. Yet long it was ere the bounds and conditions of supreme lords were so wisely determined, or quietly conserved as now they are. For at first, when as *ephori, tribuni, curatores,* etc. were erected to poise against the scale of sovereignty, much blood was shed about them, and states were put into new broils by them, and in some places the remedy proved worse than the disease. In all great distresses, the body of the people was ever constrained to rise, and by force of the major party to put an end to all intestine strifes, and make a redress

of all public grievances. But many times calamities grew to
a strange height, before so cumbersome a body could be
raised; and when it was raised, the motions of it were so distracted and irregular that after much spoil and effusion of
blood, sometimes only one tyranny was exchanged for another. Till some way was invented to regulate the motions
of the peoples moliminous[55] body, I think arbitrary rule was
most safe for the world. But now since most countries have
found ... an art and peaceable order for public assemblies,
whereby the people may assume its own power to do it self
right, without disturbance to itself or injury to princes, he is
very unjust that will oppose this art or order. That princes
may not be now beyond all limits and laws, nor yet be ...
tied upon those limits by any private parties, the whole community in its underived majesty shall convene to do justice.
And that the convention may not be without intelligence,
certain times and places and forms shall be appointed for
its reglement.[56] And that the vastness of its own bulk may
not breed confusion, by virtue of election and representation a few shall act for many, the wise shall consent for the
simple, the virtue of all shall redound to some, and the pru-
dence of some shall redound to all. And surely as this admi-
rably-composed court, which is now called a parliament, is
more regularly and orderly formed than when it was called
mickle synod or witenagemot,[57] or when this real body of
the people did throng together at it; so it is not yet perhaps
without some defects, which by art and policy might receive
farther amendment. Some divisions have ... sprung up of
late between both Houses, and some between the king and
both Houses by reason of uncertainty of jurisdiction, and
some lawyers doubt how far the parliament is able to create
new forms and precedents, and has a jurisdiction over itself.
All these doubts would be solemnly solved. But in the first
place, the true privileges of parliament belonging not only to
the being and efficacy of it, but to the honour and compli-
ment of it, would be clearly declared. For the very naming

---

55   Merriam-Webster defines as "cumbersome, weighty".
56   Merriam-Webster defines as "regulation".
57   For "mickle", Merriam-Webster defines as "great". "Synod" and "witenagemot" refer respectively to councils ecclesiastical and of Anglo-Saxon nobility.

of privileges of parliament, as if they were chimeras to the ignorant sort, and utterly unknown unto the learned, hath been entertained with scorn since the beginning of this parliament.[58]

In this large passage taken out of the Observator which concerns the original of all government, two notable propositions may be principally observed.

First, our Observator confesseth arbitrary or absolute government to be the first and the safest government for the world.

Secondly, he acknowledgeth that the jurisdiction is uncertain, and the privileges not clearly declared of limited Monarchy.

These two evident truths delivered by him he labours mainly to disguise. He seems to insinuate that arbitrary government was but in the infancy of the world, for so he terms it. But if we enquire of him, how long he will have this infancy of the world to last, he grants it continued above three thousand years, which is an unreasonable time for the world to continue under age. For the first opposers he doth find of arbitrary power were the *ephori, tribuni, curatores,* etc. The *ephori* were above three thousand years after the creation, and the *tribuni* were later. As for his *curatores,* I know not whom he means, except the master of the court of wards. I cannot English the word *curator* better. I do not believe that he can shew that any *curatores* or etceteras which he mentions were so ancient as the *ephori.* As for the *tribuni,* he mistakes much if he thinks they were erected to limit and bound monarchy. For the state of Rome was at the least aristocratical (as they call it) if not popular, when tribunes of the people were first hatched. And for the *ephori,* their power did not limit or regulate monarchy but quite take it away. For a 'Lacedemonian king' in the judgment of Aristotle 'was no king indeed, but in name only, as generalissimo of an army';[59] and the best politicians reckon the Spartan commonwealth to have been aristocratical and not monarchical. And if a limited monarchy cannot be found in Lacedaemon, I doubt our Observator will hardly find it anywhere else in the whole world—and in substance he confesseth as much, when he saith '*now* most countries have found out an art and peaceable order for public assemblies',[60] as if it were a thing but new done, and not before, for so the word *now* doth import.

The Observator in confessing the jurisdiction to be uncertain, and the

58   Henry Parker, *Observations upon some of his Majesties late Answers and Expresses,* pp. 13–15.
59   Aristotle, *Politics,* 1285ᵃ 7.
60   Parker, *Observations,* p. 14.

privileges undetermined of that court that should bound and limit monarchy doth in effect acknowledge there is no such court at all. For every court consists of jurisdictions and privileges; it is these two that create a court, and are the essentials of it. If the 'admirably composed court' of parliament have some defects which may receive amendment, as he saith, and if those defects be such as cause divisions both between the Houses, and between the king and both Houses, and these divisions be about so main a matter as jurisdictions and privileges, and power to create new privileges, all which are the fundamentals of every court (for until they be agreed upon, the act of every court may not only be uncertain, but invalid, and cause of tumults and sedition); and if 'all these doubts' and divisions have need to be 'solemnly solved', as our Observator confesseth, then he hath no reason at all to say that now the conditions of supreme lords are 'wisely determined and quietly conserved', or that now 'most countries have found out an art and peaceable order for public affairs, whereby the people may resume its own power to do it self right without injury unto princes'. For how can the 'underived majesty' of the people by assuming its own power, tell how to do herself right, or how to avoid doing injury to the prince, if her jurisdiction be uncertain, and privileges undetermined?

He tells us '*now* most countries have found an art and peaceable order for public assemblies', and to the intent 'that princes may not be *now* beyond all limits and laws the whole community in its underived majesty shall convene to do justice'. But he doth not name so much as one country or kingdom that hath found out this art, where the whole community in its underived majesty did ever convene to do justice. I challenge him, or any other for him, to name but one kingdom that hath either *now* or heretofore found out this art or peaceable order. We do hear a great rumor in this age of moderated and limited kings. Poland, Sweden, and Denmark are talked of for such, and in these kingdoms or nowhere is such a moderated government, as our Observator means, to be found. A little enquiry would be made into the manner of the government of these kingdoms. For these northern people, as Bodin observeth, breathe after liberty.

First for Poland, Boterus saith that,

> the government of it is elective altogether, and representeth rather an aristocracy than a kingdom. The nobility, who have great authority in the diets, choosing the king and limiting his authority, making his sovereignty but a slavish royalty. These diminutions of regality began first by default of King Lewis, and Jagello, who to gain the succession in the kingdom contrary to the laws, one for his daughter, and the

other for his son, departed with many of his royalties and prerogatives, to buy the voices of the nobility.[61]

The French author of the book called *The Estates of the World*, doth inform us that

> the prince's authority was more free, not being subject to any laws, and having absolute power not only of their estates but also of life and death. Since Christian religion was received, it began to be moderated, first by holy admonitions of the bishops and clergy, and then by services of the nobility in war. Religious princes gave many honours and many liberties to the clergy and nobility, and quit much of their rights, the which their successors have continued … The superior dignity is reduced to two degrees, that is, the palatinate and the chastelleine, for that kings in former times did by little and little call these men to public consultations, notwithstanding that they had absolute power to do all things of themselves—to command, dispose, recompense, and punish, of their own motions. Since they have ordained that these dignities should make the body of a senate,[62]

the king doth not challenge much right and power over his nobility, nor over their estates, neither hath he any over the clergy.

> And though the king's authority depends on the nobility for his election, yet in many things it is absolute after he is chosen. He appoints the diets at what time and place he pleaseth. He chooseth lay-councillors, and nominates the bishops, and whom he will have to be his privy council. He is absolute disposer of the revenues of the crown. He is absolute establisher of the decrees of the diets. It is in his power to advance and reward whom he pleaseth.[63]

He is lord immediate of his subjects, but not of his nobility:

> He is sovereign judge of his nobility in criminal causes. The

---

61 Giovanni Botero, *Relations of the Most Famous Kingdoms and Common-wealthes throwout the World*, p. 412.

62 Pierre d'Avity, *The Estates, Empires, and Principalities of the World*, pp. 641, 643.

63 Botero, *Relations*, p. 414.

power of the nobility daily increaseth, for that in respect of
the king's election, they neither have law, rule, nor form to
do it, neither by writing nor tradition. As the king governs
his subjects which are immediately his, with absolute authority; so the nobility dispose immediately of their vassals,
over whom every one hath more than a regal power, so as
they entreat them like slaves.[64]

There be certain men in Poland who are called 'earthly messengers or
nuntios'. They are as it were agents of jurisdictions or circles of the nobility.
These have a certain authority, and, as Boterus saith,

in the time of their diets these men assemble in a place near
to the senate house, where they choose two marshals, by
whom (but with a tribune-like authority) they signify unto
the council what their requests are. Not long since, their authority and reputation grew so mightily that they now carry themselves as heads and governors rather than officers
and ministers of the public decrees of the state. One of the
council refused his senator's place to become one of these
officers.[65]

Every palatine, the king requiring it, calls together all the nobility of his
palatinate, where having propounded unto them the matters whereon
they are to treat, and their will being known, they choose four or six out
of the company of the earthly messengers. These deputies meet and make
one body, which they call the order of knights.

This being of late years the manner and order of the government of Poland, it is not possible for the Observator to find among them that the
'whole community in its underived majesty' doth ever 'convene to do
justice', nor any election or representation of the community, or that the
people assume its own power to do it self right. The earthly messengers,
though they may be thought to represent the commons, and of late take
much upon them, yet they are elected and chosen by the nobility, as their
agents and officers. The community are either vassals to the king, or to the
nobility, and enjoy as little freedom or liberty as any nation. But it may be
said, perhaps, that though the community do not limit the king, yet the
nobility do, and so he is a limited monarch. The answer is that in truth,
though the nobility at the choosing of their king do limit his power and

64   d'Avity, *Estates*, p. 643.
65   Botero, *Relations*, p. 414. Parker, *Observations*, p. 14.

do give him an oath, yet afterwards they have always a desire to please him and to second his will, and this they are forced to do to avoid discord. For by reason of their great power they are subject to great dissensions not only among themselves but between them and the order of knights, which are the earthly messengers. Yea, the provinces are at discord one with another, and as for religion, the diversity of sects in Poland breeds perpetual jars and hatred among the people, there being as many sects as in Amsterdam itself, or any popular government can desire. The danger of sedition is the cause that though the crown depends on the election of the nobility, yet they have never rejected the king's successor or transferred the realm to any other family but once, when deposing Ladislaus for his idleness (whom yet afterward they restored) they elected Wenceslaus king of Bohemia. But if the nobility do agree to hold their king to his conditions, which is, not to conclude anything but by the advice of his council of nobles, nor to choose any wife without their leaves, then it must be said to be a commonweal, not a royalty; and the king but only the mouth of the kingdom, or as Queen Christina complained, that 'her husband was but the shadow of a sovereign'.[66]

Next, if it be considered how the nobility of Poland came to this great power, it was not by any original contract or popular convention. For it is said they have neither law, rule, nor form written or unwritten for the election of their king. They may thank the bishops and clergy, for by their holy admonitions and advice, good and religious princes, to show their piety, were first brought to give much of their rights and privileges to their subjects, devout kings were merely cheated of some of their royalties. What power soever general assemblies of the estates claim or exercise over and above the bare naked act of counselling, they were first beholding to the popish clergy for it. It is they first brought parliaments into request and power. I cannot find in any kingdom, but only where popery hath been, that parliaments have been of reputation, and in the greatest times of superstition they are first mentioned.

As for the kingdom of Denmark, I read that the senators, who are all chosen out of the nobility, and seldom exceed the number of twenty-eight, with the chief of the realm do choose their king. They have always in a manner set the king's eldest son upon the royal throne. 'The nobility of Denmark withstood the coronation of Frederick, 1559, till he swore not to put any nobleman to death until he were judged of the senate; and that all noblemen should have power of life and death over their subjects without appeal; and the king to give no office without consent of the council'. There

66 Botero, *Relations*, p. 413.

is a chancellor of the realm, before whom they do appeal from all the provinces and islands, and from him to the king himself. I hear of nothing in this kingdom that tends to popularity—no assembly of the commons, no elections, or representation of them.

Sweden is governed by a king heretofore elective, but now made hereditary in Gustavus' time. It is divided into provinces. An appeal lieth from the viscount of every territory to a sovereign judge called a *lamen*; from the *lamens* to the king's council; and from this council to the king himself.

Now let the Observator bethink himself, whether all or any of these three countries have found out any art at all whereby the people or community may assume its own power. If neither of these kingdoms have, most countries have not, nay none have. The people or community in these three realms are as absolute vassals as any in the world. The regulating power, if any be, is in the nobility, nor is it such in the nobility as it makes show for. The election of kings is rather a formality than any real power. For they dare hardly choose any but the heir, or one of the blood royal. If they should choose one among the nobility it would prove very factious; if a stranger, odious; neither safe. For the government, though the kings be sworn to reign according to the laws, and are not to do anything without the consent of their council in public affairs, yet in regard they have power both to advance and reward whom they please, the nobility and senators do comply with their kings. And Boterus concludes of the kings of Poland, who seem to be most moderated, that 'such as is their valour, dexterity, and wisdom, such is their power, authority, and government'.[67] Also Bodin saith that these three kingdoms 'are states changeable and uncertain, as the nobility is stronger than the prince, or the prince than the nobility';[68] and the people are so far from liberty, that he saith divers particular lords exact not only customs, but tributes also, which are confirmed and grow stronger both by long prescription of time and use of judgments.

THE END.

---

67   Botero, *Relations*, p. 415.
68   Bodin, *Six Bookes*, p. 166.

OBSERVATIONS ON
Mr. HOBS's LEVIATHAN:

OR, HIS ARTIFICIAL MAN
A Commonwealth.

THE PREFACE.

With no small content I read Mr. Hobbes' book *De Cive*, and his *Leviathan*, about the rights of sovereignty, which no man that I know hath so amply and judiciously handled. I consent with him about the rights of exercising government, but I cannot agree to his means of acquiring it. It may seem strange I should praise his building and yet mislike his foundation, but so it is. His *jus naturae* ["right of nature"], and his *regnum institutivum* ["kingship by institution"], will not down with me: they appear full of contradiction and impossibilities. A few short notes about them I here offer, wishing he would consider whether his building would not stand firmer upon the principles of *regnum patrimoniale* ["paternal kingship"], as he calls it, both according to Scripture and reason—since he confesseth the 'father being before the institution of a commonwealth' was originally an 'absolute sovereign' 'with power of life and death', and that 'a great family, as to the rights of sovereignty, is a little monarchy'.[1] If, according to the order of nature, he had handled paternal government before that by institution, there would have been little liberty left in the subjects of the family to consent to institution of government.

In his pleading the cause of the people, he arms them with a very large commission of array,[2] which is a right in nature for every man to war against every man when he please, and also a right for all the people to

---

1 Thomas Hobbes, *Leviathan or the Matter, Forme and Power of a Commonwealth Ecclesiastical and Civil*, p. 121 et al. Any page numbers in this chapter not otherwise footnoted refer to Hobbes' *Leviathan*.
2 *Black's Law Dictionary* defines as "A commission issued to send into every county officers to muster or set in military order the inhabitants."

govern. This latter point, although he affirm in words, yet by consequence he denies, as to me it seemeth.

He saith, a representative may be[3] of all or but of a part of the people. If it be of all, he terms it a democracy, which is the government of the people. But how can such a commonwealth be generated? For if every man covenant with every man, who shall be left to be the representative? If all must be representatives, who will remain to covenant? For he that is sovereign makes no covenant by his doctrine. It is not all that will come together that makes the democracy, but all that have power by covenant. Thus his democracy by institution fails.

The same may be said of a democracy by acquisition. For if all be conquerors, who shall covenant for life and liberty? And if all be not conquerors, how can it be a democracy by conquest?

A paternal democracy I am confident he will not affirm, so that in conclusion the poor people are deprived of their government, if there can be no democracy, by his principles.

Next, if a representative aristocratical of a part of the people be free from covenanting, then that whole assembly (call it what you will) though it be never so great, is in the state of nature, and every one of that assembly hath a right not only to kill any of the subjects that they meet with in the streets, but also they all have a natural right to cut one another's throats even while they sit together in council, by his principles. In this miserable condition of war is his representative aristocratical by institution.

A commonwealth by conquest, he teacheth, 'is then acquired when the vanquished, to avoid present death, covenanteth that so long as his life and the liberty of his body is allowed him, the victor shall have the use of it at his pleasure'.[4] Here I would know how the liberty of the vanquished can be allowed if the victor have the use of it at pleasure, or how it is possible for the victor to perform his covenant, except he could always stand by every particular man to protect his life and liberty?

In his 'review and conclusion' he resolves that 'an ordinary subject hath liberty to submit when the means of his life is within the guards and garrisons of the enemy'.[5] It seems hereby that the rights of sovereignty by institution may be forfeited, for the subject cannot be at liberty to submit to a conqueror, except his former subjection be forfeited for want of protection.

If his conqueror be in the state of nature when he conquers, he hath a

---

3   By "be", Filmer means "consist".
4   Hobbes, *Leviathan*, p. 104.
5   Hobbes, *Leviathan*, p. 390.

right without any covenant made with the conquered. If conquest be defined to be the acquiring of right of sovereignty by victory, why is it said the right is acquired in the people's submission, by which they contract with the victor, promising obedience for life and liberty? Hath not everyone in the state of nature a right to sovereignty, before conquest, which only puts him in possession of his right?

If his conqueror be not in the state of nature, but a subject by covenant, how can he get a right of sovereignty by conquest when neither he himself hath right to conquer, nor subjects a liberty to submit—since a former contract lawfully made cannot lawfully be broken by them?

I wish the title of the book had not been of a commonwealth, but of a weal public, or commonweal, which is the true word carefully observed by our translator[6] of Bodin *De Republica* into English. Many ignorant men are apt by the name of commonwealth to understand a popular government, wherein wealth and all things shall be common, tending to the levelling community in the state of pure nature.

OBSERVATIONS ON Mr. HOBS's LEVIATHAN.

I

If God created only Adam, and of a piece of him made the woman; and if by generation from them two, as parts of them, all mankind be propagated; if also God gave to Adam not only the dominion over the woman and the children that should issue from them, but also over the whole earth to subdue it, and over all the creatures on it, so that as long as Adam lived no man could claim or enjoy anything but by donation, assignation, or permission from him; I wonder how the *right of nature* can be imagined by Mr. Hobbes, which, he saith, is a liberty for 'each man to use his own power as he will himself for preservation of his own life'; 'a condition of war of everyone against everyone'; 'a right of every man to everything, even to one another's body' (p. 64), especially since himself affirms 'that originally the father of every man was also his sovereign lord with power over him of life and death'.

II

Mr. Hobbes confesseth he believes 'it was never generally so', that there was such a *jus naturae* (p. 63); and if not generally, then not at all, for one exception bars all if he mark it well. Whereas he imagines such a 'right of nature' may be now practised in America, he confesseth a government there of families, which government how 'small' or 'brutish' soever (as he calls it) is sufficient to destroy his *jus naturale* ["natural right"].

III

I cannot understand how this 'right of nature' can be conceived without imagining a company of men at the very first to have been all created together without any dependency one of another, or as 'mushrooms (*fungorum more*) they all on a sudden were sprung out of the earth without any obligation one to another', as Mr. Hobbes' words are in his book *De Cive*, ch. 8, §1; when the Scripture teacheth us otherwise, that all men came by succession and generation from one man. We must not deny the truth of the history of the creation.

IV

It is not to be thought that God would create man in a condition worse than any beasts, as if he made men to no other end by nature but to destroy one another. A right for the father to destroy or eat his children, and for children to do the like by their parents, is worse than cannibals. This horrid condition of pure nature when Mr. Hobbes was charged with, his refuge was to answer 'that no son can be understood to be in this state of pure nature'[7] (*De Cive*, ch. 1, §10)—which is all one with denying his own principle. For if men be not free-born, it is not possible for him to assign and prove any other time for them to claim a right of nature to liberty, if not at their birth.

V

But if it be allowed (which is yet most false) that a company of men were at first without a common power to keep them in awe, I do not see why such a condition must be called a state of war of all men against all men. Indeed if such a multitude of men should be created as the earth could not well nourish, there might be cause for men to destroy one another rather than perish for want of food. But God was no such niggard in the creation, and there being plenty of sustenance and room for all men, there is no cause or use of war till men be hindered in the preservation of life, so that there

---

7　Thomas Hobbes, *De Cive* (Latin version).

is no absolute necessity of war in the state of pure nature. It is the right of nature for every man to live in peace, that so he may tend the preservation of his life, which whilst he is in actual war he cannot do. War of itself as it is war preserves no man's life, it only helps to preserve and obtain the means to live. If every man tend the right of preserving life, which may be done in peace, there is no cause of war.

VI

But admit the state of nature were the state of war, let us see what help Mr. Hobbes hath for it. It is a principle of his that 'the law of nature is a rule found out by reason' (I do think it is given by God), forbidding a man 'to do that which is destructive to his life, and to omit that by which he thinks it may be best preserved' (p. 64). If the right of nature be a liberty for a man to do anything he thinks fit to preserve his life, then in the first place nature must teach him that life is to be preserved, and so consequently forbids to do that which may destroy or take away the means of life, or to omit that by which it may be preserved—and thus the right of nature and the law of nature will be all one. For I think Mr. Hobbes will not say the right of nature is a liberty for man to destroy his own life. The law of nature might better have been said to consist in a command to preserve or not to omit the means of preserving life, than in a prohibition to destroy, or to omit it.

VII

Another principle I meet with, 'if other men will not lay down their right as well as he, then there is no reason for any to divest himself of his' (p. 65). Hence it follows that if all the men in the world do not agree, no commonwealth can be established. It is a thing impossible for all the men in the world, every man with every man, to covenant to lay down their right. Nay it is not possible in the smallest kingdom, though all men should spend their whole lives in nothing else but in running up and down to covenant.

VIII

Right may be laid aside but not transferred: for 'he that renounceth or passeth away his right, giveth not to any other man a right which he had not before', and reserves a right in himself against all those with whom he doth not covenant (p. 65).

IX

> The only way to erect a common power, or a commonwealth,
> is for men to confer all their power and strength upon one
> man, or one assembly of men, that may reduce all their wills
> by plurality of voices to one will; which is to appoint one
> man or an assembly of men to bear their person, to submit
> their wills to his will. This is a real unity of them all in one
> person, made by covenant of every man with every man as
> if every man should say to every man, I authorise, and give
> up my right of governing myself to this man, or this assem-
> bly of men, on this condition, that thou give up thy right to
> him, and authorise all his actions. This done, the multitude
> so united in one person, is called a commonwealth (p. 87).

To authorise and give up his right of governing himself, to confer all his
power and strength, and to submit his will to another, is to lay down his
right of resisting. For if right of nature be a liberty to use power for preservation of life, laying down of that power must be a relinquishing of power
to preserve or defend life, otherwise a man relinquisheth nothing.

To reduce all the wills of an assembly by plurality of voices to one will, is
not a proper speech, for it is not a plurality but a totality of voices which
makes an assembly be of one will—otherwise it is but the one will of a
major part of the assembly, the negative voice of any one hinders the being
of the one will of the assembly. The negative voice of any one hinders the
being of the one will of the assembly. There is nothing more destructive to
the true nature of a lawful assembly than to allow a major part to prevail
when the whole only hath right.

For a man to give up his right to one that never covenants to protect is a
great folly, since it is neither 'in consideration of some right reciprocally
transferred to himself', nor can he hope for any other good by standing
out of the way, that the other may enjoy his own original right without
hindrance from him, by reason of so much diminution of impediments
(p. 66).

X

'The liberty', saith Mr. Hobbes,

> whereof there is so frequent and honourable mention in the
> histories and philosophy of the ancient Greeks and Romans,
> and in the writings and discourse of those that from them

> have received all their learning in the politics, is not the lib-
> erty of particular men but the liberty of the commonwealth.
> Whether a commonwealth be monarchical or popular, the
> freedom is still the same. (p. 110)

Here I find Mr. Hobbes is much mistaken. For the liberty of the Athenians
and Romans is a liberty only to be found in popular estates, and not in
monarchies. This is clear by Aristotle, who calls a city a community of freemen, meaning every particular citizen to be free. Not that every particular
man had a liberty to resist his governor or do what he list, but a liberty
only for particular men to govern and to be governed by turns, ἄρχειν
and ἄρχεσθαι are Aristotle's words.[8] This was a liberty not to be found in
hereditary monarchies. So Tacitus mentioning the several governments of
Rome, joins the consulship and liberty to be brought in by Brutus, because
by the annual election of consuls, particular citizens came in their course
to govern and to be governed. This may be confirmed by the complaint of
our author, which followeth:

> It is an easy thing for men to be deceived by the specious
> name of liberty, and for want of judgment to distinguish,
> mistake that for their private inheritance and birthright
> which is the right of the public only; and when the same
> error is confirmed by the authority of men in reputation for
> their writings on this subject, it is no wonder if it produce se-
> dition and change of government. In these western parts of
> the world, we are made to receive our opinions concerning
> the institution and rights of commonwealths from Aristotle
> and Cicero, and other men, Greeks and Romans, that liv-
> ing under popular estates, derived those rights not from the
> principles of nature, but transcribed them into their books
> out of the practice of their own commonwealths, which were
> popular. And because the Athenians were taught (to keep
> them from desire of changing their government) that they
> were freemen, and all that lived under monarchy slaves,
> therefore Aristotle puts it down in his *Politics*, 'In democracy
> liberty is to be supposed, for it is commonly held that no man
> is free in any other government'. So Cicero and other writers
> have grounded their civil doctrine on the opinions of the
> Romans, who were taught to hate monarchy, at first, by them
> that having deposed their sovereign, shared amongst them

8 1277ᵇ 14–15.

the sovereignty of Rome. And by reading of these Greek and Latin authors, men from their childhood have gotten a habit (under a false show of liberty) of favouring tumults, and of licentious controlling the actions of their sovereigns.[9]

XI

'Dominion paternal' not attained 'by generation but by contract', which is 'the child's consent, either express or by other sufficient arguments declared' (p. 102). How a child can express consent, or by other sufficient arguments declare it before it comes to the age of discretion I understand not; yet all men grant it is due before consent can be given, and I take it Mr. Hobbes is of the same mind where he teacheth that Abraham's children were bound to obey what Abraham should declare to them for God's law—which could not be but in virtue of the obedience they owed to their parents (p. 249); they *owed*, not they *covenanted* to give. Also where he saith the 'father and master being before the institution of commonweals absolute sovereigns in their own families', how can it be said that either children or servants were in the state of *jus naturae* till the institution of commonweals? It is said by Mr. Hobbes in his book *De Cive*, ch. 9, §7, the 'mother originally hath the government of her children, and from her the father derives his right, because she brings forth and first nourisheth them'. But we know that God at the creation gave the sovereignty to the man over the woman, as being the nobler and principal agent in generation. As to the objection that 'it is not known who is the father to the son but by the discovery of the mother', and that 'he is his son whom the mother will, and therefore he is the mother's', the answer is that it is not at the will of the mother to make whom she please the father, for if the mother be not in possession of a husband, the child is not reckoned to have any father at all. But if she be in the possession of a man, the child, notwithstanding whatsoever the woman discovereth to the contrary, is still reputed to be his in whose possession she is. No child naturally and infallibly knows who are his true parents, yet he must obey those that in common reputation are so, otherwise the commandment of 'honour thy father and thy mother' were in vain, and no child bound to the obedience of it.

9   Hobbes, *Leviathan*, p. 110.

XII

If the government of one man and the government of two men make two several kinds of government (p. 94), why may not the government of two and of three do the like, and make a third, and so every differing number a different kind of commonwealth? If 'an assembly of all' (as Mr. Hobbes saith) 'that will come together' be a democracy, and 'an assembly of a part only' an aristocracy, then if all that will come together be but a part only, a democracy and aristocracy are all one. And why must an assembly of part be called an aristocracy, and not a merocracy?[10]

It seems Mr. Hobbes is of the mind that there is but one kind government, and that is monarchy. For he defines a commonwealth to be one person; and an assembly of men, or 'real unity of them all in one and the same person' (p. 87), the multitude so united he calls a commonwealth. This his moulding of a multitude into one person is the generation of his great *Leviathan*, the king of the children of pride (p. 167). Thus he concludes the person of a commonwealth to be a monarch.

XIII

I cannot but wonder Mr. Hobbes should say 'the consent of a subject to sovereign power is contained in these words, "I authorise and do take upon me all his actions", in which there is no restriction at all of his own former natural liberty' (p. 112). Surely here Mr. Hobbes forgot himself, for before he makes the resignation to go in these words also, I 'give up my right of governing myself to this man'.[11] This is a restriction certainly of his own former natural liberty when he gives it away. And if a man allow his sovereign to kill him—which Mr. Hobbes seems to confess—how can he reserve a right to defend himself? And if a man have a power and right to kill himself, he doth not authorise and give up his right to his sovereign, if he do not obey him when he commands him to kill himself.

XIV

Mr. Hobbes saith 'No man is bound by the words' of his submission

> to kill himself, or any other man, and consequently that the
> obligation a man may sometimes have upon the command
> of the sovereign to execute any dangerous or dishonourable

---

10   Government by a part of the citizenry.
11   Hobbes, *Leviathan*, p. 87.

office, dependeth not on the words of our submission but on
the intention which is to be understood by the end thereof.
When therefore our refusal to obey frustrates the end for
which the sovereignty was ordained, then there is no liberty
to refuse; otherwise there is (p. 112).

If no man be bound by the words of his subjection to kill any other man,
then a sovereign may be denied the benefit of war, and be rendered unable
to defend his people—and so the end of government frustrated. If the obligation upon the commands of a sovereign to execute a dangerous or dishonourable office dependeth not on the words of our submission but on
the intention which is to be understood by the end thereof, no man, by Mr.
Hobbes' rules, is bound but by the words of his *submission*; the intention of
the *command* binds not, if the words do not. If the intention should bind,
it is necessary the sovereign must discover it, and the people must dispute
and judge it—which how well it may consist with the rights of sovereignty,
Mr. Hobbes may consider. Whereas Mr. Hobbes saith the intention is to
be understood by the ends, I take it he means the end by effect, for the end
and the intention are one and the same thing. And if he mean the effect,
the obedience must go before, and not depend on the understanding of
the effect, which can never be if the obedience do not precede it. In fine, he
resolves refusal to obey may depend upon the judging of what frustrates
the end of sovereignty, and what not, of which he cannot mean any other
judge but the people.

XV

Mr. Hobbes puts a case by way of question:

A great many men together have already resisted the sovereign power unjustly, or committed some capital crime, for
which every one of them expecteth death: whether have they
not the liberty then to join together and assist and defend
one another? Certainly they have, for they but defend their
lives, which the guilty man may as well do as the innocent.
There was indeed injustice in the first breach of their duty.
Their bearing of arms subsequent to it, though it be to maintain what they have done, is no new unjust act, and if it be
only to defend their persons, it is not unjust at all (p. 112).

The only reason here alleged for the bearing of arms, is this, that there is no
new unjust act—as if the beginning only of a rebellion were an unjust act,

and the continuance of it none at all. No better answer can be given to this case than what the author himself hath delivered in the beginning of the same paragraph in these words: 'To resist the sword of the commonwealth in defence of another man, guilty or innocent, no man hath liberty, because such liberty takes away from the sovereign the means of protecting us, and is therefore destructive of the very essence of government'. Thus he first answers the question, and then afterwards makes it, and gives it a contrary answer. Other passages I meet with to the like purpose. He saith 'a man cannot lay down the right of resisting them that assault him by force to take away his life; the same may be said of wounds, chains, and imprisonment' (p. 66); 'A covenant not[12] to defend myself from force by force, is void'; right of defending life and means of living can never be abandoned (p. 69).

These last doctrines are destructive to all government whatsoever, and even to the *Leviathan* itself. Hereby any rogue or villain may murder his sovereign, if the sovereign but offer by force to whip or lay him in the stocks, since whipping may be said to be wounding, and putting in the stocks an imprisonment. So likewise every man's goods being a means of living, if a man cannot abandon them, no contract among men, be it never so just, can be observed. Thus we are at least in as miserable condition of war as Mr. Hobbes at first by nature found us.

XVI

The kingdom of God signifies, saith Mr. Hobbes, a kingdom 'constituted by the votes of the people of Israel in a peculiar manner, wherein they choose God for their king, by covenant made with him, upon God's promising them Canaan' (p. 216). If we look upon Mr. Hobbes' text for this, it will be found that the people did not constitute by votes, and choose God for their king, but by the appointment first of God himself the covenant was to be a God to them. They did not contract with God that if he would give them Canaan they would be his subjects, and he should be their king. It was not in their power to choose whether God should be their God, yea or nay. For it is confessed He reigned naturally over all by his might. If God reigned naturally, He had a kingdom and sovereign power over His subjects, not acquired by their own consent. This kingdom, said to be constituted by the votes of the people of Israel, is but the vote of Abraham only; his single voice carried it, he was the representative of the people. For at this vote, it is confessed that the name of king is not given to God, nor of

---

12   All manuscripts omit the word "not", though it is contained in Hobbes.

kingdom to Abraham, yet the thing—if we will believe Mr. Hobbes—is all one. If a contract be the mutual transferring of right, I would know what right a people can have to transfer to God by contract. Had the people of Israel at Mount Sinai a right not to obey God's voice? If they had not such a right, what had they to transfer?

The covenant mentioned at Mount Sinai was but a conditional contract, and God but a conditional king, and though the people promised to obey God's word, yet it was more than they were able to perform, for they often disobeyed God's voice—which being a breach of the condition, the covenant was void, and God not their king by contract.

It is complained by God, 'They have rejected me that I should reign over them'.[13] But it is not said 'according to their contract'. For I do not find that the desiring of a king was a breach of their contract or covenant, or disobedience to the voice of God. There is no such law extant.

The people did not totally reject the Lord, but in part only, out of timorousness. When they saw Nahash king of the children of Ammon come against them, they distrusted that God would not suddenly provide for their deliverance, as if they had had always a king in readiness to go up presently to fight for them. This despair in them who had found so many miraculous deliverances under God's government was that which offended the Lord so highly. They did not desire an alteration of government and to cast off God's laws, but hoped for a certainer and speedier deliverance from danger in time of war. They did not petition that they might choose their king themselves. That had been a greater sin—and yet if they had, it had not been a total rejection of God's reigning over them, as long as they desired not to depart from the worship of God their king, and from the obedience of his laws. I see not that the kingdom of God was cast off by the election of Saul, since Saul was chosen by God himself, and governed according to God's laws. The government from Abraham to Saul is nowhere called the kingdom of God, nor is it said that the kingdom of God was cast off at the election of Saul.

Mr. Hobbes allows that 'Moses alone had next under God the sovereignty over the Israelites', (p. 252). But he doth not allow it to Joshua, but will have it descend to Eleazar the high priest, Aaron's son. His proof is, God expressly saith concerning Joshua, 'He shall stand before Eleazar, who shall ask counsel for him before the Lord' (after the judgment of Urim is omitted by Mr. Hobbes), 'at his word shall they go out',[14] etc. 'therefore the

---

13 1 Samuel 8:12.
14 Numbers 27:21.

supreme power of making peace and war was in the priest'.[15] Answer: the work of the high priest was only *ministerial*, not *magisterial*. He had no power to command in war, or to judge in peace. Only, when the sovereign or governor did go up to war, he enquired of the Lord by the ministry of the high priest, and, as the Hebrews say, the enquirer with a soft voice as one that prayeth for himself, asked. And forthwith the Holy Ghost came upon the priest, and he beheld the breast-plate, and saw therein by the vision of prophecy, 'go up', or 'go not up'. If this answer gave the priest sovereignty, then neither King Saul nor King David had the sovereignty, who both asked counsel of the lord by the priest.

15 Hobbes, *Leviathan*, p. 253.

OBSERVATIONS ON
Mr. Milton Against SALMASIUS.[1]

I

Among the many printed books and several discourses touching the right of kings and the liberty of the people, I cannot find that as yet the first and chief point is agreed upon or indeed so much as once disputed. The word 'king' and the word 'people' are familiar, one would think every simple man could tell what they signified. But upon examination it will be found, that the learnedest cannot agree of their meaning.

Ask Salmasius what a king is, and he will teach us that 'a king is he who hath the supreme power of the kingdom, and is accountable to none but God, and may do what he please, and is free from the laws'.[2] This definition J.M.[3] abominates as being the definition of a tyrant, and I should be of his mind if he would have vouchsafed us a better, or any other definition at all, that would tell us how any king can have a supreme power without being freed from human laws. To find fault with it without producing any other is to leave us in the dark. But though Mr. Milton brings us neither definition nor description of a king, yet we may pick out of several passages of him something like a definition, if we lay them together. He teacheth us that 'power was therefore given to a king by the people, that he might see by the authority to him committed that nothing be done against law, and that he keep our laws and not impose upon us his own. Therefore there is no regal power but in the courts of the kingdom, and by them' (p. 155).

And again he affirmeth 'the king cannot imprison, fine or punish any man, except he be first cited into some court—where not the king but the usual judges give sentence' (p. 168). And before we are told 'not the king

---

1   Claudius Salmasius, a French classical scholar who argued in his *Defensio Regia Pro Carolo I* that the rebels led by Cromwell were guilty of regicide for executing King Charles.

2   John Milton, *Pro Populo Anglicano Defensio*, p. 70. Any page numbers in this chapter not otherwise footnoted refer to Milton's *Pro Populo*, first edition.

3   John Milton.

but the authority of parliament doth set up and take away all courts' (p. 167).

Lo, here the description of a king: he is 'one to whom the people give power, to see that nothing be done against law', and yet he saith there is 'no regal power but in the courts of justice, and by them, where not the king but the usual judges give sentence'. This description not only strips the king of all power whatsoever, but puts him in a condition below the meanest of his subjects.

Thus much may show that all men are not agreed what a king is. Next, what the word people means is not agreed upon. Ask Aristotle what the people is, and he will not allow any power to be in any but in free citizens. If we demand who be free citizens, that he cannot resolve us, for he confesseth that he that is a free citizen in one city, is not so in another city. And he is of opinion that 'no artificer should be a free citizen, or have voice in a well ordered commonwealth';[4] he accounts a democracy (which word signifies the government of the people) to be a corrupted sort of government; he thinks many men by nature born to be servants, and not fit to govern as any part of the people. Thus doth Aristotle curtail the people, and cannot give us any certain rule to know who be the people. Come to our modern politicians,[5] and ask them who the people is—though they talk big of the people, yet they take up and are content with a few representors (as they call them) of the whole people, a point Aristotle was to seek in. Neither are these representors stood upon to be the whole people, but the major part of these representors must be reckoned for the whole people. Nay J.M. will not allow the major part of the representors to be the people, but the 'sounder and better part only' of them (p. 126), and in right down terms he tells us, to determine who is a tyrant he leaves 'to magistrates, at least to the uprighter sort of them, and of the people, though in number less by many, to judge as they find cause' (p. 7). If the 'sounder, the better, and the uprighter' part have the power of the people, how shall we know, or who shall judge who they be?

II

One text is urged by Mr. Milton for the people's power: Deuteronomy 17:14—'When thou art come into the land which thy Lord thy God giveth thee, and shalt say I will set a king over me, like as all the nations about

4   1278ᵃ 8–9.
5   Political scientists.

me'. It is said, by the *Tenure of Kings*[6] 'these words confirm us that the right of choosing, yea, of changing their own government is by the grant of God himself in the people'.[7] But can the foretelling or forewarning of the Israelites of a wanton and wicked desire of theirs, which God himself condemned, be made an argument that God gave or granted them a right to do such a wicked thing? Or can the narration and reproving of a future fact be a donation and approving of a present right, or the permission of a sin be made a commission for the doing of it? The author of his book against Salmasius falls so far from making God the donor or grantor, that he cites him only for a witness: '*Teste ipso Deo penes populos arbitrium semper fuisse, vel ea, quae placeret forma reipub. Utendi, vel hanc in aliam mutandi; de Hebraeis hoc diserte dicit Deus: de reliquis non abnuit*': that here in this text 'God himself being witness, there was always a power in the people either to use what form of government they pleased, or of changing it into another. God saith this expressly of the Hebrews, and denies it not of others'.[8] Can any man find that God in this text expressly saith that there was always a right in the people to use what form of government they please? The text not warranting this right of the people, the foundation of the defence of the people is quite taken away—there being no other grant or proof of it pretended.

2. Where it is said that the Israelites desired a king, though then under another form of government, in the next line but one it is confessed they had a king at the time when they desired a king, which was God himself, and his viceroy Samuel, and so saith God: 'They have not rejected thee, but they have rejected me, that I should not reign over them'. Yet in the next verse God saith, as 'they have forsaken me, so do they also unto thee'.[9] Here is no show of any other form of government but monarchy. God by the mediation of Samuel reigned, who 'made his sons judges over Israel'.[10] When one man constitutes judges we may call him a king, or if the having of judges do alter the government then the government of every kingdom is altered from monarchy. Where judges are appointed by kings, it is now reckoned one of the duties of kings to judge by their judges only.

3. Where it is said, 'he shall not multiply to himself horses, nor wives, nor riches, that he might understand that he had no power over others, who

---

6   *The Tenure of Kings and Magistrates*, published in *The Works of John Milton* vol.5 (1649)
7   Milton, *Tenure*, p. 14.
8   Milton, *Pro Populo*, p.76.
9   1 Samuel 8:7–8.
10   1 Samuel 8:1.

could decree nothing of himself *extra legem*[11] ["outside the law"], if it had said *contra legem Dei* ["against the law of God"], it had been true, but if it meant *extra legem humanam* ["outside human law"], it is false.

4. If there had been any right given to the people, it seems it was to the elders only. For it is said it was 'the elders of Israel gathered together'[12] petitioned for a king. It is not said it was all the people, nor that the people did choose the elders, who were the fathers and heads of families authorized by the judges.

5. Where it is said, 'I will set a king over me like as all the nations about me',[13] 'to set a king' is not to choose a king but by some solemn public act of coronation or otherwise to acknowledge their allegiance to the king chosen. It is said thou shalt 'set him king whom the Lord thy God shall choose'.[14] The elders did not desire to choose a king like other nations, but they say 'now make us a king to judge us like all the nations'.[15]

III

As for David's covenant with the elders when he was anointed, it was not to observe any laws or conditions made by the people, for ought appears, but to keep God's laws and serve Him, and to seek the good of the people as they were to protect him.

6. The Reubenites and Gadites promise their obedience, not according to their laws or conditions agreed upon, but in these words: 'All that thou commandest us we will do, and whithersoever thou sendest us we will go; as we harkened to Moses in all things, so will we harken unto thee. Only the Lord thy God be with thee as He was with Moses'.[16] Where is there any condition of any human law expressed? Though the rebellious tribes offered conditions to Rehoboam, where can we find that 'for like conditions not performed, all Israel deposed Samuel'? I wonder Mr. Milton should say this, when within a few lines after he professeth that 'Samuel had governed them uprightly'.[17]

---

11   Milton, *Pro Populo*, p.76.
12   1 Samuel 8:4.
13   Deuteronomy 17:14.
14   Deuteronomy 17:15.
15   1 Samuel 8:5.
16   Joshua 1:16–17.
17   Milton, *Tenure*, p. 15.

IV

Jus regni ["law of the realm"] is much stumbled at, and the definition of a king which saith 'his power is supreme in the kingdom, and he is accountable to none but to God, and that he may do what he please, and is not bound by laws'. It is said if this definition be good, no man is or ever was, who may be said to be a tyrant (p. 14). For 'when he hath violated all divine and human laws, nevertheless he is a king, and guiltless *jure regio* ["by royal right"]'.[18] To this may be answered that the definition confesseth he is accountable to God, and therefore not guiltless if he violate divine laws. Human laws must not be shuffled in with divine, they are not of the same authority. If humane laws bind a king, it is impossible for him to have supreme power amongst men. If any man can find us out such a kind of government wherein the supreme power can be without being freed from human laws, they should first teach us that. But if all sorts of popular government that can be invented cannot be one minute without an arbitrary power, freed from all human laws, what reason can be given why a royal government should not have the like freedom? If it be tyranny for one man to govern arbitrarily, why should it not be far greater tyranny for a multitude of men to govern without being accountable or bound by laws? It would be further enquired how it is possible for any government at all to be in the world without an arbitrary power. It is not power except it be arbitrary. A legislative power cannot be without being absolved from human laws. It cannot be showed how a king can have any power at all but an arbitrary power. We are taught that 'power was therefore given to a king by the people, that he might see by the authority to him committed that nothing be done against law, and that he keep our laws, and not impose upon us his own. Therefore there is no royal power but in the courts of the kingdom, and by them' (p. 155). And again it is said 'the king cannot imprison, fine or punish any man except he be first cited into some court, where not the king but the usual judges give sentence' (p. 168). And before, we are told, 'not the king, but the authority of parliament doth set up and take away all courts' (p. 167).

Lo, here we have Mr. Milton's perfect definition of a king: he is one to whom the people gave 'power to see that nothing be done against law, and that he keep our laws, and not impose his own'. Whereas all other men have the faculty of seeing by nature, the king only hath it by the gift of the people. Other power he hath none. He may see the judges keep the laws if they will; he cannot compel them, for he may not imprison, fine, nor pun-

---

18 Milton, *Pro Populo*, p.72.

ish any man. The courts of justice may, and they are set up and put down by the parliament. Yet in this very definition of a king we may spy an arbitrary power in the king, for he may wink if he will—and no other power doth this description of a king give, but only a power to see. Whereas it is said Aristotle 'doth mention an absolute kingdom for no other cause but to shew how absurd, unjust and most tyrannical it is'.[19] There is no such thing said by Aristotle, but the contrary, where he saith that 'a king according to law makes no sort of government';[20] and after he had reckoned up five sorts of kings he concludes that there were in a manner but two sorts, the Lacedemonian king and the absolute king, whereof the first was but as general in an army, and therefore no king at all, and then fixes and rests upon the 'absolute king, who ruleth according to his own will'.[21]

V

If it be demanded what is meant by the word people? 1. Sometimes it is *populus universus* ["the whole people"], and then every child must have his consent asked, which is impossible. 2. Sometimes it is *pars major* ["the greater part"], and sometimes it is pars *potior et senior* ["the better and sounder part"]. How the major part, where all are alike free, can bind the minor part, is not yet proved.

But it seems the major part will not carry it, nor be allowed except they be the 'better part and the sounder part'.[22] We are told 'the sounder part implored the help of the army when it saw itself and the commonwealth betrayed', and that the 'soldiers judged better than the great council, and by arms saved the commonwealth, which the great council had almost damned by their votes' (p. 7).

Here we see what the people is—to wit, 'the sounder part of which the army is the judge'. Thus upon the matter the soldiers are the people—which being so, we may discern where the liberty of the people lieth, which we are taught to consist 'all for the most part in the power of the people's choosing what form of government they please' (p. 61). A miserable liberty, which is only to choose to whom we will give our liberty, which we may not keep. See more concerning the people, in a book entitled *The Anarchy*, (pp. 8, 9, 10, 11, 12, 13, 14).[23]

---

19   Milton, *Pro Populo*, p. 88.
20   Aristotle, *Politics*, 1287[a] 3–4.
21   Aristotle, Politics, 1287[a] 9–10.
22   Milton, *Pro Populo*, p. 356.
23   pp. 74–80 above.

VI

We are taught that 'a father and a king are things most diverse. The father begets us, but not the king; but we create the king. Nature gives a father to the people, the people gives themselves a king. If the father kill his son he loseth his life, why should not the king also?' (p. 34).

Answer: father and king are not so diverse. It is confessed that at first they were all one, for there is confessed *paternum imperium et haereditarium* ["a paternal and hereditary empire"] (p. 141), and this fatherly empire, as it was of itself *hereditary*, so it was *alienable* by parent, and *seizable* by an usurper as other goods are. And thus every king that now is hath a paternal empire, either by inheritance, or by translation, or usurpation. So a father and a king may be all one.

A father may die for the murder of his son where there is a superior father to them both, or the right of such a supreme father. But where there are only father and sons, no sons can question the father for the death of their brother. The reason why a king cannot be punished is not because he is excepted from punishment, or doth not deserve it, but because there is no superior to judge him but God only to whom he is reserved.

VII

It is said thus, 'He that takes away from the people the power of choosing for themselves what form of government they please, he doth take away that wherein all civil liberty almost consists' (p. 65). If almost all liberty be in choosing of the kind of government, the people have but a poor bargain of it—who cannot exercise their liberty but in chopping and changing their government, and have liberty only to give away their liberty, than which there is no greater mischief, as being the cause of endless sedition.

VIII

'If there be any statute in our law by which thou canst find that tyrannical power is given to a king, that statute—being contrary to God's will, to nature and reason—understand that by that general and primary law of ours, that statute is to be repealed, and not of force with us' (p. 153). Here if any man may be judge what law is contrary to God's will, or to nature, or to reason, it will soon bring in confusion. Most men that offend, if they be to be punished or fined, will think that statute that gives all fines and forfeitures to a king to be a tyrannical law. Thus most statutes would be judged void, and all our forefathers taken for fools or madmen to make all our laws to give all penalties to the king.

IX

The sin of the children of Israel did lie not in desiring a king, but in desiring such a king like as the nations round about had. They distrusted God almighty that governed them by the monarchical power of Samuel, in the time of oppression, when God provided a judge for them. But they desired a perpetual and hereditary king that they might never want. In desiring a king they could not sin, for it was but desiring what they enjoyed by God's special providence.

X

Men are persuaded that in making of a covenant, something is to be performed on both parts by mutual stipulation, which is not always true. For we find God made a covenant with Noah and his seed, with all the fowl and the cattle, not to destroy the earth any more by a flood. This covenant was to be kept on God's part. Neither Noah, nor the fowl, nor the cattle, were to perform any thing by this covenant. On the other side, Genesis 17:9, 10, God covenants with Abraham, saying 'Thou shalt keep my covenant … every male-child among you shall be circumcised'. Here it is called God's covenant, though it be to be performed only by Abraham. So a covenant may be called the king's covenant, because it is made to him, and yet to be performed only by the people. So also, 2 Kings 11:17, 'Jehoiada made a covenant between the Lord and the king and the people, that they should be the Lord's people; between the king also and the people'—which might well be that the people should be the king's servants, and not for the king's covenanting to keep any human laws. For it is not likely the king should either covenant or take any oath to the people when he was but seven years of age, and that never any king of Israel took a coronation oath that can be showed. When Jehoiada showed the king to the rulers in the house of the Lord, he took an oath of the people. He did not article with them, but—saith the next verse—commanded them to keep a 'watch of the king's house', and that they should 'compass the king round about, every man with his weapons in his hand: and he that cometh within the ranges, let him be slain'.[24]

---

24   2 Kings 11:5–8.

XI

To the text, 'Where the word of a king is, there is power, and who may say unto him, what doest thou?'[25] J.M. gives this answer: 'It is apparent enough that the preacher in this place gives precepts to every private man, not to the great Sanhedrin, nor to the senate … shall not the nobles, shall not all the other magistrates, shall not the whole people dare to mutter, so oft as the king pleaseth to dote?'[26] We must here note that the great council and all other magistrates or nobles, or the whole people, compared to the king are all but private men if they derive their power from him. They are magistrates under him, and out of his presence. For when he is in place they are but so many private men. J.M. asks, 'Who swears to a king, unless the king on the other side be sworn to keep God's laws and the laws of the country?'[27] We find that the rulers of Israel took an oath at the coronation of Jehoash. But we find no oath taken by that king—no not so much as to God's laws, much less to the laws of the country.

XII

'A tyrant is he, who regarding neither law nor the common good, reigns only for himself and his faction' (p. 19). In his *Defence*[28] he expresseth himself thus, 'he is a tyrant who looks after only his own, and not his people's profit. *Ethics*, book 10'[29] (p. 189).

1. If it be tyranny not to regard the law, then all courts of equity and pardons for any offences must be taken away. There are far more suits for relief against the laws than there be for the observation of the laws. There can be no such tyranny in the world as the law, if there were no equity to abate the rigour of it. *Summum jus* ["supreme law"] is *summa injuria* ["supreme injustice"]. If the penalties and forfeitures of all laws should still be exacted by all kings, it would be found that the greatest tyranny would be for a king to govern according to law. The fines, penalties, and forfeitures of all laws are due to the supreme power only, and were they duly paid they would far exceed the taxes in all places. It is the chief happiness of a kingdom, and their chief liberty, not to be governed by the laws only.

2. 'Not to regard the common good but to reign only for himself', is the supposition of an impossibility in the judgment of Aristotle, who teacheth

25   Ecclesiastes 8:4.
26   Milton, *Pro Populo*, p. 80.
27   Milton, *Pro Populo*, p. 80.
28   Milton, *Pro Populo*.
29   Aristotle, *Nicomachean Ethics*.

us that 'the despotical power cannot be preserved, except the servant, or he in subjection, be also preserved'.[30] The truth of this strongly proves that it is in nature impossible to have a form of government that can be for the destruction of a people, as tyranny is supposed. If we will allow people to be governed, we must grant they must in the first place be preserved, or else they cannot be governed.

Kings have been and may be vicious men, and the government of one not so good as the government of another. Yet it doth not follow that the form of government is or can be in its own nature ill, because the governor is so. It is anarchy, or want of government, that can totally destroy a nation. We cannot find any such government as tyranny mentioned or named in Scripture, or any word in the Hebrew tongue to express it. After such time as the cities of Greece practised to shake off monarchy, then and not till then, (which was after Homer's time) the name of tyrant was taken up for a word of disgrace for such men as by craft or force wrested the power of a city from a multitude to one man only—and not for the *exercising*, but for the *ill obtaining* of the government. But now every man that is but thought to govern ill, or to be an ill man, is presently termed a tyrant, and so judged by his subjects. Few remember the prohibition, Exodus 22:28, 'Thou shalt not revile the gods, nor curse the ruler of thy people', and fewer understand the reason of it. Though we may not one judge another, yet we may speak evil or revile one another, in that which hath been lawfully judged, and upon a trial wherein they have been heard and condemned. This is not to judge, but only to relate the judgment of the ruler. To speak evil, or to revile a supreme judge, cannot be without judging him who hath no superior on earth to judge him—and in that regard must always be presumed innocent, though never so ill, if he cannot lawfully be heard.

J.M. that will have it tyranny in a king not to regard the laws, doth himself give as little regard to them as any man, where he reckons that 'contesting for privileges, customs, forms, and that old entanglement of iniquity, their gibberish laws', are 'the badges of ancient slavery': *Tenure* (p. 3); 'a disputing precedents, forms and circumstances', (p. 5).

J.M. is also of opinion that 'if at any time our forefathers, out of baseness, have lost anything of their right, that ought not hurt us. They might if they would promise slavery for themselves. For us certainly they could not, who have always the same right to free ourselves that they had to give themselves to any man in slavery'.[31] This doctrine well practised, layeth all open to constant anarchy.

---

30   Aristotle, *Politics*, 1278^b 36–8.
31   Milton, *Pro Populo*, p. 412.

Lastly, if any desire to know what the liberty of the people is which J.M. pleads for, he resolves us, saying that 'he that takes away from the people the right of choosing what form of government they please, takes away truly that in which all liberty doth almost consist'.[32] It is well said by J.M. that all liberty doth *almost* consist in choosing their form of government. For there is another liberty exercised by the people, which he mentions not—which is the liberty of the people's choosing their religion. Every man may be of any religion, or of no religion. Greece and Rome have been as famous for polytheism, or multitudes of gods, as of governors; and imagining aristocracy and democracy in heaven, as on earth.

32 Milton, *Pro Populo*, p. 192.

OBSERVATIONS UPON
H. Grotius
DE JURE BELLI & PACIS.

In most questions of weight and difficulty concerning the right of war, or peace, or supreme power, Grotius hath recourse to the law of nature or of nations, or to the primitive will of those men who first joined in society. It is necessary therefore a little to lay open the variety or contrariety in the civil and canon law, and in Grotius himself, about the law of nature and nations, not with a purpose to raise any contention about words or phrases, but with a desire to reconcile or expound the sense of different terms.

Civilians,[1] canonists, politicians and divines are not a little perplexed in distinguishing between the law of nature and the law of nations. About *jus naturae* and *jus gentium* there is much dispute by such as handle the original of government, and of property and community.

The civil law in one text allows a threefold division of law into *jus naturae*, *jus gentium*, and *jus civile*. But in another text of the same law we find only a twofold division, into *jus civile*, and *jus gentium*. This latter division the law takes from Gaius, the former from Ulpian, who will have *jus naturale* to be 'that which nature hath taught all creatures': '*quod natura omnia animalia docuit*'.[2] But for this he is confuted by Grotius, Salmasius, and others who restrain the law of nature only to men using reason, which makes it all one with the law of nations—to which the canon law consents, and saith that '*jus naturale est commune omnium nationum*'[3] ["natural law is common to all nations"]. 'That which natural reason appoints all men to use, is the law of nations', saith Theophilus in the text of the civil law, and in the second book of the Institutes, ch. 1, *jus naturae* is confounded with *jus gentium*.

As the civilians sometimes confound and sometimes separate the law of nature and the law of nations, so other-whiles they make them also contrary one to the other. 'By the law of nature all men are born free': '*jure*

---

1 Merriam-Webster defines as "a specialist in Roman or modern civil law".
2 *Corpus Iuris Civilis, Digestorum et Pandectorum*, i, 1.
3 *Corpus Iuris Canonici, Decreti prima pars*, §1.

naturali omnes liberi nascuntur'; but servitude is by the law of nations: '*jure gentium servitus invasit*'[4] ["servitude entered by the laws of nations"], saith Ulpian.

And the civil law not only makes the law of nature and of nations contrary, but also will have the law of nations contrary to itself. 'War', saith the law, 'was brought in by the law of nations': '*ex jure gentium introducta bella*'.[5] And yet the law of nations saith 'since nature hath made us all of one kindred, it follows it is not lawful for one man to lie in wait for another': '*cum inter nos cognitionem quandam natura constituit, consequens est hominem homini insidiare nefas esse*',[6] saith Florentinus.

Again, the civil law teacheth that 'from the law of nature proceeds the conjunction of man and woman, the procreation and education of children'.[7] But as for 'religion to God, and obedience to parents'[8] it makes it to be by the law of nations.

To touch now the canon law, we may find in one place that 'men are governed either by the law of nature, or by customs': '*homines reguntur naturali jure, aut moribus*'.[9] The law of nature they call 'a divine law, the customs a human law': '*leges aut divinae sunt aut humanae; divinae naturae, humanae moribus constant*'.[10] But in the next place the canon law makes *jus* to be either '*naturale, aut civile, aut gentium*'.[11] Though this division agree in terms with that of Ulpian in the civil law, yet in the explication of the terms there is diversity. For what one law makes to belong to the law of nature, the other refers to the law of nations—as may easily appear to him that will take the pains to compare the civil and canon law in these points.

A principal ground of these diversities and contrarieties of divisions was an error which the heathens taught, that 'all things at first were common', and that 'all men were equal'. This mistake was not so heinous in those ethnic[12] authors of the civil laws, who wanting the guide of the history of Moses were fain to follow poets and fables for their leaders. But for Christians, who have read the Scriptures, to dream either of a community of all things, or an equality of all persons, is a fault scarce pardonable.

To salve these apparent contrarieties of community and property, of

4   *Digest*, i, 4.
5   *Digest*, i, 5.
6   *Digest*, i, 3.
7   *Digest*, i, 1.
8   *Digest*, i, 2.
9   *Decreti*, §1.
10   *Decreti*, §1.
11   *Decreti*, §1.
12   Pagan.

equality and subjection, the law of *jus gentium* was first invented. When that could not satisfy, to mend the matter this *jus gentium* was divided into a natural law of nations, and an human law of nations; and the law of nature into a primary and a secondary law of nature—distinctions which make a great sound, but edify not at all if they come under examination.

If there hath been a time when all things were common and all men equal, and that it be otherwise now, we must needs conclude that the law by which all things were common, and men equal, was contrary to the law by which now things are proper[13] and men subject.

If we will allow Adam to have been lord of the world and of his children, there will need no such distinctions of the law of nature and of nations. For the truth will be that whatsoever the heathens comprehended under these two laws, is comprised in the moral law.

That the law of nature is one and the same with the moral may appear by a definition given by Grotius. The 'law of nature', saith he, 'is the dictate of reason, shewing that in every action by the agreeing or disagreeing of it with natural reason there is a moral honesty or dishonesty, and consequently that such an action is commanded or forbidden by God the author of nature' (Grotius 1, i, x, 1). I cannot tell how Grotius would otherwise have defined the moral law. And the canon law grants as much, teaching that 'the law of nature is contained in the law and the gospel'[14] 'whatsoever ye will that men do', etc., Matthew 7.

The term of *jus naturae* is not originally to be found in Scripture. For though Thomas Aquinas takes upon him to prove out of the second[15] to the Romans, that there is a *jus naturae*, yet St. Paul doth not use those express terms. His words are 'the gentiles which have not the law, do by nature the things contained in the law, these, having not the law are a law unto themselves'.[16] He doth not say nature is a law unto them, but they are a law unto themselves. As for that which they call the law of nations, it is not a law distinct, much less opposite to the law of nature. But it is a small branch or parcel of that great law, for it is nothing but the law of nature or the moral law between nations. The same commandment that forbids one private man to rob another, or one corporation to hurt another corporation, obliges also one king not to rob another king, and one commonwealth not to spoil another. The same law that enjoins charity to all men,

---

13   "Proper" in the sense of *proprius*, i.e. "one's own, particular, private".
14   *Decreti*, §1.
15   Second epistle.
16   Romans 2:14.

even to enemies, binds princes and states to show charity to one another, as well as private persons.

And as the common or civil laws of each kingdom which are made against treason, theft, murder, adultery, or the like, are all and every one of them grounded upon some particular commandment of the moral law; so all the laws of nations must be subordinate and reducible to the moral law.

The law of nature or the moral law is like the main ocean, which though it be one entire body, yet several parts of it have distinct names according to the diversity of the coasts on which they border. So it comes to pass that the law of nations, which is but a part of the law of nature, may be sub-divided almost *in infinitum*, according to the variety of the persons or matters about which it is conversant.

The law of nature or the divine law is general, and doth only comprehend some principles of morality notoriously known of themselves, or at the most is extended to those things which by necessary and evident inference are consequent to those principles. Besides these, many other things are necessary to the well governing of a commonwealth, and therefore it was necessary that by human reason something more in particular should be determined concerning those things which could not be defined by natural reason alone. Hence it is that human laws be necessary as comments upon the text of the moral law—and of this judgment is Aquinas, who teacheth that

> *necessitas legis humanae manat ex eo, quod lex naturalis, vel divina, generalis est, et solum complectitur quaedam principia morum per se nota, et ad summum extenditur ad ea quae necessaria et evidenti elatione ex illis principiis consequuntur: praeter illa vero multa alia sunt necessaria in republica ad ejus rectam gubernationem: et ideo necessarium fuit ut per humanam rationem aliqua magis in particulari determinarentur circa ea quae per solam rationem naturalem definiri non possunt*

> ["the necessity of human law emanates from this: the natural or divine law is general, and includes certain self-evident moral principles, and is extended at most to what follows evidently and necessarily from those principles. But besides these much else is necessary for the right government of a state. And thus it was necessary that through human reason some things should be determined more particularly concerning that which cannot be defined through natural reason alone."] (Ludovicus Molina, *De Justitia*).

Thus much may suffice to show the distractions in and between the civil and common laws about the law of nature and nations. In the next place we are to consider how Grotius distinguisheth these laws.

To maintain the community of things to be natural, Grotius hath framed new divisions of the law of nature. First, in his preface to his books *De Jure Belli et Pacis*, he produceth a definition of the law of nature in such doubtful, obscure and reserved terms, as if he were diffident of his undertaking. Next, in his first book and first chapter he gives us another distribution which differs from his doctrine in his preface.

In his preface his principle is that the 'appetite of society, that is to say, of community, is an action proper to man'. Here he presently corrects himself with an exception, that 'some other creatures are found to desire society', and withal he answers the objections thus—that 'this desire of society in brute beasts comes from some external principle'.[17] What he means by *principium intelligens extrinsecum*' ["intelligent external principle"] I understand not, nor doth he explain, nor is it material, nor is the argument he useth to any purpose. For admitting all he saith to be true, yet his principle fails, for the question is not from what principle this desire of society proceeds in beasts, but whether there be such a desire or no. Besides, here he takes the appetite of society and community to be all one, whereas many live in society which live not in community.

Next he teacheth that 'the keeping of society (*custodia societatis*) which in a rude manner', saith he, 'we have now expressed, is the fountain of that law which is properly so called'. I conceive by the law properly so called he intends the law of nature, though he express not so much; and to this appetite of sociable community he refers *alieni abstinentia* ["abstaining from (that of) others"]. But herein it may be he forgets himself, for where there is community there is neither *meum* ["mine"] nor *tuum* ["thine"], nor yet *alienum* ["another's"]—and if there be no *alienum* there can be no *alieni abstinentia*. To the same purpose he saith that 'by the law of nature men must stand to bargains': '*juris naturae sit stare pactis*'.[18] But if all things were common by nature, how could there be any bargain?

Again, Grotius tells us that 'from this signification of the law there hath flowed another larger', which consists, saith he, 'in discerning what delights us or hurts us, and in judging how things should be wisely distributed to each one'. This latter he calls the 'looser law of nature'; the former, '*jus sociale*, the law of nature, strictly, or properly taken'. 'And these two laws of nature should have place', saith he, 'though men should deny there were a

17   Hugo Grotius, *De Jure Belli ac Pacis*, prolegomena 6–7.
18   Grotius, *De Jure*, prolegomena 15.

God. But to them that believe there is a God, there is another original of law beside the natural, coming from the free will of God, to the which our own understanding tells us we must be subject'.

Thus have I gathered the substance of what is most material concerning the law of nature in his preface.

If we turn to the book itself, we have a division of the law into

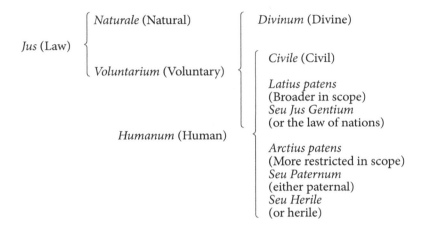

In the definition of *jus naturale* he omits those subtleties of *jus naturae proprie dictum* ["the law of nature properly so-called"], and *quod laxius ita dicitur* ["what is more freely so-called"], which we find in his preface, and gives such a plain definition as may fitly agree to the moral law. By this it seems the law of nature and the moral law are one and the same.

Whereas he affirmeth that

> the actions about which the law of nature is conversant are lawful or unlawful of themselves, and therefore are necessarily commanded or forbidden by God—by which mark this law of nature doth not only differ from human law but from the divine voluntary law, which doth not command or forbid those things which of themselves and by their own nature are lawful or unlawful, but makes them unlawful by forbidding them and due by commanding them.[19]

19   Grotius, *De Jure*, 1, i, x, 2.

in this he seems to make the law of nature to differ from God's volun-
tary law,; whereas in God necessary and voluntary are all one. Salmasius
De Usuris[20] in the twentieth chapter condemns this opinion of Grotius.
Though he name him not, yet he means him, if I mistake not.

   In the next place I observe his saying that some things are by the law of
nature not *proprie* ["properly"] but *reductive* ["by reducing"]; and that the
law of

> nature deals not only with those things which are beside the
> will of man but also with many things which follow the act
> of man's will. So dominion, such as is now in use, man's will
> brought in. But now that it is brought in, it is against the law
> of nature to take that from thee against thy will which is in
> thy dominion.[21]

Yet for all this Grotius maintains that 'the law of nature is so immutable
that it cannot be changed by God himself'.[22] He means to make it good
with a distinction: 'some things', saith he, 'are by the law of nature, but not
simply, but according to the certain state of things. So the common use
of things was natural as long as dominion was not brought in, and right
for every man to take his own by force before laws were made'. Here if
Grotius would have spoken plain, instead of 'but not simply, but according
to the certain state of things', he would have said 'but not immutably, but
for a certain time'. And then this distinction would have run thus: 'some
things are by the law of nature, but not immutably, but for a certain time'.
This must needs be the naked sense of his distinction, as appears by his
explication in the words following, where he saith that 'the common use
of things was natural so long as dominion was not brought in'. Dominion,
he saith, was brought in by the will of man, whom by this doctrine Grotius
makes to be able to change that law which God himself cannot change,
as he saith. He gives a double ability to man: first, to make that no law of
nature which God made to be the law of nature; and next, to make that a
law of nature which God made not. For now that dominion is brought in,
he maintains, it is against the law of nature to take that which is in another
man's dominion.

   Besides, I find no coherence in these words: 'by the law of nature it was
right for every man to take his own by force, before laws made', since by the
law of nature no man had anything of his own, and until laws were made

---

20   Claudius Salmasius, *De Usuris Liber*.
21   Grotius, *De Jure*, 1, i, x, 3–4.
22   Grotius, *De Jure*, 1, i, x, 5.

there was no property according to his doctrine.

'*Jus humanum voluntarium latius patens*' ["voluntary human law, broader in scope"], he makes to be the law of nations, which, saith he, 'by the will of all or many nations hath received a power to bind'. He adds 'of many' because there is, as he grants, 'scarce any law to be found common to all nations besides the law of nature—which also is wont to be called the law of nations, being common to all nations'. Nay, as he confesseth 'often that is the law in one part of the world which in another part of the world is not the law of nations'.[23]

By these sentences it seems Grotius can scarce tell what to make to be the law of nations or where to find it.

Whereas he makes the law of nations to have a binding power from the will of men, it must be remembered that it is not sufficient for men to have a will to bind, but it is necessary also to have a power to bind.

Though several nations have one and the same law—for instance, let it be granted that theft is punished by death in many countries—yet this doth not make it to be a law of nations, because each nation hath it but as a natural or civil law of their own country, and though it have a binding power from the will of many nations, yet because each nation hath but a will and power to bind themselves, and may without prejudice, consent, or consulting of any neighbour-nation alter this law if they find cause, it cannot properly be called the law of nations. That which is the foundation of the law of nations is to have it concern 'such things as belong to the mutual society of nations among themselves', as Grotius confesseth (book 2, ch. 8)—and not of such things as have no further relation than to the particular benefit of each kingdom. For, as private men must neglect their own profit for the good of their country, so particular nations must sometimes remit part of their benefit for the good of many nations.

True it is that in particular kingdoms and commonwealths there be civil and national laws, and also customs that obtain the force of laws. But yet such laws are ordained by some supreme power, and the customs are examined, judged, and allowed by the same supreme power. Where there is no supreme power that extends over all or many nations but only God himself, there can be no laws made to bind nations, but such as are made by God himself. We cannot find that God made any laws to bind nations, but only the moral law. As for the judicial law, though it were ordained by God, yet it was not the law of nations but of one nation only, and fitted to that commonwealth.

If any think that the customs wherein many nations do consent may be called the law of nations, as well as the customs of any one nation may be esteemed for national laws, they are to consider that it is not the being of a custom that makes it lawful—for then all customs, even evil customs, would be lawful. But it is the approbation of the supreme power that gives a legality to the custom. Where there is no supreme power over many nations, their customs cannot be made legal.

The doctrine of Grotius is that

> God immediately after the creation did bestow upon man-kind in general a right over things of inferior nature ... From whence it came to pass that presently every man might snatch what he would for his own use, and spend what he could—and such an universal right was then instead of property. For what every one so catched another could not take from him but by injury (*De Jure Belli*, book 2, ch. 2).

How repugnant this assertion of Grotius is to the truth of holy Scripture, Mr. Selden teacheth us in his *Mare Clausum*[24] (book 1, ch. 4), saying that Adam 'by donation from God', Genesis 1:28,

> was made the general lord of all things, not without such a private dominion to himself as (without his grant) did exclude his children. And by donation and assignation, or some kind of cession (before he was dead or left any heir to succeed him) his children had their distinct territories by right of private dominion. Abel had his flocks and pastures for them. Cain had his fields for corn, and the land of Nod where he built himself a city.[25]

This determination of Mr. Selden's being consonant to the history of the Bible, and to natural reason, doth contradict the doctrine of Grotius. I cannot conceive why Mr. Selden should afterwards affirm that 'neither the law of nature nor the divine law do command or forbid either communion of all things or private dominion, but permitteth both'.[26]

As for the general community between Noah and his sons which Mr. Selden will have to be granted to them, Genesis 9:2, the text doth not warrant it. For although the sons are there mentioned with Noah in the blessing, yet it may best be understood with a subordination or a benediction

---

24   John Selden, *Mare Clausum Seu De Dominio Maris Libri Duo*.

25   Selden, *Mare Clausum*, translated as *Of the Dominion, or Ownership of the Sea*, p. 19.

26   Selden, *Dominion*, p. 20.

in succession. The blessing might truly be fulfilled if the sons, either under or after their father, enjoyed a private dominion. It is not probable that the private dominion which God gave to Adam—and by his donation, assignation, or cession to his children—was abrogated, and a community of all things instituted between Noah and his sons. At the time of the flood, Noah was left the sole heir of the world. Why should it be thought that God would disinherit him of his birthright, and make him of all the men in the world the only tenant in common with his children? If the blessing given to Adam, Genesis 1:28, be compared to that given to Noah and his sons, Genesis 9:2, there will be found a considerable difference between those two texts. In the benediction of Adam we find expressed a 'subduing of the earth, and a dominion over the creatures', neither of which are expressed in the blessing of Noah, nor the earth there once named. It is only said, the 'fear of you shall be upon the creatures, and into your hands are they delivered'. Then immediately it follows, 'Every moving thing shall be meat for you, as the green herb'. The first blessing gave Adam dominion over the earth and all creatures, the latter allows Noah liberty to use the living creatures for food. Here is no alteration or diminishing of his title to a property of all things, but an enlargement only of his commons.

But whether, with Grotius, community came in at the creation, or, with Mr. Selden, at the Flood, they both agree it did not long continue. '*Sed veri non est simile hujusmodi communionem diu obtinuisse*' ["but it is not true that this same sort of common ownership prevailed for long"], is the confession of Mr. Selden. It seems strange that Grotius should maintain that community of all things should be by the law of nature, of which God is the author, and yet such community should not be able to continue. Doth it not derogate from the providence of God Almighty to ordain a community which could not continue? Or doth it make the act of our forefathers, in abrogating the natural law of community by introducing that of property, to be a sin of a high presumption?

The prime duties of the second table[27] are conversant about the right of property. But if property be brought in by a human law, as Grotius teacheth, then the moral law depends upon the will of man. There could be no law against adultery or theft if women and all things were common.

Mr. Selden saith that the law of nature or of God '*nec vetuit, nec jubebat, sed permisit utrumque, tam nempe rerum communionem quam privatum dominium*'[28] ["neither forbade nor commanded, but permitted each, namely as much common as private ownership of things"]. And yet for

---

27   Commandments 5–10 of the Decalogue.
28   Selden, *Dominion*, p. 20.

property (which he terms '*primaeva rerum dominia*' ["primeval owner-ship of things"]) he teacheth that 'Adam received it from God': *a numine acceperat*. And for community he saith: 'We meet with evident footsteps of the community of things in that donation of God by which Noah and his three sons are made *domini pro indiviso rerum omnium*'[29] ["lords in common of all things"]. Thus he makes the private dominion of Adam as well as the common dominion of Noah and his sons to be both by the will of God. Nor doth he shew how Noah, or his sons, or their posterity, had any authority to alter the law of community which was given them by God.

'In distributing territories', Mr. Selden saith, 'the consent as it were of mankind (passing their promise which should also bind their posterity) did intervene. So that men departed from their common right of commu-nion of those things which were so distributed to particular lords or mas-ters.'[30] This distribution by consent of mankind we must take upon credit, for there is not the least proof offered for it out of antiquity.

How the consent of mankind could bind posterity when all things were common is a point not so evident. Where children take nothing by gift or by descent from their parents, but have an equal and common interest with them, there is no reason in such cases that the acts of the fathers should bind the sons.

I find no cause why Mr. Selden should call community a pristine right; since he makes it but to begin in Noah, and to end in Noah's children, or grand children at the most; for he confesseth the earth '*a Noachidis secu-lis aliquot post diluvium esse divisam*'[31] ["was divided by Noah's posterity sometime after the Flood"].

That ancient tradition which by Mr. Selden's acknowledgment hath ob-tained reputation everywhere, seems most reasonable, in that he tells us that

> Noah himself, as lord of all, was author of the distribution of the world, and of private dominion, and that by the appoint-ment of an oracle from God he did confirm this distribution by his last will and testament, which at his death he left in the hands of his eldest son Shem. And also warned all his sons that none of them should invade any of their brothers' dominions, or injure one another, because from thence dis-cord and civil war would necessarily follow.[32]

29 Selden, *Dominion*, p. 17.
30 Selden, *Dominion*, p. 21.
31 Selden, *Dominion*, p. 18.
32 Selden, *Dominion*, p. 19.

Many conclusions in Grotius his book *De Jure Belli ac Pacis* are built upon the foundation of these two principles:

> 1. The first is that '*communis rerum usus naturalis fuit*'[33] ["the use of things in common was natural"].

> 2. The second is that '*dominium quale nunc in usu est, voluntas humana introduxit*'[34] ["human will introduced the kind of ownership now in use"].

Upon these two propositions of natural community and voluntary property depend divers dangerous and seditious conclusions, which are dispersed in several places. In the fourth chapter of the first book, the title of which chapter is of the war of subjects against their superiors, Grotius handleth the question 'Whether the law of not resisting superiors do bind us in most grievous and most certain danger,'[35] and his determination is that

> This law of not resisting superiors seems to depend upon the will of those men who at first joined themselves in a civil society, from whom the right of government doth come to them that govern. If those had been at first asked if their will were to impose this burden upon all, that they should choose rather to die than in any case by arms to repel the force of superiors, I know not whether they would answer that it was their will unless perhaps with this addition: if resistance cannot be made but with the great disturbance of the commonwealth, and destruction of many innocents.[36]

Here we have his resolution that in great and certain danger men may resist their governors, if it may be without disturbance of the commonwealth. If you would know who should be judge of the greatness and certainty of the danger, or how we may know it, Grotius hath not one word of it. So that for ought appears to the contrary, his mind may be that every private man may be judge of the danger—for other judge he appoints none. It had been a foul fault in so desperate a piece of service as the resisting of superiors, to have concealed the lawful means by which we may judge of the greatness or certainty of public danger before we lift up our hands against authority,

---

33 Grotius, *De Jure*, 1, i, x, 7.
34 Grotius, *De Jure*, 1, i, x, 4.
35 Grotius, *De Jure*, 1, iv, vii, 1.
36 Grotius, *De Jure*, 1, iv, vii, 2.

considering how prone most of us are to censure and mistake those things for great and certain dangers which in truth many times are no dangers at all, or at the most but very small ones; and so flatter ourselves that by resisting our superiors, we may do our country laudable service without disturbance of the commonwealth, since the effects of sedition cannot be certainly judged of but by the events only.

Grotius proceeds to answer an objection against this doctrine of resisting superiors. 'If', saith he,

> any man shall say that this rigid doctrine of dying rather than resisting any injuries of superiors is no human but a divine law, it is to be noted that men at first, not by any precept of God, but of their own accord, led by experience of the infirmities of separated families against violence, did meet together in civil society, from whence civil power took beginning. Which therefore St. calls an human ordinance, although elsewhere it be called a divine ordinance, because God approveth the wholesome institutions of men. God in approving a human law is to be thought to approve it as human, and in a human manner.[37]

And again in another place he goeth further, and teacheth us that 'if the question happen to be concerning the primitive will of the people, it will not be amiss for the people that now are, and which are accounted the same with them that were long ago, to express their meaning in this matter which is to be followed, unless it certainly appear that the people long ago willed otherwise' (book 2, ch. 2).

For fuller explication of his judgment about resisting superiors, he concludes thus:

> The greater the thing is which is to be preserved, the greater is the equity which reacheth forth an exception against the words of the law. Yet I dare not (saith Grotius) without difference condemn either single men or a lesser part of the people, who in the last refuge of necessity do so use this equity as in the meantime they do not forsake the respect of the common good.[38]

---

37 Grotius, *De Jure*, 1, iv, vii, 3.
38 Grotius, *De Jure*, 1, iv, vii, 4.

Another doctrine of Grotius is that 'the empire which is exercised by kings doth not cease to be the empire of the people'.[39] 'That kings who in a lawful manner succeed those who were elected have the supreme power by an usufructuary right only, and no property'.

Furthermore he teacheth that 'the people may choose what form of government they please, and their will is the rule of right: *Populus eligere potest qualem vult gubernationis formam, neque ex praestantia formae, sed ex voluntate jus metiendum est*' (book 1, ch. 3).

Also that:

> The people choosing a king may reserve some acts to them-
> selves and may bestow others upon the king with full au-
> thority if either an express partition be appointed, or if the
> people being yet free do command their future king by way
> of a standing command, or if anything be added by which it
> may be understood that the king may be compelled or else
> punished.[40]

In these passages of Grotius which I have cited, we find evidently these doctrines:

> 1. That civil power depends on the will of the people.

> 2. That private men or petty multitudes may take up arms
> against their princes.

> 3. That the lawful kings have no property in their kingdoms,
> but an usufructuary right only as if the people were the lords
> and kings but their tenants.

> 4. That the law of not resisting superiors is a human law, de-
> pending on the will of the people at first.

> 5. That the will of the first people, if it be not known, may be
> expounded by the people that now are.

No doubt but Grotius foresaw what uses the people might make of these doctrines by concluding if the chief power be in the people that then it is lawful for them to compel and punish kings as oft as they misuse their power. Therefore he tells us he 'rejects the opinion of them who every-where and without exception will have the chief power to be so the peo-

---

39   Grotius, *De Jure*, 2, xvi, xvi, 1.
40   Grotius, *De Jure*, 1, iii, xvii, 1.

ple's that it is lawful for them to compel and punish kings as oft as they misuse their power'. And 'this opinion', he confesseth, 'if it be altogether received, hath been and may be the cause of many evils'. This cautelous[41] rejection, qualified with these terms of *everywhere, without exception*, and *altogether*, makes but a mixed negation—partly negative and partly affirmative (which our lawyers call a negative pregnant[42]). Which brings forth this modal proposition, *that in some places with exception, and in some sort the people may compel and punish their kings.*

But let us see how Grotius doth refute the general opinion that people may correct kings. He frames his argument in these words:

> It is lawful for every man to yield himself to be a private servant to whom he please. What should hinder but that also it may be lawful for a free people so to yield themselves to one or more, that the right of governing them be fully set over without retaining any part of the right? And you must not say 'that this may not be presumed', for we do not now seek what in a doubtful case may be presumed, but what by right may be done.[43]

Thus far is the argument, in which the most that is proved (if we gratify him and yield his whole argument for good) is this, *that the people may grant away their power without retaining any part.* But what is this to what the people *have* done? For though the people may give away their power without reservation of any part to themselves, yet if they have not so done, but have reserved a part, Grotius must confess that the people may compel and punish their kings if they transgress. So that by his favour, the point will be not what by right may be done, but what in this doubtful case *hath* been done—since by his own rule it is the will and meaning of the first people that joined in society that must regulate the power of their successors.

But on Grotius' side it may be urged that in all presumption the people have given away their whole power to kings, unless they can prove they

41 *Merriam-Webster* defines as "crafty, cunning".
42 *Nolo's Plain-English Law Dictionary* defines as "a denial of wrongdoing that implies the opposite by denying only a qualification of the allegation, not the allegation itself. For example, if a defendant who is accused of embezzling a million dollars in 2007 denies the allegation by saying, 'I did not embezzle a million dollars in 2007,' the denial is pregnant with the possibility that the defendant may have embezzled a different sum of money in a different year."
43 Grotius, *De Jure*, 1, iii, viii, 1.

have reserved a part. For if they will have any benefit of a reservation or exception, it lies on their part to prove their exception, and not on the kings' part who are in possession.

This answer, though in itself it be most just and good, yet of all men Grotius may not use it. For he saves the peoples labour of proving the primitive reservation of their forefathers, by making the people that now are competent expositors of the meaning of those first ancestors, who may justly be presumed not to have been either so improvident for themselves or so negligent of all their posterity, when by the law of nature they were free and had all things common, as at an instant without any condition or limitation to give away that liberty and right of community and to make themselves and their children eternally subject to the will of such governors as might misuse them without control.

On the behalf of the people, it may be further answered to Grotius that although our ancestors had made an absolute grant of their liberty, without any condition expressed, yet it must be necessarily implied that it was upon condition to be well governed, and that the non-performance of that implied condition makes the grant void. Or, if we will not allow an implicit condition, then it may be said that the grant in itself was a void grant for being unreasonable and a violation of the law of nature, without any valuable consideration. What sound reply Grotius can return to such answers I cannot conceive, if he keep himself to his first principle of natural community.

As Grotius' argument against the people is not sound, so his answer to the argument that is made for the people is not satisfactory. It is objected that 'he that ordains, is above him that is ordained'. Grotius answers:

> *verum duntaxat est in ea constitutione cujus effectus perpetuo pendet a voluntate constituentis, non etiam in ea quae ab initio est voluntatis, postea vero effectum habet necessitates: quomodo mulier virum sibi constituit, cui parere semper habet necesse.*[44]

> ["it is true only in a grant of authority in which the effect continually depends on the will of the one granting, and not true where it depends on the grantor's will but afterward holds necessarily: in the same way as the wife takes to herself a husband whom she holds it necessary to always obey."]

---

44 Grotius, *De Jure*, 1, iii, viii, 13.

The reply may be that by Grotius' former doctrine the very effect of the constitution of kings by the people depends perpetually upon the will of them that constitute, and upon no other necessity. He will not say that it is by any necessity of the law of nature, or by any positive law of God. He teacheth that: '*Non Dei praecepto, sed sponte*' ["not by the command of God, but by their own free will"], men entered into civil society; that it is an human ordinance; that God doth only approve it '*ut humanum*', ["as human"] and '*humano modo*'[45] ["in a human way"]. He tells us further that '*populus potest eligere qualem vult gubernationis formam, et ex voluntate jus metiendum est*'[46] ["the people can choose what form of government it wish, and from its will is right to be measured"]; that the people may give the king as little power as they will and for as little time as they please; that they may make temporary kings, as directors and protectors—'*jus quovis tempore revocabile, id est precarium*' ["a right revocable at any time whatsoever, that is, a borrowed right"]; as the Vandals in Africa and the Goths in Spain would depose their kings as oft as they displeased them, '*horum enim actus irriti possunt reddi ab his qui potestatem revocabiliter dederunt, ac proinde non idem est effectus nec jus idem*'[47] ["for their acts can be declared void by these who gave them revocable power, and hence it is neither the same effect, nor the same right"]. Here he doth teach in plain words, the effect doth depend upon the will of the people. By this we may judge how improperly he useth the instance of a woman that appoints herself a husband, whom she must always necessarily obey—since the necessity of the continuance of the wife's obedience depends upon the law of God, which hath made the bond of matrimony indissolvable. Grotius will not say the like for the continuance of the subject's obedience to the prince, neither will they say that women may choose husbands as he tells us the people may choose kings, by giving their husbands as little power and for as little a time as they please.

Next it is objected that tutors who are set over pupils may be removed if they abuse their power. Grotius answers: '*In tutore hoc procedit qui superiorem habet, at in imperiis quia progressus non datur in infinitum*' ["this happens in the case of a tutor who has a superior, but in matters of governance it happens because progress is not infinite"], '*omnino in aliqua persona aut coetu consistendum est*': 'we must stay in some one person, or in a multitude, whose faults (because they have no superior judge above them) God hath witnessed that He will have a particular care of, either to

---

45 Grotius, *De Jure*, 1, iv, vii, 3.
46 Grotius, *De Jure*, 1, iii, viii, 2.
47 Grotius, *De Jure*, 1, iii, xi, 3.

revenge them if He judge it needful, or to tolerate them either for punishment or trial of the people'. It is true in kingdoms we cannot proceed *in infinitum*. Yet we may and must go to the highest, which by Grotius' rule is the people, because they first made kings. So that there is no need to stay *in aliqua persona*, but *in coetu*, in the people—so that by his doctrine kings may be punished by the people, but the faults of the people must be left to the judgment of God.

I have briefly presented here the desperate inconveniences which attend upon the doctrine of the natural freedom and community of all things. These and many more absurdities are easily removed if on the contrary we maintain the natural and private dominion of Adam to be the fountain of all government and property. And if we mark it well we shall find that Grotius doth in part grant as much. The ground why those that now live do obey their governors is the will of their forefathers, who at the first ordained princes—and in obedience to that will the children continue in subjection. This is according to the mind of Grotius, so that the question is not *whether* kings have a fatherly power over their subjects, but *how* kings came first by it. Grotius will have it that our forefathers, being all free, made an assignment of their power to kings. The other opinion denies any such general freedom of our forefathers, but derives the power of kings from the original dominion of Adam.

This natural dominion of Adam may be proved out of Grotius himself, who teacheth that '*generatione jus acquiritur parentibus in liberos*'[48] ["by generation, right is acquired over children by their parents"], and that 'naturally no other can be found but the parents to whom the government should belong', and the right of ruling and compelling them doth belong to parents. And in another place he hath these words, speaking of the fifth commandment: '*Parentum nomine qui naturales sunt magistratus, etiam alios rectores par est intelligi quorum authoritas societatem humanam continet*'[49] ["by the name of parents, who are natural rulers, is also to be understood other governors, whose authority binds human society"]. And if parents be natural magistrates, children must needs be born natural subjects.

But although Grotius acknowledges parents to be natural magistrates, yet he will have it that children when they come to full age and are separated from their parents are free from natural subjection. For this he offers proof out of Aristotle and out of Scripture.

First, for Aristotle. We must note he doth not teach that every separation

48   Grotius, *De Jure*, 2, v, ii, 1.
49   Grotius, *De Jure*, 2, xx, xxx, 2.

of children of full age is an obtaining of liberty, as if that men when they come to years might voluntarily separate themselves and cast off their natural obedience. But Aristotle speaks only of a passive separation. For he doth not say that children are subject to parents until they *do separate*, but he saith until they *be separated*, χωρισθῇ, in the verb of the passive voice. That is, until *by law* they be separated. For the law (which is nothing else but the will of him that hath the power of the supreme father) doth in many cases, for the public benefit of society, free children from subjection to the subordinate parent. So that the natural subjection by such emancipation of children is not extinguished, but only assumed and regulated by the parent paramount.

Secondly, Grotius cites Numbers 30 to prove that the 'power of the fathers over the sons and daughters, to dissolve their vows, was not perpetual, but during the time only whilst the children were part of the father's family'.[50] But if we turn to the chapter, we may find that Grotius either deceives himself or us. For there is not one word in that chapter concerning the vows of sons, but of daughters only, being in their father's family. And the being of the daughter in the father's house meaneth only the daughter's being a virgin and not married, which may be gathered by the argument of the whole chapter—which taketh particular order for the vows of women of all estates. First, for virgins, in the third verse. Secondly, for wives in general, in the sixth verse. Thirdly, for widows and women divorced, in the ninth verse. There is no law for virgins out of their fathers' houses; we may not think they would have been omitted if they had been free from their fathers. We find no freedom in the text for women till after marriage—and if they were married, though they were in their fathers' houses, yet the fathers had no power of their vows, but their husbands.

If by the law of nature departure from the father's house had emancipated children, why doth the civil law, contrary to the law of nature, give power and remedy to fathers to recover by action of law their children that depart, or are taken away from them without their consent? Without the consent of parents the civil law allows no emancipation.

Concerning subjection of children to parents, Grotius distinguisheth three several times:

The first is the time of 'imperfect judgment'.

The second is the time of 'perfect judgment', but 'whilst the son remains part of the father's family'.

The third is 'the time after he hath departed out of his father's family'.

50   Grotius, *De Jure*, 2, v, vii.

In the first time, he saith, 'all the actions of children are under the dominion of the parents'.[51]

During the second time,

> when they are of the age of mature judgment they are under their father's command in those actions only which are of moment for their parents' family. In other actions the children have a power or moral faculty of doing, but they are bound in those also to study always to please their parents. But since this duty is not by force of any moral faculty, as those former are, but only of piety, observance, and duty of repaying thanks, it doth not make any thing void which is done against it, as neither a gift of any thing is void being made by any owner whatsoever against the rules of parsimony.[52]

> [...]

> In both these times, the right of ruling and compelling is (as Grotius acknowledgeth) comprehended so far forth as children are to be compelled to their duty, or amended. Although the power of a parent doth so follow the person of a father that it cannot be pulled away and transferred upon another, yet the father may naturally pawn, or also sell his son if there be need.[53]

In the third time, he saith, 'the son is in all things free and of his own authority, always that duty remaining of piety and observance, the cause of which is perpetual'.[54] In this triple distinction, though Grotius allow children in some cases during the second, and in all cases during the third time to be free and of their own power by a moral faculty, yet, in that he confesseth in all cases children are bound to study always to please their parents,—'the cause of which', as he saith, 'is perpetual'—I cannot conceive how in any case children can naturally have any power or moral faculty of doing what they please without their parents' leave, since they are always bound to study to please their parents. And though by the laws of some nations children when they attain to years of discretion have power and liberty in many actions, yet this liberty is

51 Grotius, *De Jure*, 2, v, ii, 1.
52 Grotius, *De Jure*, 2, v, iii.
53 Grotius, *De Jure*, 2, v, iv-v.
54 Grotius, *De Jure*, 2, v, vi.

granted them by positive and human laws only—which are made by the supreme fatherly power of princes, who regulate, limit, or assume the authority of inferior fathers for the public benefit of the commonwealth. So that naturally the power of parents over their children never ceaseth by any separation, but only by the permission of the transcendent fatherly power of the supreme prince, children may be dispensed with, or privileged in some cases, from obedience to subordinate parents.

Touching the point of dissolving the vows of children, Grotius in his last edition of his book hath corrected his first. For in the first he teacheth 'that the power of the father was greater over the daughter dwelling with him than over the son, for her vow he might make void, but not his'. But instead of these words, in his last edition he saith 'that the power over the son or daughter to dissolve vows was not perpetual but did endure as long as the children were a part of their father's family'.[55] About the meaning of the text out of which he draws this conclusion, I have already spoken.[56]

Three ways Grotius propoundeth whereby supreme power may be had:

> First, by full right of property.
>
> Secondly, by an usufructuary right.
>
> Thirdly, by a temporary right.

The Roman dictators, saith he,

> had supreme power by a temporary right. As well those kings who are first elected, as those that in a lawful right succeed to kings elected, have supreme power by an usufructuary right. Some kings that have got supreme power by a just war, or into whose power some people, for avoiding a greater evil, have so yielded themselves, as that they have excepted nothing, have a full right of property.[57]

Thus we find but two means acknowledged by Grotius whereby a king may obtain a full right of property in a kingdom. That is, either by a just war or by donation of the people.

How a war can be just without a precedent title in the conqueror, Grotius doth not show. And if the title only make the war just, then no other right can be obtained by war than what the title bringeth. For a just war doth

---

55 Grotius, *De Jure*, 2, v, vii.
56 p. 147 above.
57 Grotius, *De Jure*, 1, iii, xi, 1.

only put the conqueror in possession of his old right, but not create a new. The like which Grotius saith of succession may be said of war. 'Succession', saith he, 'is no title of a kingdom, which gives a form to the kingdom, but a continuation of the old, for the right which began by the election of the family is continued by succession, wherefore so much as the first election gave, so much the succession brings'.[58] So to a conqueror that hath a title, war doth not give, but put him in possession of a right, and except the conqueror had a full right of property at first, his conquest cannot give it him. For if originally he and his ancestors had but an usufructuary right, and were outed of the possession of the kingdom by an usurper, here, though the re-conquest be a most just war, yet shall not the conqueror in this case gain any full right of property, but must be remitted to his usufructuary right only. For what justice can it be that the injustice of a third person— an usurper—should prejudice the people to the divesting of them of that right of property which was reserved in their first donation to their elected king, to whom they gave but an usufructuary right, as Grotius conceiveth? Wherefore it seems impossible that there can be a just war whereby a full right of property may be gained, according to Grotius' principles. For if a king come in by conquest, he must either conquer them that have a governor, or those people that have none. If they have no governor, then they are a free people, and so the war will be unjust to conquer those that are free, especially if the freedom of the people be by the primary law of nature as Grotius teacheth. But if the people conquered have a governor, that governor hath either a title or not. If he hath a title, it is an unjust war that takes the kingdom from him. If he hath no title, but only the possession of a kingdom, yet it is unjust for any other man that wants a title also, to conquer him that is but in possession. For it is a just rule that 'where the cases are alike, he that is in possession is in the better condition': '*in pari causa possidentis melior conditio*' (book 2, ch. 23). And this by the law of nature, even in the judgment of Grotius. But if it be admitted that he that attempts to conquer have a title and he that is in possession hath none, here the conquest is but in nature of a possessory action, to put the conqueror in possession of a primer right and not to raise a new title. For war begins where the law fails: '*ubi judicia deficiunt incipit bellum*' (book 2, ch. 1). And thus upon the matter I cannot find in Grotius's book *De Jure Belli* how that any case can be put wherein by a just war a man may become a king *pleno jure proprietatis* ["by full right of property"].

All government and supreme power is founded upon public subjection, which is thus defined by Grotius: '*Publica subjectio est, qua se populus ho-*

mini alicui, aut pluribus hominibus, aut etiam populo alteri in ditionem dat'
["public subjection is when the people gives itself into the authority of one
or more men, or even of another people"] (book 2, ch. 5). If subjection be
the gift of the people, how can supreme power, *pleno jure*, in full right, be
got by a just war?

As to the other means whereby kings may get supreme power in full right
of property, Grotius will have it to be 'when some people, for avoiding a
greater evil, do so yield themselves into another's power as that they do
except nothing'.[59] It would be considered how, without war, any people can
be brought into such danger of life as that because they can find no other
ways to defend themselves, or because they are so pressed with poverty as
they cannot otherwise have means to sustain themselves, they are forced
to renounce all right of governing themselves and deliver it to a king.

But if such a case cannot happen but by war only, which reduceth a people to such terms of extremity as compels them to an absolute abrenun-
ciation of all sovereignty, then war—which causeth that necessity—is the
prime means of extorting such sovereignty, and not the free gift of the
people, who cannot otherwise choose but give away that power which they
cannot keep.

Thus upon the reckoning, the two ways propounded by Grotius are but
one way—and that one way, in conclusion, is no way whereby supreme
power may be had in full right of property. His two ways are, a just war,
or a donation of the people. A just war cannot be without a title, no title
without the donation of the people, no donation without such a necessity
as nothing can bring upon the donors but a war. So that howsoever Grotius in words acknowledges that kings may have full right of property, yet by
consequence he denies it by such circular suppositions as by coincidence
destroy each other. And in effect he leaves all people a right to plead in bar
against the right of property of any prince, either *per minas*, ["by threats"]
or *per dures* ["by duress"].

Many times, saith Grotius, it happens that war is grounded upon 'ex-
pletive justice, *justitiam expletricem*', which is 'when a man cannot obtain
what he ought, he takes that which is as much in value, which in moral
estimation is the same'.[60] For in war, when the same province cannot be
recovered to the which a man hath a title, he recovers another of the like
value. This recovery cannot give a full right of property, because the justice
of such a war reacheth no farther than to a compensation for a former
right to another thing, and therefore can give no new right.

59   Grotius, *De Jure*, 1, iii, xi, 1.
60   Grotius, *De Jure*, 2, vii, ii, 1.

I am bound to take notice of a case put by Grotius amongst those causes which he thinks should move the people to renounce all their right of
governing and give it to another. 'It may also happen', saith he, 'that a father of a family possessing large territories will not receive any man to
dwell within his land upon any other condition'.[61] And in another place he
saith that 'all kings are not made by the people',[62] which may be sufficiently understood by the example of a father of a family receiving strangers
under the law of obedience. In both these passages we have a close and
curt acknowledgment that a father of a family may be an absolute king
over strangers, without choice of the people. Now I would know whether
such fathers of families have not the same absolute power over their own
children without the people's choice, which he allows them over strangers.
If they have, I cannot but call them absolute proprietary kings, though
Grotius be not willing to give them that title in plain terms. For indeed,
to allow such kings were to condemn his own principle that 'dominion
came in by the will of the people',[63] and so consequently to overthrow his
usufructuary kings—of whom I am next to speak.

Grotius saith that 'the law of obeying or resisting princes depends upon
the will of them who first met in civil society, from whom power doth flow
to kings';[64] and that 'men of their own accord came together into civil society, from whence springs civil power';[65] and 'the people may choose what
form of government they please'.[66] Upon these suppositions he concludes
that kings elected by the people have but an usufructuary right, that is, a
right to take the profit or fruit of the kingdom, but not a right of property
or power to alienate it. But why doth he call it an usufructuary right? It
seems to me a term too mean or base to express the right of any king, and
is derogatory to the dignity of supreme majesty. The word usufructuary
is used by the lawyers to signify him that hath the use, profit, or fruit of
some corporal thing that may be used without the property, for of fungible
things (*res fungibles*, the civilians[67] call them) that are spent or consumed
in the use, as corn, wine, oil, money, there cannot be an usufructuary right.

It is to make a kingdom all one with a farm, as if it had no other use but
to be let out to him that can make most of it. Whereas in truth it is the
part and duty of a king to govern, and he hath a right so to do, and to that

---

61   Grotius, *De Jure*, 1, iii, viii, 3.
62   Grotius, *De Jure*, 1, viii, iii, 13.
63   Grotius, *De Jure*, 1, i, x, 4.
64   Grotius, *De Jure*, 1, iv, vii, 2.
65   Grotius, *De Jure*, 1, iv, vii, 3.
66   Grotius, *De Jure*, 1, iii, viii, 2.
67   *Merriam-Webster* defines as "a specialist in Roman or modern civil law".

end supreme power is given unto him. The taking of the profit or making use of the patrimony of the crown is but as a means only to enable him to perform that work of government.

Besides, Grotius will not only have an elected king but also his lawful successors to have but an usufructuary right, so that though a king hath a crown to him and to his heirs, yet he will allow him no property, because he hath no power to alienate it. For he supposeth the primary will of the people to have been to bestow supreme power to go in succession, and not to be alienable. But for this he hath no better proof than a naked presumption, '*in regnis quae populi voluntate delata sunt, concedo non esse praesumendum eam fuisse populi voluntatem, aut alienatio imperii sui regi permitteretur*'[68] ["in kingdoms which were granted by the will of the people, I admit that it should not be presumed that it was the will of the people to permit to the king the alienation of his own power"].

But though he will not allow kings a right of property in their kingdoms, yet a right of property there must be in some body, and in whom but in the people? For he saith, 'the empire which is exercised by kings doth not cease to be the empire of the people'.[69] His meaning is, the use is the king's, but the property is the people's.

But if the power to alienate the kingdom be in him that hath the property, this may prove a comfortable doctrine to the people. But yet to allow a right of succession in kings and still to reserve a right of property in the people may make some contradiction. For the succession must either hinder the right of alienation which is in the people, or the alienation must destroy that right of succession which, by Grotius' confession, may attend upon elected kings.

Though Grotius confess that supreme power be '*unum quiddam* ["a unity"], and in itself indivisible', yet he saith, 'sometimes it may be divided either by parts potential, or subjective'.[70] I take his meaning to be that the government or the governed may be divided. An example he gives of the Roman Empire which was divided into the east and west. But whereas he saith '*fieri potest*', etc. It may be, the people choosing a king may reserve some actions to themselves, and in others they may give full power to the king,[71] the example he brings out of Plato of the Heraclides doth not prove it, and it is to dream of such a form of government as never yet had name, nor was ever found in any settled kingdom, nor can possibly be without

68 Grotius, *De Jure*, 1, iii, xiii, 1.
69 Grotius, *De Jure*, 2, xvi, xvi, 1.
70 Grotius, *De Jure*, 1, iii, xvii, 1.
71 Grotius, *De Jure*, 1, iii, xvii, 1.

strange confusion.

If it were a thing so voluntary and at the pleasure of men when they were free to put themselves under subjection, why may they not as voluntarily leave subjection when they please, and be free again? If they had a liberty to change their natural freedom into a voluntary subjection, there is stronger reason that they may change their voluntary subjection into natural freedom—since it is as lawful for men to alter their wills as their judgments.

Certainly it was a rare felicity that all the men in the world at one instant of time should agree together in one mind to change the natural community of all things into private dominion. For without such an unanimous consent it was not possible for community to be altered. For if but one man in the world had dissented, the alteration had been unjust, because that man by the law of nature had a right to the common use of all things in the world, so that to have given a property of any one thing to any other had been to have robbed him of his right to the common use of all things. And of this judgment the Jesuit Ludovicus Molina seems to be in his book *De Justitia*, where he saith, '*si aliquis de cohabitantibus*, etc. If one of the neighbours will not give his consent to it, the commonwealth should have no authority over him, because then every other man hath no right or authority over him, and therefore can they not give authority to the commonwealth over him'.

If our first parents, or some other of our forefathers did voluntarily bring in property of goods and subjection to governors, and it were in their power either to bring them in or not, or having brought them in, to alter their minds and restore them to their first condition of community and liberty, what reason can there be alleged that men that now live should not have the same power? So that if any one man in the world, be he never so mean or base, will but alter his will and say he will resume his natural right to community, and be restored unto his natural liberty, and consequently take what he please, and do what he list, who can say that such a man doth more than by right he may? And then it will be lawful for every man, when he please, to dissolve all government, and destroy all property.

Whereas Grotius saith that by the law of nature all things were at first common and yet teacheth that after property was brought in it was against the law of nature to use community, he doth thereby not only make the law of nature changeable, which he saith God cannot do, but he also makes the law of nature contrary to itself.

OBSERVATIONS UPON ARISTOTLE'S Politicks, TOUCHING Forms of Government.

THE PREFACE.

In every alteration of government there is something new, which none can either divine or judge of till time hath tried it. We read of many several ways of government. But they have all, or most of them, been of particular cities, with none or very small territories at first belonging to them. At this present the government of the Low Countries and of Switzerland are not appropriated either of them to any one city, for they are compounded of several petty principalities which have special and different laws and privileges each of them. Insomuch that the United Provinces and united cantons are but confederacies and leaguers, and not two entire common-weals; associates only for mutual defence. Nay, the cantons of Switzerland are not only several republics, but reputed to have different forms of commonweals—some being said to be aristocratically governed, and others democratically, as the mountaineers. And some of the cantons are papists, and some Protestants, and some mixed of both. We do not find that any large or great dominion or kingdom united in one government and under the same laws, was ever reduced at once to any kind of popular government, and not confined to the subjection of one city. This being a thing not yet done, requires the abler men to settle such a peaceable government as is to be desired, there being no precedent in the case. All that can be done in it is at first to enquire into such governments as have been existent in the world. As a preface to such an enquiry the sacred Scripture (if it be but for the antiquity of it) would be consulted, and then Aristotle—the grand master of politics. And after him the Greek and Latin historians that lived in popular times would be diligently examined. To excite others of greater abilities to an exacter disquisition, I presume to offer a taste of some doctrines of Aristotle, which are ushered in with a briefer touch of the holy Scriptures.

It is not probable that any sure direction of the beginning of government can be found either in Plato, Aristotle, Cicero, Polybius, or in any other of the heathen authors, who were ignorant of the manner of the creation of the world. We must not neglect the Scriptures and search in philosophers for the grounds of dominion and property, which are the main principles of government and justice. The first government in the world was monarchical, in the father of all flesh. Adam being commanded to multiply and people the earth, and to subdue it, and having dominion given him over all creatures, was thereby the monarch of the whole world. None of his posterity had any right to possess anything but by his grant or permission, or by succession from him. The 'earth', saith the psalmist, 'hath he given to the children of men'[1]—which shows the title comes from fatherhood. There never was any such thing as an independent multitude, who at first had a natural right to a community. This is but a fiction or fancy of too many in these days, who please themselves in running after the opinions of philosophers and poets to find out such an original of government as might promise them some title to liberty, to the great scandal of Christianity and bringing in of atheism—since a natural freedom of mankind cannot be supposed without the denial of the creation of Adam. And yet this conceit of original freedom is the only ground upon which not only the heathen philosophers but also the authors of the principles of the civil law, and Grotius, Selden, Hobbes, Ashcam, and others, raise and build their doctrines of government and of the several sorts or kinds, as they call them, of commonwealths.

Adam was the father, king, and lord over his family. A son, a subject, and a servant or a slave, were one and the same thing at first. The father had power to dispose or sell his children or servants. Whence we find that at the first reckoning up of goods in Scripture, the manservant and the maidservant are numbered among the possessions and substance of the owner, as other goods were. As for the names of subject, slave, and tyrant, they are not found in Scripture, but what we now call a subject or a slave is there named no other than a servant. I cannot learn that either the Hebrew, Greek, or Latin have any proper and original word for a tyrant or a slave. It seems these are names of later invention, and taken up in disgrace of monarchical government.

I cannot find any one place or text in the Bible where any power or commission is given to a people either to govern themselves, or to choose themselves governors, or to alter the manner of government at their pleasure. The power of government is settled and fixed by the commandment of 'honour thy father'. If there were a higher power than the fatherly, then

1   Psalms 95:16.

this commandment could not stand and be observed. Whereas we read in Scripture of some actions of the people in setting up of kings, further than to a naked declaration by a part of the people of their obedience, such actions could not amount—since we find no commission they have to bestow any right. A true representation of the people to be made is as impossible as for the whole people to govern. The names of an aristocracy, a democracy, a commonweal, a state, or any other of like signification, are not to be met either in the law or gospel.

That there is a ground in nature for monarchy, Aristotle himself affirmeth, saying the first kings were fathers of families. As for any ground of any other form of government, there hath been none yet alleged but a supposed natural freedom of mankind, the proof whereof I find none do undertake, but only beg it to be granted. We find the government of God's own people varied under the several titles of patriarchs, captains, Judges, and kings. But in all these the supreme power rested still in one person only. We nowhere find any supreme power given to the people or to a multitude in Scripture, or ever exercised by them. The people were never the Lord's anointed, nor called gods, nor crowned, nor had the title of nursing fathers, Genesis 35:11. The supreme power being an indivisible beam of majesty cannot be divided among, or settled upon a multitude. God would have it fixed in one person, not sometimes in one part of the people and sometimes in another, and sometimes—and that for the most part—nowhere, as when the assembly is dissolved it must rest in the air or in the walls of the chamber where they were assembled.

If there were any thing like a popular government among God's people it was about the time of the Judges, when there was 'no king in Israel'.[2] For they had then some small show of government, such as it was, but it was so poor and beggarly that the Scripture brands it with this note, that 'every man did what was right in his own eyes, because there was no king in Israel'. It is not said 'because there was no government', but because there was no king. It seems no government but the government of a king, in the judgment of the Scriptures, could restrain men from doing what they listed. Where every man doth what he pleaseth, it may be truly said there is no government. For the end of government is that every man should not do what he pleaseth or be his own judge in his own case. For the scripture to say there was no king is to say there was no form of government in Israel.

And what the Old Testament teacheth us, we have confirmed in the New.

2 Judges 17:6.

If St. Paul had only said 'let every soul be subject to the higher powers'[3] and said no more, then men might have disputed whether St. Paul by 'higher powers' had not meant as well other governors as kings, or other forms of government as monarchy. But the good luck is, St. Paul hath been his own interpreter or comment. For after the general doctrine of obedience to be given by all men to the higher powers, he proceeds next to charge it home and lay it to the conscience under pain of damnation, and applies it to each particular man's conscience, saying, 'wilt thou not be afraid of the power?'—which power he expounds in the singular number, restraining it to one person, saying, 'he is the minister of God to thee': it is not, 'they are the ministers to thee'. And then again, 'he beareth not the sword in vain'; and then a third time in the same verse, lest thou shouldest forget it, he saith, for 'he is the minister of God, a revenger to wrath, etc., upon thee'. If St. Paul had said, 'they are the ministers of God', or 'they bear not the sword in vain', it might be doubted whether 'they' were meant of kings only, or of other governors also. But this scruple is taken away by the apostle himself. And as St. Paul hath expounded what he means by higher powers, so St. Peter also doth the like. For the self-same word that St. Paul useth for 'higher' in St. Peter is translated 'supreme', so that though in our English Bibles the words differ, yet in the original they are both the same. So that St. Paul might have been Englished, 'let every soul be subject to the supreme power', or St. Peter might have been translated, 'whether to the king as to the higher'. Yet there is this difference, that whereas St. Paul useth the word in the plural number, St. Peter hath it in the singular, and with application to the king.

It will be said, though St. Peter make the king supreme, yet he tells us the king is a 'human ordinance', or a creature of the people's. But it is answered, kings may be called an human ordinance for being made of one of the people, and not by the people—and so are human in regard of their material cause, not of their efficient. If St. Peter had meant that kings had been made by the people, he must also have meant that governors had been made by the people, for he calls the governors as well an ordinance of man, as the king. For his words are, 'submit yourselves to every ordinance of man for the Lord's sake, whether it be to the king as supreme, or whether it be to governors'. But St. Peter showeth that governors are not made by the people, for he saith 'they that are sent by him' (not by them) 'for the punishment of evil doers'.[4] So that the governors are sent by the king, and not by the people. Some would have 'sent by him' to be 'sent by

3   Romans 13:1.
4   1 Peter 2:13.

God', but the relative must be referred to the next antecedent, which is the king, and not God. Besides, if governors be sent by God, and kings by the people, then governors would be supreme, which is contrary to St. Peter's doctrine; and it will follow that the people have not the power of choosing representors to govern, if governors must be sent of God.

The safest sense of St. Peter's words is: submit your selves to all human laws whether made by the king or by his subordinate governors. So the king may be called a human ordinance, as being all one with a speaking law. The word in the original is, be subject to every humane creation. It is more proper to call a law made by a king a creation of an ordinance, than the people's choosing or declaring of a king, a creation of him.

But take the words in what sense soever you will, it is most evident that St. Peter in this place takes no notice of any government or governors, but of a king, and governors sent by him, but not by the people. And it is to be noted that St. Peter and St. Paul, the two chief of the apostles, wrote their epistles at such a time when the name of a popular government, or of the power of the people of Rome, was at least so much in show and in name that many do believe that notwithstanding the emperors by strong hand usurped a military power, yet the government was for a long time in most things then in the senate and people of Rome. But for all this, neither of the two apostles take any notice of any such popular government—no, nor our Saviour himself, who divides all between God and Caesar, and allows nothing that we can find for the people.

OBSERVATIONS UPON ARISTOTLE'S Politicks.

What cannot be found in Scripture many do look for in Aristotle. For if there be any other form of government besides monarchy, he is the man best able to tell what it is, and to let us know by what name to call it, since the Greek tongue is most happy in compounding names most significant to express the nature of most things. The usual terms in this age—of aristocracy and democracy—are taken up from him to express forms of government most different from monarchy. We must therefore make inquiry into Aristotle touching these two terms.

True it is, Aristotle seems to make three sorts of government which he distinguisheth by 'the sovereignty of one man, or of a few, or of many, for the common good'[5] (book 3, ch. 7). 'These', he saith, 'are right or perfect governments, but those that are for the private good of one, or of a few, or

5   Ἀνάγκη δ' εἶναι κύριον ἢ ἕνα, ἢ ὀλίγους, ἢ τοὺς πολλοὺς πρὸς τὸ κοινὸν συμφέρον. 1279ᵃ 27–9.

of a multitude, are transgressions.'[6] The government of a monarchy for the common good he calls a kingdom. The government

> of a few more than one, an aristocracy, either because the best men govern or because it is for the best of the governed. When a multitude governs for the common good, it is called by the common name of all governments, a polity. It is possible that one or a few may excel in virtue, but it is difficult for many to excel in all virtue except in war-like affairs, for this is natural in a multitude. Therefore, in this sort of government their principal use is to war one for another, and to possess the arms or ammunition. The transgressions of government before spoken of are these: tyranny is the transgression of the kingdom, and democracy is the transgression of the polity. For tyranny is a monarchy for the benefit of the monarch; the oligarchy for the profit of the rich; the democracy for the benefit of the poor. None of these are for the common good (book 3, ch. 7).[7]

Here Aristotle, if he had stood to his own principles, should have said 'an oligarchy should be for the benefit of a few, and those the best, and not for the benefit of the rich; and a democracy for the benefit of many, and not of the poor only'; for so the opposition lieth. But then Aristotle saw his democracy would prove to be no transgression, but a perfect polity, and his oligarchy would not be for the benefit of a few, and those the best men. For they cannot be the best men that seek only their private profit. In this chapter the mind of Aristotle about the several kinds of government is clearliest delivered, as being the foundation of all his books of *Politics*. It is the more necessary to make a curious observation of these his doctrines. In the first place, he acknowledgeth the government of one man, or of a monarchy, and that is a perfect form of government.

Concerning monarchy, Aristotle teacheth us the beginning of it. For, saith he, the 'first society made of many houses is a colony, which seems most naturally to be a colony of families or foster-brethren of children and children's children. And therefore at the beginning cities were, and now

6　　Ταύτας μὲν ὀρθὰς ἀναγκαῖον εἶναι [30] τὰς πολιτείας, τὰς δὲ πρὸς τὸ ἴδιον ἢ τοῦ ἑνὸς ἢ τῶν ὀλίγων ἢ τοῦ πλήθους παρεκβάσεις. ἢ γὰρ οὐ πολίτας φατέον εἶναι τοὺς μετέχοντας, ἢ δεῖ κοινωνεῖν τοῦ συμφέροντος. καλεῖν δ᾽ εἰώθαμεν τῶν μὲν μοναρχιῶν τὴν πρὸς τὸ κοινὸν ἀποβλέπουσαν συμφέρον βασιλείαν... 1279ᵃ 29–31.

7　　1279ᵃ 34–1279ᵇ 10.

nations, under the government of kings. The eldest in every house is king, and so for kindred sake it is in colonies'[8] (book 1, ch. 2).

Thus he deduced the original of government from the power of the fatherhood, not from the election of the people. This it seems he learnt of his master Plato, who in his third book of *Laws* affirms that the true and first reason of authority is that the father and mother, and simply those that beget and engender, do command and rule over all their children. Aristotle also tells us from Homer, 'that every man gives laws to his wife and children.'[9]

In the fourth book of his *Politics*, ch. 2, he gives to monarchy the title of the 'first and divinest sort of government', defining tyranny to be 'a transgression from the first and divinest.'[10]

Again, Aristotle in the eighth book of his *Ethics*, in the twelfth chapter saith that of 'the right kinds of government, a monarchy was the best, and a popular estate the worst.'[11]

Lastly, in the third book of his *Politics* and the sixteenth chapter concerning monarchy, he saith that 'a perfect kingdom is that wherein the king rules all things according to his own will' 'for he that is called a king according to the law makes no kind of government.'[12]

Secondly, he saith there is a government of a *few* men, but doth not tell us how many those few men may or must be. Only he saith they must be more than one man, but how many, that he leaves uncertain.

This perfect government of a few any man would think Aristotle should have called an oligarchy, for that this word properly signifies so much. But instead of the government of a few, Aristotle gives it a quite other name and terms it an aristocracy, which signifies the power of the best. The reason why it is called an aristocracy, saith Aristotle, is for that there the best men govern, or (because that is not always true) 'for that it is for the best of the governed'. By this latter reason any government, and most especially

---

8   Μάλιστα δὲ κατὰ φύσιν ἔοικεν ἡ κώμη ἀποικία οἰκίας εἶναι, οὓς καλοῦσί τινες ὁμογάλακτας, παῖδάς τε καὶ παίδων παῖδας. διὸ καὶ τὸ πρῶτον ἐβασιλεύοντο αἱ πόλεις, καὶ νῦν ἔτι τὰ ἔθνη: ἐκ βασιλευομένων γὰρ συνῆλθον: πᾶσα γὰρ οἰκία βασιλεύεται ὑπὸ τοῦ πρεσβυτάτου, ὥστε καὶ αἱ ἀποικίαι, διὰ τὴν συγγένειαν. 1252^b 16–21.

9   θεμιστεύει δὲ ἕκαστος παίδων ἠδ᾽ ἀλόχων. 1252^b 22–23.

10   Ἀνάγκη γὰρ τὴν μὲν τῆς πρώτης καὶ θειοτάτης παρέκβασιν εἶναι χειρίστην. 1289^a 39–41.

11   τούτων δὲ βελτίστη μὲν ἡ βασιλεία, χειρίστη δ᾽ ἡ τιμοκρατία. 1160^a 35–6.

12   Περὶ δὲ τῆς παμβασιλείας καλουμένης αὕτη δ᾽ ἐστὶ καθ᾽ ἣν ἄρχει πάντων κατὰ τὴν ἑαυτοῦ βούλησιν ὁ βασιλεύς [...] ὁ μὲν γὰρ κατὰ νόμον λεγόμενος βασιλεὺς οὐκ ἔστιν εἶδος, καθάπερ εἴπομεν, πολιτείας. 1287^a 8–10, 3–4.

a monarchy, may be called an aristocracy—because the end of monarchy is for the best of the governed, as well as the end of an aristocracy. So that of these two reasons for calling the government of a few an aristocracy the first is seldom true, and the latter is never sufficient to frame a distinction. This Aristotle himself confesseth in his next chapter, saying 'that the causes aforesaid do not make a difference, and that it is poverty and riches, and not few and many, that make the difference between an oligarchy and democracy. There must be an oligarchy where rich men rule, whether they be few or many: and wheresoever the poor have the sovereignty, there must be a democracy'.[13]

Now if Aristotle will allow riches and poverty to make a difference between an oligarchy and a democracy, these two must likewise make the difference between an aristocracy and a polity, for the only difference Aristotle makes between them is in their ends, and not in their matter. For the same few men may make an aristocracy if their end be the common good, and they may be an oligarchy if they aim only at their private benefit.

Thus is Aristotle distracted and perplexed how to distinguish his aristocracy, whether by the smallness of their number or by the greatness of their estates. Nay, if we look into Aristotle's *Rhetorics* (book 1, ch. 8) we shall find a new conceit, not only about aristocracy but also about the sorts of government. For whereas he has taught us in his *Politics* that there be three sorts of right or perfect government and as many sorts of wrong, which he calls transgressions or corruptions, he comes in his *Rhetorics* and teacheth us that there be four sorts of government:

1. A democracy, where magistracies are distributed by lots.

2. In an oligarchy by their wealth.

3. In an aristocracy by their instructions in the law. It is necessary for these to appear the best, from whence they have their name.[14]

4. A monarchy according to the name, wherein one is lord over all.[15]

13   Διὸ καὶ οὐ συμβαίνει τὰς ῥηθείσας αἰτίας αἰτίας γίνεσθαι διαφορᾶς ᾧ δὲ διαφέρουσιν ἥ τε δημοκρατία καὶ ἡ ὀλιγαρχία ἀλλήλων πενία καὶ πλοῦτός ἐστιν, etc. 1279ᵇ 38–1280ᵃ 1.
14   ἔστιν δὲ δημοκρατία μὲν πολιτεία ἐν ᾗ κλήρῳ διανέμονται τὰς ἀρχάς, ὀλιγαρχία δὲ ἐν ᾗ οἱ ἀπὸ τιμημάτων, ἀριστοκρατία δὲ ἐν ᾗ κατὰ τὴν παιδείαν. 1365ᵇ 31.
15   Μοναρχία δὲ ἐστὶ κατὰ τοὔνομα ἐν ᾗ εἷς ἁπάντων κύριός ἐστιν. 1366ᵃ 1.

Here we see aristocracy is not distinguished by smallness of number, nor by riches, but by skill in the laws. For he saith those that are instructed in the laws govern in an aristocracy,[16] a point not dreamt of in his *Politics*. By which it seems Aristotle himself did not know well what he would have to be an aristocracy. And as he cannot teach us truly what an aristocracy is, so he is to seek to tell us where any aristocracy ever was. Even himself seems to doubt whether there be any such form of government, where he saith in his third book of *Politics*, ch. 5, it is impossible for any mechanical man to be a citizen in an aristocracy, 'if there be any such government as they call aristocratical'.[17]

His 'if' makes him seem to doubt of it. Yet I find him affirm that the commonwealth of Carthage was aristocratical. He doth not say it was an aristocracy, for he confesseth it had many of the transgressions which other commonwealths had, and did incline either to a democracy or an oligarchy: 'the government of Carthage did transgress from an aristocracy to an oligarchy'[18] (book 2, ch. 11).

And he concludes that if by misfortune there should happen any discord among the Carthaginians themselves, there would be no medicine by law found out to give it rest. Wherein methinks Aristotle was a kind of prophet, for the discords between the citizens of Carthage were the main cause that Hannibal lost not only Italy, but Carthage itself.

By these few collections we may find how uncertain Aristotle is in determining what an aristocracy is, or where or when any such government was. It may justly be doubted whether there ever was or can be any such government.

Let us pass from his aristocracy to his third sort of perfect or right government, for which he finds no particular name, but only the common name of all government, *politia*. It seems the Greeks were wonderfully to seek, that they of all men should not be able to compound a name for such a perfect form of government. Unless we should believe that they esteemed this kind of commonwealth so superlatively excellent, as to be called, κατ' ἐξοχὴν, the government of all governments, or polity of polities.

But howsoever Aristotle in his books of *Politics* vouchsafe us not a name, yet in his books of *Ethics* he affirmeth it may very properly be called 'a

16   οἱ γὰρ ἐμμεμενηκότες ἐν τοῖς νομίμοις ἐν τῇ ἀριστοκρατίᾳ ἄρχουσιν. 1278ᵃ 18.

17   Ἔι τίς ἐστιν ἣν καλοῦσιν ἀριστοκρατικήν. 1278ᵃ 19.

18   Παρεκβαίνει δὲ τῆς ἀριστοκρατίας ἡ τάξις τῶν Καρχηδονίων μάλιστα πρὸς τὴν ὀλιγαρχίαν. 1273ᵃ 21–2.

timocratical government, where magistrates are chosen by their wealth'[19] (book 8, ch. 12). But why Aristotle should give it such a name I can find no reason. For a polity by his doctrine is the government of many, or of a multitude, and the multitude he will have to be the poorer sort, insomuch that except they be poor he will not allow it to be the government of a multitude, though they be never so many. For he makes poverty the truest note of a popular estate, and as if to be poor and to be free were all one, he makes liberty likewise to be a mark of popular estate, for in his fourth book, and fourth chapter, he resolves that 'a popular state is where free men govern, and an oligarchy where rich men rule'[20]—as if rich men could not be free-men. Now how magistrates should be chosen for their wealth, ἀπὸ τιμημάτων among all poor men, is to me a riddle.

Here I cannot but wonder why all our modern politicians,[21] who pretend themselves Aristotelians, should forsake their great master and account a democracy a right or perfect form of government, when Aristotle brands it for a transgression, or a depraved or corrupted manner of government. They had done better to have followed Aristotle, who (though other Grecians could not, yet he) could find out the name of a timocracy for a right popular government. But it may be our politicians forbear to use the word timocracy because he affords an ill character of it, saying that of all the right kinds of government a 'monarchy was the best, and a timocracy the worst'.[22] Yet afterwards Aristotle in the same chapter makes amends for it in saying a 'democracy is the least vicious, because it doth but a little transgress from a timocracy'.

But not to insist longer on the name of this nameless form of government, let inquiry be made into the thing itself, that we may know what Aristotle saith is the 'government of many, or of a multitude, for the common good'.

This many or multitude is not the whole people, nor the major part of the people, or any chosen by the people to be their representors. No, Aristotle never saith or meaneth any such thing. For he tells us 'the best city doth not make any artificer, or handicraftsman a citizen'.[23]

And if these be excluded out of the number of citizens, there will be but a few left in every city to make his timocratical government, since artificers or mercenary men make far the greatest part of a city; or to say 'a city is

19   Τρίτη δὲ ἀπὸ τιμημάτων, ἣν τιμοκρατικὴν λέγειν οἰκεῖον φαίνεται. 1160ᵃ 33–4.

20   Ὅτι δῆμος μέν ἐστιν ὅταν οἱ ἐλεύθεροι κύριοι ὦσιν, ὀλιγαρχία δ᾽ ὅταν οἱ πλούσιοι. 1290ᵇ 1–2.

21   Political scientists.

22   βελτίστη μὲν ἡ βασιλεία, χειρίστη δ᾽ ἡ τιμοκρατία. 1160ᵃ 35–6.

23   Ἡ δὲ βελτίστη πόλις οὐ ποιήσει βάναυσον πολίτην. 1278ᵃ 8–9.

a community of free men,'[24] and yet to exclude the greatest part of the inhabitants from being citizens, is but a mockery of freedom. For any man would think that a city being a society of men assembled to the end to live well, that such men without whom a city cannot subsist, and who perform necessary works, and minister to all in public, should not be barred from being citizens. Yet says Aristotle, 'all those are not to be deemed citizens without whom a city cannot subsist,'[25] except they abstain from necessary works; for he resolves it 'impossible for him to exercise the work of virtue, that useth a mechanical or mercenary trade.'[26]

And he makes it one of his conclusions that 'in ancient times among some men no public workman did partake of the government until the worst of democracies were brought in.'[27]

Again, Aristotle will have his best popular government consist of free men, and accounts the poorer sort of people to be free men. How then will he exclude poor artificers, who work for the public, from participating of the government?

Further, it is observable in Aristotle that, quite contrary to the signification of the Greek names, the government of a multitude may be termed an oligarchy if they be rich, and the rule of a few a democracy if they be poor and free.

After much uncertainty of the nature of this politic government which wants a name, Aristotle at last resolves that this general commonweal or *politia* is compounded of a 'democracy and oligarchy', for, 'to speak plainly, a polity is a mixture of a democracy and an oligarchy.'[28]

That is, one perfect form is made of two imperfect ones. This is rather a confounding than compounding of government, to patch it up of two corrupt ones by appointing an oligarchical penalty for the rich magistrates that are chosen by election, and a democratical fee for the poor magistrates that are chosen by lot.

Lastly, it is to be noted that Aristotle doth not offer to name any one city or commonweal in the world where ever there was any such government as he calls a polity. For him to reckon it for a perfect form of government, and of such excellency as to carry the name from all other, and yet never to

24 Ἡ δὲ πόλις κοινωνία τῶν ἐλευθέρων ἐστίν. 1279ᵃ 21.

25 Οὐ πάντας θετέον πολίτας ὧν ἄνευ οὐκ ἂν εἴη πόλις. 1278ᵃ 3–4.

26 Οὐ γὰρ οἷόν τ' ἐπιτηδεῦσαι τὰ τῆς ἀρετῆς ζῶντα βίον βάναυσον ἢ θητικόν. 1278ᵃ 20–1.

27 Διὸ παρ' ἐνίοις οὐ μετεῖχον οἱ δημιουργοὶ τὸ παλαιὸν ἀρχῶν, πρὶν δῆμον γενέσθαι τὸν ἔσχατον. 1277ᵇ 1–3.

28 Ἔστι γὰρ ἡ πολιτεία ὡς ἁπλῶς εἰπεῖν μίξις ὀλιγαρχίας καὶ δημοκρατίας. 1293ᵇ 33–4.

have been extant in the world, may seem a wonder, and a man may be excused for doubting or for denying any such form to be possible in nature, if it cannot be made manifest what it is, nor when, nor where it ever was.

In conclusion, since Aristotle reckons but three kinds of perfect government, which are, first, a monarchy of one; secondly, an aristocracy of a few; thirdly, a polity of a multitude; and if these two latter cannot be made good by him, there will remain but one right form of government only, which is monarchy. And it seems to me that Aristotle in a manner doth confess as much where he informs us 'that the first commonweals among the Grecians, after kingdoms, was made of those that waged war'²⁹ (book 4, ch. 13)—meaning that the Grecians, when they left to be governed by kings, fell to be governed by an army. Their monarchy was changed into a stratocracy,³⁰ and not into an aristocracy or democracy. For if unity in government, which is only found in monarchy, be once broken, there is no stay or bound, until it come to a constant standing army. For 'the people or multitude', as Aristotle teacheth us, 'can excel in no virtue but military', and that 'that is natural to them', and therefore in a popular estate 'the sovereign power is in the sword and those that are possessed of the arms'.³¹ So that any nation or kingdom that is not charged with the keeping of a king must perpetually be at the charge of paying and keeping of an army.

These brief observations upon Aristotle's perfect forms of government may direct what to judge of those corrupted or imperfect forms which he mentions, for *rectum est index sui et obliqui* ["what is right is a guide to itself and to what is crooked"], and he reckons them to be all one in matter and form, and to differ only in their end—the end of the perfect forms being for the good of the governed, and of the imperfect for the benefit only of the governors. Now since Aristotle could not tell how to define or describe his right or perfect forms of government, it cannot be expected he can satisfy us concerning those he calls imperfect. Yet he labours and bestirs himself mainly in the business, though to little purpose. For howsoever the title of his book be πολιτικῶν, of *Politics*, and that he mentions πολιτεία for a special form of government, which hath the common name of a polity, yet when he comes to dispute in particular of government he argues only about democracies and oligarchies, and therein he is copi-

---

29   καὶ ἡ πρώτη δὲ πολιτεία ἐν τοῖς Ἕλλησιν ἐγένετο μετὰ τὰς βασιλείας ἐκ τῶν πολεμούντων. 1297ᵇ 16–17.

30   Rule by military.

31   Πλείους δ' ἤδη χαλεπὸν ἠκριβῶσθαι πρὸς πᾶσαν ἀρετήν, ἀλλὰ μάλιστα τὴν πολεμικήν· αὕτη γὰρ ἐν πλήθει γίγνεται· διόπερ κατὰ ταύτην τὴν πολιτείαν κυριώτατον τὸ προπολεμοῦν καὶ μετέχουσιν αὐτῆς οἱ κεκτημένοι τὰ ὅπλα. 1279ᵃ 40–1279ᵇ 4.

ous because only those which he calls corrupt forms of governments were common in Greece in his days. As for an aristocracy or a polity which he mentions, they are only speculative notions or airy names, invented to delude the world and to persuade the people that under those quaint terms there might be found some subtle government which might at least equal, if not excel, monarchy. And the inventers of those fine names were all but rebels to monarchy, by Aristotle's confession, where he saith 'the first commonweals of Greece, after kings were left, were made of those that waged war' (book 4, ch. 13).

As Aristotle is irresolute to determine what are truly perfect aristocracies and polities, so he is to seek in describing his imperfect forms of government, as well oligarchies as democracies. And therefore he is driven to invent several sorts of them, and to confound himself with subdivisions. We will allege some of his words.

> The cause why there be many kinds of commonweals is for that there are many parts of every city. Sometimes all these parts are in a commonweal, sometimes more of them, sometimes fewer. Whence it is manifest that there are many commonweals differing from each other in kind, because the parts of them differ after the same manner. For a commonweal is the order of magistrates distributed either according to the power of them that are partakers of it, or according to some other common equality belonging to poor and rich, or some other thing common to both. It is therefore necessary that there be so many commonweals as there are orders, according to the excellencies and differences of parts. But it seemeth principally there are but two chief kinds of commonweals, the democracy and the oligarchy. For they make the aristocracy a branch of oligarchy, as if it were a kind of oligarchy; and that other which is properly a policy, to be a branch of democracy. So they are wont to esteem of commonweals. But it is both truer and better that there being two right forms, or one, that all the other be transgressions.[32]

Here we find Aristotle of several minds. Sometimes he is for many commonweals, sometimes for two, or sometimes for one. As for his many commonweals, if he allow them according to the several parts of a city, he may as well make three thousand kinds of commonweals, as three. If two artificers and three soldiers should govern, that should be one kind of

32   1289^b 27–1290^a 26.

commonweal. If four husbandmen, and five merchants, that would be a second sort; or six tailors, and ten carpenters, a third sort; or a dozen sailors, and a dozen porters, a fourth; and so *in infinitum*. For Aristotle is not resolved how many parts to make of a city or how many combinations of those parts, and therefore in his reckoning of them he differs from himself, sometimes makes more, sometimes fewer parts, and oft concluding at the end of his account with *etceteras*, and confessing that one and the same man may act several parts—as he that is a soldier may be a husbandman and an artificer. And in his fourth book and fourth chapter he seems to reckon up eight parts of a city, but in the tale of them he misses or forgets the sixth: 1. He names the plowman. 2. The artificer. 3. The tradesman or merchant. 4. The mercenary hireling. 5. The soldier (here Aristotle falls foul upon Plato for making but four parts of a city: 1. The weaver. 2. The plowman. 3. The tailor. 4. The carpenter. Afterwards, as if these were not sufficient, he addeth the smith and the feeder of necessary cattle, the merchant, and the ingrosser or retailer). Whilst Aristotle was busy in this reprehension of Plato, he forgets himself and skips over his sixth part of a city, and names the 7. rich men, 8. the magistrates. In the same chapter he offers at another division of the parts of a city or commonweal, first dividing it into a populacy, and nobility. The people he divides first into 'husbandmen. 2. Into artificers. 3. Into merchants or those that use buying or selling. 4. Into those that frequent the seas', of whom 'some follow the war, others seek for gain'; some are 'carriers or transporters', others 'fishermen. 5. Handicraftsmen that possess so little goods that they cannot be idle. 6. Those that are not free on both sides, and any other such like multitude of people'. The kinds of noblemen are distinguished 'by riches, by lineage, by virtue, by learning, and other suchlike things'.

That there may be more parts of a commonweal than are here numbered, Aristotle confesseth or supposeth; and of a multitude of parts, and of a multitude of mixtures of such parts may be made a world of forms of oligarchies and democracies.

This confusion of the parts and kinds of commonweals drove Aristotle rather to rest upon the division of rich and poor for the main parts of a commonweal, than any other. The distinction of a few and of a multitude, or the whole people, might seem more proper to distinguish between an oligarchy and a democracy. But the truth is, Aristotle looking upon the cities of Greece and finding that in every of them, even in Athens itself, there were many of the people that were not allowed to be citizens and to participate in the government, and that many times he was a citizen in one sort of government who was not a citizen in another, and that citizens differed according to every commonweal; he considered that if he should place a right in the whole people either to govern or to choose their form of government or the parties that should govern, he should hereby condemn the government of all the cities in Greece, and especially of aristocracy, which, as he saith, allows no artificer to be a citizen. And besides, he should thereby confute a main principle of his own *Politics*, which is that some men are born slaves by nature—which quite contradicts the position that all men are born equal and free. And therefore Aristotle thought it fitter to allow all imaginable forms of government, that so he might not disparage any one city, than to propound such a form as might condemn and destroy all the rest.

Though Aristotle allow so many several forms of corrupted governments, yet he insists upon no one form of all those that he can define or describe, in such sort that he is able to say that any one city in all Greece was governed just according to such a form. His diligence is only to make as many forms as the giddy or inconstant humour of a city could happen upon. He freely gives the people liberty to invent as many kinds of government as they please, provided he may have liberty to find fault with every one of them. It proved an easier work for him to find fault with every form, than to tell how to amend any one of them. He found so many imperfections in all sorts of commonweals that he could not hold from reproving them before ever he tells us what a commonweal is or how many sorts there are. And to this purpose he spends his whole second book in setting out and correcting the chief commonweals of Greece, and among others the Lacedemonian, the Cretan, and Carthaginian commonweals, which three he esteems to be much alike, and better than any other. Yet he spares not to lay open their imperfections, and doth the like to the Athenian. Wherein he breaks the rule of method, by delivering the faults of commonweals before he teach us what a commonweal is. For in his first book he speaks only of the parts of which a city or a commonweal is made, but tells us not what a city or commonweal is until he come to his third book, and there in handling the sorts of government he observes no method at all, but in a disorderly way flies backward and forward from one sort to another. And howsoever there may be observed in him many rules of policy touching government in general, yet without doubt where he comes to discourse of particular forms he is full of contradiction, or confusion, or both. It is true, he is brief and difficult. The best right a man can do him is to confess he understands him not. Yet a diligent reader may readily discern so many irregularities and breaches in Aristotle's books of *Politics* as tend to such distraction or confusion that none of our new politicians can make advantage of his principles for the confirmation of an original power by nature in the people, which is the only theme now in fashion. For Aristotle's discourse is of such commonweals as were founded by particular persons—as the Chalcedonian by Phaleas, the Milesian by Hippodamas, the Lacedemonian by Lycurgus, the Cretan by Minos, the Athenian by Solon, and the like. But the natural right of the people to found or elect their kind of government is not once disputed by him. It seems the 'underived majesty'[33] of the people was such a metaphysical piece of speculation as our grand philosopher was not acquainted with. He speaks very contemptuously of the multitude in several places. He affirms that 'the people are base or wicked judges in their own cases'[34] (book 3, ch. 9) and that 'many of them differ nothing from beasts'[35] (book 3, ch. 11). And again he saith 'the common people or freemen are such as are neither rich nor in reputation for virtue, and it is not safe to commit to them great governments, for by reason of their injustice and unskilfulness they would do much injustice and commit many errors, and it is pleasanter to the multitude to live disorderly than soberly'[36] (book 6, ch. 4). If Aristotle had believed a public interest to have been in the people to the enabling them to be their own carvers in point of government, he would never have entangled himself with such intricate and ambiguous forms of commonweals as himself cannot tell how to explain, nor any of his commentators how to understand or make use of.

This one benefit I have found by reading Aristotle, that his books of *Politics* serve for an admirable commentary upon that text of Scripture which saith 'in those days there was no king in Israel; every man did that which was right in his own eyes'.[37] For he grants a liberty in every city for any man or multitude of men either by cunning or force to set up what government they please, and he will allow some name or other of a commonweal, which in effect is to allow every man to do what he lists, if he be able. Hence it is that by the confession of Aristotle 'the first commonweals in Greece, after kings were given over, were made of those that waged war'. Those several kinds of commonweals were all summed up into the government of an army. For 'it is', saith Aristotle, 'in their power who manage arms to continue or not continue the form of government whereby the estate is governed'[38] (book 7, ch. 9), which is nothing else but a stratocracy,

33   Henry Parker, *Observations upon some of His Majesties Late Answers and Expresses*, p. 15.

34   οἱ πλεῖστοι φαῦλοι κριταὶ περὶ τῶν οἰκείων. 1280ᵃ 15–16.

35   τί διαφέρουσιν ἔνιοι τῶν θηρίων. 1281ᵇ 19–20.

36   ἥδιον γὰρ τοῖς πολλοῖς τὸ ζῆν ἀτάκτως ἢ τὸ σωφρόνως. 1319ᵇ 31–2.

37   Judges 17:6.

38   Ὁι γὰρ τῶν ὅπλων κύριοι καὶ τοῦ μένειν ἢ μὴ μένειν κύριοι τὴν πολιτείαν. 1329ᵃ 11–12.

or military government. We cannot much blame Aristotle for the uncertainty and contrariety in him about the sorts of government if we consider him as a heathen. For it is not possible for the wit of man to search out the first grounds or principles of government (which necessarily depend upon the original of property) except he know that at the creation one man alone was made, to whom the dominion of all things was given and from whom all men derive their title. This point can be learnt only from the Scriptures. As for the imaginary contract of people, it is a fancy not improbable only, but impossible, except a multitude of men at first had sprung out and were engendered of the earth, which Aristotle knows not whether he may believe or no (book 2, ch. 8). If justice (which is to give every man his due) be the end of government, there must necessarily be a rule to know how any man at first came to have a right to anything to have it truly called his. This is a point Aristotle disputes not, nor so much as ever dreamt of an original contract among people. He looked no farther in every city then to a scambling[39] among the citizens, whereby everyone snatched what he could get, so that a violent possession was the first and best title that he knew.

The main distinction of Aristotle touching perfect or right forms of government from those that are imperfect or corrupt consists solely in this point, that where the profit of the governed is respected there is a right government, but where the profit of the governors is regarded there is a corruption or transgression of government. By this it is supposed by Aristotle that there may be a government only for the benefit of the governors. This supposition to be false may be proved from Aristotle himself; I will instance about the point of tyranny.

'Tyranny', saith Aristotle, 'is a despotical or masterly monarchy' (book 3, ch. 7). Now he confesseth that 'in truth the masterly government is profitable both to the servant by nature and the master by nature' (book 4, ch. 10), and he yields a solid reason for it, saying, 'It is not possible, if the servant be destroyed, that the mastership can be saved' (book 3, ch. 6). Whence it may be inferred that if the masterly government of tyrants cannot be safe without the preservation of them whom they govern, it will follow that a tyrant cannot govern for his own profit only. And thus his main definition of tyranny fails, as being grounded upon an impossible supposition by his own confession. No example can be shewed of any such government that ever was in the world as Aristotle describes a tyranny to be. For under the worst of kings, though many particular men have unjustly suffered, yet the multitude or the people in general have found

39   Free-for-all.

benefit and profit by the government.

It being apparent that the different kinds of government in Aristotle arise only from the difference of the number of governors—whether one, a few, or many—there may be as many several forms of governments as there be several numbers, which are infinite. So that not only the several parts of a city or commonweal but also the several numbers of such parts may cause multiplicity of forms of government by Aristotle's principles.

It is further observable in assemblies that it is not the whole assembly but the major part only of the assembly that hath the government. For 'that which pleaseth the most is always ratified', saith Aristotle (book 4, ch. 4). By this means one and the same assembly may make at one sitting several forms of commonweals. For in several debates and votes the same number of men, or all the self-same men do not ordinarily agree in their votes; and the least disagreement, either in the persons of the men or in their number, alters the form of government. Thus in a commonweal one part of the public affairs shall be ordered by one form of government, and another part by another form, and a third part by a third form, and so *in infinitum*. How can that have the denomination of a form of government, which lasts but for a moment only, about one fraction of business? For in the very instant, as it were in the twinkling of an eye, while their vote lasteth the government must begin and end.

To be governed is nothing else but to be obedient and subject to the will or command of another: it is the will in a man that governs. Ordinarily men's wills are divided according to their several ends or interests, which most times are different and many times contrary the one to the other. And in such cases where the wills of the major part of the assembly do unite and agree in one will, there is a monarchy of many wills in one, though it be called an aristocracy or democracy in regard of the several persons. It is not the many bodies, but the one will or soul of the multitude that governs. 'Where one is set up out of many the people becometh a monarch, because many are lords not separately but altogether as one. Therefore such a people, as if it were a monarch, seeks to bear rule alone'[40] (book 4, ch. 4).

It is a false and improper speech to say that a whole multitude, senate, council, or any multitude whatsoever doth govern where the major part only rules; because many of the multitude that are so assembled are so far from having any part in the government that they themselves are governed against and contrary to their wills. There being in all government

---

40   Μόναρχος γὰρ ὁ δῆμος γίνεται, σύνθετος εἷς ἐκ πολλῶν: οἱ γὰρ πολλοὶ κύριοί εἰσιν οὐχ ὡς ἕκαστος ἀλλὰ πάντες. [...] ὁ δ' οὖν τοιοῦτος δῆμος, ἅτε μόναρχος ὤν, ζητεῖ μοναρχεῖν. 1292ᵃ 11–13, 15–16.

various and different debates and consultations, it comes to pass oft-times that the major part in every assembly differs according to the several humours or fancies of men. Those who agree in one mind, in one point, are of different opinions in another. Every change of business or new matter begets a new major part, and is a change both of the government and governors. The difference in the number or in the qualities of the persons that govern is the only thing that causes different governments, according to Aristotle, who divides his kinds of government to the number of one, a few, or many. As amongst the Romans their tribunitial laws had several titles according to the names of those tribunes of the people that preferred and made them, so in other governments the body of their acts and ordinances is composed of a multitude of momentary monarchs, who by the strength and power of their parties or factions are still under a kind of a civil war, fighting and scratching for the legislative miscellany or medley of several governments. If we consider each government according to the nobler part of which it is composed, it is nothing else but a monarchy of monothelites[41] or of many men of one will, most commonly in one point only. But if we regard only the baser part or bodies of such persons as govern, there is an interrupted succession of a multitude of short-lived governments, with as many intervals of anarchy. So that no man can say at any time that he is under any form of government, for in a shorter time than the word can be spoken, every government is begun and ended. Furthermore in all assemblies, of what quality soever they be, whether aristocratical or democratical, as they call them, they all agree in this one point, to give that honourable regard to monarchy, that they do interpret the major or prevailing part in every assembly to be but as one man, and so do feign to themselves a kind of monarchy.

Though there be neither precept nor practice in Scripture, nor yet any reason alleged by Aristotle for any form of government but only monarchy, yet it is said that it is evident to common sense that of old time Rome, and in this present age Venice and the Low Countries, enjoy a form of government different from monarchy. Hereunto it may be answered that a people may live together in society and help one another, and yet not be under any form of government; as we see herds of cattle do, and yet we may not say they live under government. For government is not a society only to live, but to live well and virtuously. This is acknowledged by Aristotle who teacheth that 'the end of a city is to live blessedly and honestly. Political communities are ordained for honest actions, but not for living

---

41   The theological doctrine that in Christ there is but one will though two natures.

together only'.[42]

Now there be two things principally required to a blessed and honest life—religion towards God, and peace towards men; that is, 'a quiet and peaceable life in all godliness and honesty', 1 Timothy 2:2. Here then will be the question: whether godliness and peace can be found under any government but monarchy, or whether Rome, Venice, or the Low Countries did enjoy these under any popular government. In these two points let us first briefly examine the Roman government, which is thought to have been the most glorious.

For religion, we find presently after the building of the city by Romulus, the next king, Numa, most devoutly established a religion and began his kingdom with the service of the gods. He forbade the Romans to make any images of God, which law lasted and was observed 170 years; there being in all that time no image or picture of God in any temple or chapel of Rome. Also, he erected the pontifical college and was himself the first bishop or *pontifex*. These bishops were to render no account either to the senate or commonalty. They determined all questions concerning religion, as well between priests as between private men. They punished inferior priests if they either added or detracted from the established rites or ceremonies, or brought in any new thing into religion. The chief bishop, *pontifex maximus*, taught every man how to honour and serve the gods. This care had monarchy of religion.

But after the expulsion of kings, we do not find during the power of the people any one law made for the benefit or exercise of religion. There be two tribunitian laws concerning religion, but they are merely for the benefit of the power of the people and not of religion. L. Papirius, a tribune, made a law called *Lex Papiria*, that it should not be lawful for any to consecrate either houses, grounds, altars, or any other things without the determination of the people. Domitius Ænobarbus, another tribune, enacted a law called *Domitia Lex*, that the pontifical college should not, as they were wont, admit whom they would into the order of priesthood, but it should be in the power of the people. And because it was contrary to their religion that church dignities should be bestowed by the common people, hence for very shame he ordained that the lesser part of the people, namely seventeen tribes, should elect whom they thought fit, and afterwards the party elected should have his confirmation or admission from the college.

---

42   Τέλος μὲν οὖν πόλεως τὸ εὖ ζῆν, ταῦτα δὲ τοῦ τέλους χάριν. πόλις δὲ ἡ γενῶν καὶ κωμῶν κοινωνία ζωῆς τελείας καὶ αὐτάρκους, τοῦτο δ' ἐστίν, ὡς φαμέν, τὸ ζῆν εὐδαιμόνως καὶ καλῶς. τῶν καλῶν ἄρα πράξεων χάριν θετέον εἶναι τὴν πολιτικὴν κοινωνίαν ἀλλ' οὐ τοῦ συζῆν. 1280ᵇ 39–1281ᵃ 4.

Thus by a committee of seven tribes taken out of thirty-five, the ancient form of religion was altered and reduced to the power of the lesser part of the people. This was the great care of the people to bring ordination and consecration to the laity.

The religion in Venice and the Low Countries is sufficiently known; much need not be said of them. They admirably agree under a seeming contrariety. It is commonly said that one of them hath all religions, and the other no religion; the atheist of Venice may shake hands with the sectary of Amsterdam. This is the liberty that a popular estate can brag of: every man may be of any religion, or no religion, if he please. Their main devotion is exercised only in opposing and suppressing monarchy. They both agree to exclude the clergy from meddling in government, whereas in all monarchies both before the law of Moses and under it, and ever since, all barbarians, Grecians, Romans, infidels, Turks, and Indians, have with one consent given such respect and reverence to their priests as to trust them with their laws. And in this our nation, the first priests we read of before Christianity were the Druids, who, as Caesar saith, 'decided and determined controversies in murder, in case of inheritance, of bounds of lands, as they in their discretion judged meet; they grant rewards and punishments'.[43] It is a wonder to see what high respect even the great Turk giveth to his mufti, or chief bishop, so necessary is religion to strengthen and direct laws.

To consider of the point of peace, it is well known, that no people ever enjoyed it without monarchy. Aristotle saith the Lacedemonians 'preserved themselves by warring, and after they had gotten to themselves the empire then were they presently undone, for that they could not live at rest nor do any better exercise than the exercise of war'[44] (book 2, ch. 7). After Rome had expelled kings it was in perpetual war till the time of the emperors. Once only was the temple of Janus shut,[45] after the end of the first Punic War, but not so long as for one year, but for some months. It is true, as Orosius saith, that 'for almost 700 years, that is, from Tullus Hostilius to Augustus Caesar, only for one summer the bowels of Rome did not sweat blood'.[46] On the behalf of the Romans it may be said that though the bowels of Rome did always sweat blood, yet they did obtain most glorious victories abroad. But it may be truly answered, if all the Roman conquests had no other foundation but injustice, this alone soils all the glory of her war-

---

43   Caesar, *De Bello Gallico*, 6.13.

44   1271^b 3–6.

45   The gates of the temple of Janus were shut only during times of peace.

46   Orosius, *Historiarum adversus paganos*, iv, 12, 9.

like actions. The most glorious war that ever Rome had was with Carthage, the beginning of which war Sir Walter Raleigh proves to have been most unjustly undertaken by the Romans, in confederating with the Mamertines and aiding of rebels, under the title of protecting their confederates. Whereas kings many times may have just cause of war for recovering and preserving their rights to such dominions as fall to them by inheritance or marriage, a popular estate, that can neither marry nor be heir to another, can have no such title to a war in a foreign kingdom. And to speak the truth, if it be rightly considered the whole time of the popularity of Rome the Romans were no other than the only prosperous and glorious thieves and robbers of the world.

If we look more narrowly into the Roman government, it will appear that in that very age wherein Rome was most victorious and seemed to be most popular, she owed most of her glory to an apparent kind of monarchy. For it was the kingly power of the consuls, who, as Livy saith, had the same royal jurisdiction or absolute power that the kings had, not any whit diminished or abated, and held all the same regal ensigns of supreme dignity, which helped Rome to all her conquests. Whiles the tribunes of the people were struggling at home with the senate about election of magistrates, enacting of laws and calling to account, or such other popular affairs, the kingly consuls gained all the victories abroad. Thus Rome at one and the same time was broken and distracted into two shews of government—the popular, which served only to raise seditions and discords within the walls, whilst the regal achieved the conquests of foreign nations and kingdoms. Rome was so sensible of the benefit and necessity of monarchy that in her most desperate condition and danger, when all other hopes failed her, she had still resort to the creation of a dictator who for the time was an absolute king, and from whom no appeal to the people was granted—which is the royallest evidence for monarchy in the world. For they who were drawn to swear they would suffer no king of Rome, found no security but in perjury and breaking their oath by admitting the kingly power in spite of their teeth, under a new name of a dictator or consul—a just reward for their wanton expelling their king for no other crime they could pretend but pride, which is most tolerable in a king of all men. And yet we find no particular point of pride charged upon him but that he enjoined the Romans to labour in cleansing and casting of ditches, and paving their sinks—an act both for the benefit and ornament of the city, and therefore commendable in the king. But the citizens of Rome, who had been conquerors of all nations round about them, could not endure of warriors to become quarriers and day-labourers. Whereas it is said that Tarquin was expelled for the rape committed by his son on

Lucrece, it is unjust to condemn the father for the crime of his son. It had been fit to have petitioned the father for the punishment of the offender. The fact of young Tarquin cannot be excused, yet without wrong to the reputation of so chaste a lady as Lucrece is reputed to be, it may be said, she had a greater desire to be thought chaste than to be chaste. She might have died untouched, and unspotted in her body if she had not been afraid to be slandered for inchastity. Both Dionysius Halicarnasseus, and Livy, who both are her friends, so tell the tale of her as if she had chosen rather to be a whore than to be thought a whore. To say truth, we find no other cause of the expulsion of Tarquin than the wantonness and licentiousness of the people of Rome.

This is further to be considered in the Roman government, that all the time between their kings and their emperors there lasted a continued strife between the nobility and commons, wherein by degrees the commons prevailed at last so to weaken the authority of the consuls and senate that even the last sparks of monarchy were in a manner extinguished, and then instantly began the civil war which lasted till the regal power was quickly brought home and settled in monarchy. So long as the power of the senate stood good for the election of consuls, the regal power was preserved in them, for the senate had their first institution from monarchy. It is worth the noting that in all those places that have seemed to be most popular, that weak degree of government that hath been exercised among them, hath been founded upon and been beholden unto monarchical principles both for the power of assembling and manner of consulting. For the entire and gross body of any people is such an unwieldy and diffused thing as is not capable of uniting, or congregating, or deliberating in an entire lump, but in broken parts, which at first were regulated by monarchy.

Furthermore it is observable that Rome in her chief popularity was oft beholden for her preservation to the monarchical power of the father over the children. By means of this fatherly power, saith Bodin, the Romans flourished in all honour and virtue, and oftentimes was their commonweal thereby delivered from most imminent destruction, when the fathers drew out of the consistories their sons being tribunes publishing laws tending to sedition. Amongst others Cassius 'threw his son headlong out of the consistory, publishing the law *agraria* (for the division of lands) in the behoof of the people, and after by his own private judgment put him to death'[47]—the magistrates, sergeants, and people standing thereat astonished, and not daring to withstand his fatherly authority, although they would with all their power have had that law for division of lands; which is

---

47 Jean Bodin, *The Six Bookes of a Commonweale*, tr. Richard Knolles, p. 23.

sufficient proof this power of the father not only to have been sacred and inviolable, but also to have been lawful for him either by right or wrong to dispose of the life and death of his children, even contrary to the will of the magistrates and people.

It is generally believed that the government of Rome, after the expulsion of kings, was popular. Bodin endeavours to prove it, but I am not satisfied with his arguments, and though it will be thought a paradox, yet I must maintain, it was never truly popular.

First, it is difficult to agree, what a popular government is. Aristotle saith it is where many or a multitude do rule; he doth not say where the people, or the major part of the people, or the representors of the people govern.

Bodin affirms, 'if all the people be interested in the government it is a popular estate', (book 2, ch. 1), but after in the same chapter he resolves that 'it is a popular estate when all the people, or the greater part thereof hath the sovereignty',[48] and he puts the case that if there be three-score thousand citizens, and forty thousand of them have the sovereignty, and twenty thousand be excluded, it shall be called a popular estate. But I must tell him, though fifty-nine thousand, nine hundred and ninety-nine of them govern, yet it is no popular estate. For if but one man be excluded, the same reason that excludes that one man may exclude many hundreds, and many thousands, yea, and the major part itself. If it be admitted that the people are or ever were free by nature, and not to be governed but by their own consent, it is most unjust to exclude any one man from his right in government; and to suppose the people so unnatural as at the first to have all consented to give away their right to a major part (as if they had liberty given them only to give away, and not to use it themselves) is not only improbable, but impossible. For the whole people is a thing so uncertain and changeable that it alters every moment, so that it is necessary to ask of every infant so soon as it is born its consent to government, if you will ever have the consent of the whole people.

Moreover, if the arbitrary trial by a jury of twelve men be a thing of that admirable perfection and justice as is commonly believed, wherein the negative voice of every single person is preserved, so that the dissent of any of the twelve frustrates the whole judgment; how much more ought the natural freedom of each man be preserved by allowing him his negative voice, which is but a continuing him in that estate wherein, it is confessed, nature at first placed him? Justice requires that no one law should bind all, except all consent to it. There is nothing more violent and contrary to nature, than to allow a major part, or any other greater part less than the

48   Bodin, *Six Bookes*, p. 184.

whole, to bind all the people.

The next difficulty to discovering what a popular estate is, is to find out where the supreme power in the Roman government rested. It is Bodin's opinion, that 'in the Roman state the government was in the magistrates, the authority and council in the senate, but the sovereign power and majesty in the people' (book 2, ch. 1). So in his first book his doctrine is that 'the ancient Romans said "*imperium in magistratibus, authoritatem in senatu, potestatem in plebe, majestatem in populo jure esse dicebant*" ["command was said to be in the magistrates, authority in the senate, power in the plebs, and majesty in the people"]'.[49] These four words *command, authority, power,* and *majesty* signify ordinarily one and the same thing, to wit, the sovereignty, or supreme power, I cannot find that Bodin knows how to distinguish them. For they were not distinct faculties placed in several subjects, but one and the same thing diversely qualified. For *imperium, authoritas, potestas,* and *majestas* were all originally in the consuls, although for the greater show the consuls would have the opinion and consent of the senate—who were never called together nor had their advice asked, but when and in what points only it pleased the consuls to propound. So that properly *senatusconsultum* ["a decree of the senate"] was only a decree of the consuls with the advice of the senators. And so likewise the consuls, when they had a mind to have the countenance of an ampler council, they assembled the centuries, who were reckoned as the whole people and were never to be assembled but when the consuls thought fit to propound some business of great weight unto them. So that *jussus populi*—the command of the people—which Bodin so much magnifies, was properly *jussus consulum*—the command of the consuls, by the advice or consent of the assembly of the centuries, who were a body composed of the senators and the rest of the patricians, knights, and gentlemen, or whole nobility together with the commons. For the same men who had voices in senate had also their votes allowed in the assembly of the centuries, according to their several capacities.

It may further appear that the Roman government was never truly popular, for that in her greatest show of popularity there were to be found above ten servants for every citizen or freeman, and of those servants not one of them was allowed any place or voice in government. If it be said that the Roman servants were slaves taken in war, and therefore not fit to be freemen; to this it may be answered that if the opinion of our modern politicians be good, which holds that all men are born free by nature, or if but the opinion of Aristotle be sound, who saith that 'by nature some men are servants and some are masters',[50] then it may be unnatural or unjust to make all prisoners in war servants, or (as they are now called) slaves—a term not used in the popular governments, either of Rome or Greece. For in both languages the usual word that doth answer to our late term of slave is but *servus* in Latin, and δοῦλος in Greek. Besides, if the wars of the Romans by which they gained so many servants were unjust, as I take all offensive war to be without a special commission from God, and as I believe all the Roman wars were that were made for the enlargement of their empire, then we may conclude that the Romans were the notablest plagiaries[51] or men-stealers in the world.

But to allow the lesser part of the people of Rome, who called themselves citizens, to have had a just right to exclude all servants from being a part of the people of Rome, let us enquire whether the major part of those whom they allowed to be citizens had the government of Rome—whereby we may discover easily how notoriously the poorer and greater part of the citizens were gulled of their share in government. There were two famous manners of their assembling the people of Rome. The first was by classes, as they called them, which were divided into centuries. The second was by tribes, or wards. The former of these was a ranking of the people according to their abilities or wealth; the latter according to the place or ward wherein every citizen dwelt. In the assemblies of neither of these, had the major part of the people the power of government, as may thus be made appear.

First, for the assembly of the centuries, there were six degrees or classes of men according to their wealth. The first classis was of the richest men in Rome, none whereof were under 200 pounds in value. The valuation of the second classis was not under fourscore pounds; and so the third, the fourth, and the fifth classis were each a degree one under another. The sixth classis contained the poorer sort and all the rabble. These six classes were subdivided into hundreds, or centuries.

The first classis had	98
The second classis had	22
The third classis had	20
The fourth classis had	22
The fifth classis had	30
The sixth classis had	1
Total	**193**

50   1255ᵃ 1–2.
51   *Merriam Webster* defines plagiary thus: *Plagiarius*, the Latin source of "plagiary," literally means "kidnapper."

The classes and centuries being thus ordered, when the assembly came to give their votes, they did not give their voices by the poll, which is the true popular way; but each century voted by itself. Each century having one voice, the major part of the centuries carried the business. Now there being fourscore and eighteen centuries in the first classis—in which all the patricians, senators, noblemen, knights, and gentlemen of Rome, were enrolled—being more in number, and above half the centuries, must needs have the government if they agreed all together in their votes, because they voted first. For when ninety-seven centuries had agreed in their votes, the other centuries of the inferior classis were never called to vote. Thus the nobles and richer men who were but few in comparison of the common people did bear the chief sway, because all the poorer sort, or proletarian rabble, were clapped into the sixth classis—which in reckoning were allowed but the single voice of one century, which never came to voting, whereas in number they did far exceed all the five other classes or centuries. And if they had been allowed the liberty of other citizens they might have been justly numbered for a thousand centuries or voices in the assembly. This device of packing so many thousands into one century did exclude far the greatest part of the people from having a part in the government.

Next, for the assembly of the people of Rome by tribes, it must be considered, that the tribes did not give their voices by the poll all together, which is the true way of popular voting, but each tribe or ward did vote by itself, and the votes of the major part (not of the people but) of the tribes did sway the government. The tribes being unequal, as all divisions by wards usually are, because the number of the people of one tribe is not just the same with the number of the people of each other tribe; whence it followed that the major number of the tribes might possibly be the minor number of the people, which is a destroying of the power of the major part of the people.

Add hereunto that the nobility of Rome were excluded from being present at the assembly of the tribes, and so the most considerable part of the people was wanting. Therefore it could not be the voices of the major part of the people, where a great part of the people were allowed no voices at all. For it must be the major part of the *whole* and not of a *part* of the people that must denominate a popular government.

Moreover, it must be noted that the assembly of the tribes was not originally the power of the people of Rome, for it was almost forty years after the rejection of kings before an assembly of tribes were thought on, or spoken of. For it was the assembly of the people by centuries that agreed to the expulsion of kings and creating of consuls in their room. Also the famous laws of the twelve tables were ratified by the assembly of the centuries. This assembly by centuries, as it was more ancient than that by tribes, so it was more truly popular, because all the nobility as well as the commons had voices in it. The assembly by tribes was pretended at first only to elect tribunes of the people and other inferior magistrates to determine of lesser crimes that were not capital but only finable, and to decree that peace should be made. But they did not meddle with denouncing war to be made, for that high point did belong only to the assembly of the centuries, and so also did the judging of treason and other capital crimes. The difference between the assembly of the tribes and of the centuries is very material, for though it be commonly thought that either of these two assemblies were esteemed to be the people, yet in reality it was not so. For the assembly of the centuries only could be said to be the people, because all the nobility were included in it as well as the commons, whereas they were excluded out of the assembly of the tribes. And yet in effect the assembly of the centuries was but as the assembly of the lords or nobles only, because the lesser and richer part of the people had the sovereignty, as the assembly of the tribes was but the commons only.

In maintenance of the popular government of Rome, Bodin objects that there could be no regal power in the two consuls, 'who could neither make law, nor peace, nor war'.[52] The answer is, though there were two consuls yet but one of them had the regality, for they governed by turns, one consul one month, and the other consul another month; or the first one day, and the second another day. That the consuls could make no laws is false. It is plain by Livy that they had the power to make laws, or war, and did execute that power, though they were often hindered by the tribunes of the people. Not for that the power of making laws or war was ever taken away from the consuls, or communicated to the tribunes, but only the exercise of the consular power was suspended by a seeming humble way of intercession of the tribunes. The consuls by their first institution had a lawful right to do those things, which yet they would not do by reason of the shortness of their reigns, but chose rather to countenance their actions with the title of a decree of the senate (who were their private council) yea, and sometimes with the decree of the assembly of the centuries (who were their public council). For both the assembling of the senate and of the centuries was at the pleasure of the consuls, and nothing was to be propounded in either of them but at the will of the consuls—which argues a sovereignty in them over the senate and centuries. The senate of Rome was like the House of Lords, the assembly of the tribes resembled the House of Commons, but

---

the assembling of the centuries was a body composed of lords and commons united to vote together.

The tribunes of the people bore all the sway among the tribes. They called them together when they pleased, without any order, whereas the centuries were never assembled without ceremony and religious observation of the birds by the augurs, and by the approbation of the senate, and therefore were said to be *auspicate* ["auspicious"], and *ex authoritate patrum* ["from the authority of the patricians"].

These things considered, it appears that the assembly of the centuries was the only legitimate and great meeting of the people of Rome. As for any assembling or electing of any trustees or representors of the people of Rome in nature of the modern parliaments, it was not in use or ever known in Rome.

Above two hundred and twenty years after the expulsion of kings a sullen humour took the commons of Rome, that they would needs depart the city to Janiculum, on the other side of Tiber. They would not be brought back into the city until a law was made that a *plebiscitum*, or a decree of the commons, might be observed for a law. This law was made by the dictator Hortensius to quiet the sedition by giving a part of the legislative power to the commons in such inferior matters only as by toleration and usurpation had been practised by the commons. I find not that they desired an enlargement of the points which were the object of their power, but of the persons or nobility that should be subject to their decrees. The great power of making war, of creating the greater magistrates, of judging in capital crimes, remained in the consuls with the senate and assembly of the centuries.

For further manifestation of the broken and distracted government of Rome, it is fit to consider the original power of the consuls, and of the tribunes of the commons, who are ordinarily called the tribunes of the people.

First, it is undeniable that upon the expulsion of kings, kingly power was not taken away but only made annual and changeable between two consuls, who in their turns and by course had the sovereignty and all regal power. This appears plainly in Livy, who tells us that Valerius Publicola being consul, he himself alone ordained a law and then assembled a general session.

Terentilius Harsa inveighed and complained against 'the consuls' government as being so absolute, and in name only less odious than that of kings, but in fact more cruel. For instead of one lord the city had received twain, having authority beyond all measure, unlimited and infinite'. Sextius and Licinius complain that there would never be any indifferent course so long as the nobles kept the sovereign place of command, and the sword to strike, whilst the poor commons have only the buckler. Their conclusion was that 'it remains that the commons bear the office of consuls too, for that were a fortress of their liberty. From that day forward shall the commons be partakers of those things wherein the nobles now surpass them, namely sovereign rule and authority'.[53]

The law of the twelve tables affirms, *Regio imperio duo sunto, iique consules appellantor*:[54] 'let two have regal power, and let them be called consuls'. Also, the judgment of Livy is that 'the sovereign power was translated from consuls to decemvirs, as before from kings to consuls'.[55] These are proofs sufficient to show the royal power of the consuls.

About sixteen years after the first creation of consuls, the commons finding themselves much run into debt by wasting their estates in following the wars, and so becoming, as they thought, oppressed by usury, and cast into prison by the judgment and sentence of the consuls, they grievously complained of usury and of the power of the consuls, and by sedition prevailed, and obtained leave to choose among themselves magistrates called tribunes of the people, who by their intercession might preserve the commons from being oppressed and suffering wrong from the consuls. And it was further agreed that the persons of those tribunes should be sacred, and not to be touched by any. By means of this immunity of the bodies of the tribunes from all arrests or other violence, they grew in time by degrees to such boldness that by stopping the legal proceedings of the consuls (when they pleased to intercede) they raised such an anarchy oft-times in government that they themselves might act and take upon them what power soever they pleased (though it belonged not to them). This gallantry of the tribunes was the cause that the commons of Rome, who were diligent pretenders to liberty, and the great masters of this part of politics, were thought the only famous preservers and keepers of the liberty of Rome. And to do them right, it must be confessed they were the only men that truly understood the rights of a negative voice. If we will allow every man to be naturally free till they give their consent to be bound, we must allow every particular person a negative voice. So that when as all have equal power, and are as it were fellow magistrates or officers, each man may impeach or stop his fellow-officers in their proceedings. This is grounded upon the general reason of all them which have any thing in common, where he which forbiddeth, or denieth, hath most right—be-

53   Livy, *Ab Urbe Condita*, 6.37.
54   Cicero, *De Republica*, 3.3.
55   Livy, 3.33.

cause his condition in that case is better than his which commandeth, or moveth to proceed. For every law or command is in itself an innovation, and a diminution of some part of popular liberty—for it is no law except it restrain liberty. He that by his negative voice doth forbid or hinder the proceeding of a new law doth but preserve himself in that condition of liberty wherein nature hath placed him, and whereof he is in present possession. The condition of him thus in possession being the better, the stronger is his prohibition, any single man hath a juster title to his negative voice than any multitude can have to their affirmative. To say the people are free, and not to be governed but by their own consent, and yet to allow a major part to rule the whole, is a plain contradiction, or a destruction of natural freedom. This the commons of Rome rightly understood—and therefore the transcendent power of the negative voice of any one tribune, being able of itself to stay all the proceedings not of the consuls and senate only, and other magistrates, but also of the rest of his fellow tribunes, made them seem the powerfullest men in all Rome. And yet in truth they had no power or jurisdiction at all, nor were they any magistrates, nor could they lawfully call any man before them. For they were not appointed for administration of justice, but only to oppose the violence and abuse of magistrates by interceding for such as appealed, being unjustly oppressed. For which purpose at first they sat only without the door of the senate, and were not permitted to come within the doors. This negative power of theirs was of force only to hinder but not to help the proceedings in courts of justice; to ungovern, and not to govern the people. And though they had no power to make laws, yet they took upon them to propound laws, and flattered and humoured the commons by the agrarian and frumentarian laws. By the first they divided the common fields and conquered lands among the common people; and by the latter they afforded them corn at a cheaper or lower price. By these means these demagogues or tribunes of the commons led the vulgar by the noses, to allow whatsoever usurpations they pleased to make in government.

The royal power of the consuls was never taken away from them by any law that I hear of, but continued in them all the time of their pretended popular government, to the very last—though repined at, and opposed in some particulars by the commons.

The no-power or negative power of the tribunes did not long give content to the commons, and therefore they desired that one of the consuls might be chosen out of the commonalty. The eager propounding of this point for the commons, and the diligent opposing of it by the nobility or senate, argues how much both parties regarded the sovereign power of a consul. The dispute lasted fourscore years within two. The tribunes, pressing it upon all advantages of opportunity, never gave over till they carried it by strong hand, or stubbornness, hindering all elections of the *curule* or greater magistrates for five years together; whereby the nobles were forced to yield the commons a consul's place, or else an anarchy was ready to destroy them all. And yet the nobility had for a good while allowed the commons military tribunes with consular power, which in effect or substance was all one with having one of the consuls a commoner, so that it was the bare name of a consul which the commons so long strived for with the nobility. In this contention, some years consuls were chosen, some years military tribunes, in such confusion that the Roman historians cannot agree among themselves what consuls to assign or name for each year, although they have Capitoline tables, Sicilian and Greek registers, and calendars, fragments of Capitoline marbles, linen books or records to help them. A good while the commons were content with the liberty of having one of the consuls a commoner. But about fourscore years after they enjoyed this privilege, a desire took them to have it enacted that a decree of the commons, called a *plebiscitum*, might be observed for a law. Hortensius the dictator yielded to enact it, thereby to bring back the seditious commons, who departed to Janiculum on the other side of Tiber, because they were deeply engaged in debt in regard of long seditions and dissensions. The eleventh book of Livy, where this sedition is set down, is lost; we have only a touch of it in Florus his epitome, and St. Augustine mentions the plundering of many houses by the commons at their departing. This sedition was above 220 years after the expulsion of kings, in all which time the people of Rome got the spoil of almost all Italy and the wealth of very many rich cities. And yet the commons were in so great penury, and overwhelmed with debts, that they fell to plunder the rich houses of the citizens, which sounds not much for the honour of a popular government. This communicating of a legislative power to the commons, touching power of enfranchising allies, judgments penal, and fines, and those ordinances that concerned the good of the commons—called *plebiscita*—was a dividing of the supreme power and the giving a share of it to others as well as to the consuls, and was in effect to destroy the legislative power. For to have two supremes is to have none, because the one may destroy the other, and is quite contrary to the indivisible nature of sovereignty. The truth is, the consuls having but annual sovereignty, were glad for their own safety, and ease in matters of great importance and weight, to call together sometimes the senate, who were their ordinary council, and many times the centuries of the people, who were their council extraordinary, that by their advice they might countenance and strengthen such actions as were full of danger and envy. And thus the consuls by weakening their original power brought the government to confusion, civil dissension, and utter ruin. So dangerous a thing it is to show favour to common people, who interpret all graces and favours for their rights and just liberties. The consuls following the advice of the senate or people, did not take away their right of governing no more than kings lose their supremacy by taking advice in parliaments.

Not only the consuls but also the praetors and censors (two great offices, ordained only for the ease of the consuls, from whom an appeal lay to the consuls) did in many things exercise an arbitrary or legislative power in the absence of the consuls. They had no laws to limit them. For, many years after the creation of consuls, ten men were sent into Greece to choose laws. And after the twelve tables were confirmed, whatsoever the praetors—who were but the consuls' substitutes—did command, was called *jus honorarium* ["an honorary law"]; and they were wont at the entrance into their office to collect and hang up for public view a form of administration of justice which they would observe. And though the *edictum praetoris* ["edict of the praetor"] expired with the praetor's office, yet it was called *edictum perpetuum*.

What peace the Low Countries have found since their revolt is visible. It is near about an hundred years since they set up for themselves, of all which time only twelve years they had a truce with the Spaniard. Yet in the next year after the truce was agreed upon, the war of Juliers broke forth, which engaged both parties. So that upon the matter, they have lived in a continual war for almost one hundred years. Had it not been for the aid of their neighbours, they had been long ago swallowed up, when they were glad humbly to offer their new hatched commonweal and themselves vassals to the Queen of England, after that the French king Henry III had refused to accept them as his subjects. That little truce they had was almost as costly as a war, they being forced to keep about thirty thousand soldiers continually in garrison. Two things they say they first fought about, religion and taxes—and they have prevailed it seems in both, for they have gotten all the religions in Christendom, and pay the greatest taxes in the world. They pay tribute half in half for food, and most necessary things, paying as much for tribute as the price of the thing sold. Excise is paid by all retailers of wine and other commodities. For each tun of beer six shillings; for each cow for the pail two stivers every week; for oxen, horses, sheep, and other beasts sold in the market the twelfth part at least; be they never so oft sold by the year to and fro, the new master still pays as much. They pay five stivers for every bushel of their own wheat, which they use to grind in public mills. These are the fruits of the Low Country war.

It will be said that Venice is a commonwealth that enjoys peace. She indeed of all other states hath enjoyed of late the greatest peace. But she owes it not to her kind of government but to the natural situation of the city, having such a bank in the sea of near three score miles, and such marshes towards the land as make her unapproachable by land or sea. To these she is indebted for her peace at home—and what peace she hath abroad she buys at a dear rate. And yet her peace is little better than a continued war. The city always is in such perpetual fears, that many besieged cities are in more security. A senator or gentleman dares not converse with any stranger in Venice, shuns acquaintance, or dares not own it. They are no better than banditos to all human society. Nay, no people in the world live in such jealousy one of another. Hence are their intricate solemnities or rather lotteries in election of their magistrates, which in any other place would be ridiculous and useless. The senators or gentlemen are not only jealous of the common people, whom they keep disarmed, but of one another. They dare not trust any of their own citizens to be a leader of their army, but are forced to hire and entertain foreign princes for their generals, excepting their citizens from their wars and hiring others in their places. It cannot be said that people live in peace which are in such miserable fears continually.

The Venetians at first were subject to the Roman Emperor, and for fear of the invasion of the Huns forsook Padua and other places in Italy, and retired with all their substance to those islands where now Venice stands. I do not read they had any leave to desert the defence of their prince and country where they had got their wealth, much less to set up a government of their own. It was no better than a rebellion or revolting from the Roman Empire. At first they lived under a kind of oligarchy, for several islands had each a tribune, who all met. and governed in common. But the dangerous seditions of their tribunes put a necessity upon them to choose a duke for life, who for many hundreds of years had an absolute power—under whose government Venice flourished most, and got great victories and rich possessions. But by insensible degrees the great council of the gentlemen have for many years been lessening the power of their dukes, and have at last quite taken it away. It is a strange error for any man to believe that the government of Venice hath been always the same that it is now. He that reads but the history of Venice may find for a long time a sovereign power in their dukes, and that for these last two hundred years, since the diminishing of that power, there have been no great victories and conquests obtained by that estate.

That which exceeds admiration is that Contarini hath the confidence to affirm the present government of Venice to be a mixed form of monarchy, democracy, and aristocracy. For whereas he makes the duke to have the person and show of a king; he after confesseth that the duke can do nothing at all alone, and being joined with other magistrates he hath no more authority than any of them. Also, the power of the magistrates is so small that no one of them, how great soever he be, can determine of anything of moment without the allowance of the council. So that this duke is but a man dressed up in purple, a king only in pomp and ornament, in power but a senator, within the city a captive, without a traitor, if he go without leave. As little reason is there to think a popular estate is to be found in the great council of Venice, or S.P.Q.V. For it doth not consist of the fortieth part of the people, but only of those they call patricians or gentlemen. For the commons neither by themselves nor by any chosen by them for their representors, are admitted to be any part of the great council. And if the gentlemen of Venice have any right to keep the government in their own hands and to exclude the commons, they never had it given them by the people, but at first were beholding to monarchy for their nobility. This may further be noted: that though Venice of late enjoyed peace abroad, yet it had been with that charge—either for fortification and defence, or in bribery so excessive (whereby of late upon any terms they purchased their peace)—that it is said their taxes are such that Christians generally live better under the Turk than under the Venetians. For there is not a grain of corn, a spoonful of wine, salt, eggs, birds, beasts, fowl, or fish sold, that payeth not a certain custom. Upon occasions the labourers and craftsmen pay a rate by the poll monthly. They receive incredible gains by usury of the Jews, for in every city they keep open shops of interest, taking pawns after fifteen in the hundred, and if at the year's end it be not redeemed it is forfeited, or at the least sold at great loss. The revenues which the very courtesans pay for toleration maintains no less than a dozen of galleys.

By what hath been said, it may be judged how unagreeable the popular government of Rome heretofore, and of Venice and the United Provinces[56] at present are, either for religion or peace (which two are principal ingredients of government), and so consequently not fit to be reckoned for forms—since whatsoever is either good or tolerable in either of their governments is borrowed or patched up of a broken and distracted monarchy. Lastly, though Venice and the Low Countries are the only remarkable places in this age that reject monarchy, yet neither of them pretend their government to be founded upon any original right of the people, or have the common people any power amongst them, or any chosen by them. Never was any popular estate in the world famous for keeping themselves in peace; all their glory hath been for quarrelling and fighting.

Those that are willing to be persuaded that the power of government

56 The Dutch Republic.

is originally in the people, finding how impossible it is for any people to exercise such power, do surmise that though the people cannot govern, yet they may choose representors or trustees, that may manage this power for the people—and such representors must be surmised to be the people. And since such representors cannot truly be chosen by the people, they are fain to divide the people into several parts, as of provinces, cities, and borough towns, and to allow to every one of those parts to choose one representor or more of their own. And such representors, though not any of them be chosen by the whole or major part of the people, yet still must be surmised to be the people. Nay, though not one of them be chosen either by the people or the major part of the people of any province, city, or borough for which they serve, but only by a smaller part, still it must be said to be the people. Now when such representors of the people do assemble or meet, it is never seen that all of them can at one time meet together, and so there never appears a true or full representation of the whole people of the nation, the representors of one part or other being absent. But still they must be imagined to be the people. And when such imperfect assemblies be met—though not half be present—they proceed, and though their number be never so small, yet it is so big that in the debate of any business of moment, they know not how to handle it without referring it to a fewer number than themselves, though themselves are not so many as they should be. Thus those that are chosen to represent the people are necessitated to choose others to represent the representors themselves. A trustee of the north doth delegate his power to a trustee of the south; and one of the east may substitute one of the west for his proxy. Hereby it comes to pass that public debates which are imagined to be referred to a general assembly of a kingdom, are contracted into a particular or private assembly—than which nothing can be more destructive or contrary to the nature of public assemblies. Each company of such trustees hath a prolocutor or speaker, who by the help of three or four of his fellows that are most active, may easily comply in gratifying one the other. So that each of them in their turns may sway the trustees, whilst one man, for himself or his friend, may rule in one business, and another man for himself or his friend prevail in another cause, till such a number of trustees be reduced to so many petty monarchs as there be men of it. So in all popularities where a general council or great assembly of the people meet, they find it impossible to dispatch any great action, either with expedition or secrecy, if a public free debate be admitted; and therefore are constrained to epitomize and sub-epitomize themselves so long, till at last they crumble away into the atoms of monarchy, which is the next degree to anarchy—for anarchy is nothing else but a broken monarchy, where every man is his own monarch or governor.

Whereas the power of the people in choosing both their government and governors is of late highly magnified, as if they were able to choose the best and excellentest men for that purpose, we shall find it true what Aristotle hath affirmed, that 'to choose well is the office of him that hath knowledge, none can choose a geometrician but he that hath skill in geometry'[57] (book 3, ch. 11). For, saith he, 'all men esteem not excellency to be one and the same'[58] (book 3, ch. 17).

A great deal of talk there is in the world of the freedom and liberty that they say is to be found in popular commonweals. It is worth the enquiry how far and in what sense this speech of liberty is true: 'true liberty is for every man to do what he list, or to live as he please, and not to be tied to any laws'. But such liberty is not to be found in any commonweal, for there are more laws in popular estates than anywhere else, and so consequently less liberty; and government, many say, was invented to take away liberty, and not to give it to every man. Such liberty cannot be; if it should, there would be no government at all. Therefore Aristotle (book 6, ch. 4): 'It is profitable not to be lawful to do everything that we will, for power to do what one will cannot restrain that evil that is in every man'.[59] So that true liberty cannot, nor should not be in any estate. But the only liberty that the talkers of liberty can mean is a liberty for some men 'to rule and to be ruled',[60] for so Aristotle expounds it; one while to govern, another while to be governed; to be a king in the forenoon, and a subject in the afternoon. This is the only liberty that a popular estate can brag of, that where a monarchy hath but one king, their government hath the liberty to have many kings by turns. If the common people look for any other liberty, either of their persons or their purses, they are pitifully deceived. For a perpetual army and taxes are the principal materials of all popular regiments: never yet any stood without them, and very seldom continued with them. Many popular estates have started up, but few have lasted—'it is no hard matter for any kind of government to last one, or two, or three days'[61] (book 6, ch. 5). For all such as out of hope of liberty attempt to erect new forms of government, he gives this prudent lesson: 'We must look well into the continuance of time, and remembrance of many years, wherein the means tending to establish community had not lain hid if they had been good

---

57   1282^a 8–10.
58   1288^a 23–4.
59   1318^b 38–1319^a 1.
60   1277^b 14.
61   1319^b 35–6.

and useful. For almost all things have been found out, albeit some have not been received, and other some have been rejected after men have had experience of them'[62] (book 2, ch. 5).

It is believed by many that at the very first assembling of the people it was unanimously agreed in the first place that the consent of the major part should bind the whole; and that though this first agreement cannot possibly be proved, either how, or by whom it should be made, yet it must necessarily be believed or supposed because otherwise there could be no lawful government at all. That there could be no lawful government, except a general consent of the whole people be first surmised, is no sound proposition. Yet true it is that there could be no popular government without it. But if there were at first a government without being beholden to the people for their consent, as all men confess there was, I find no reason but that there may be so still, without asking leave of the multitude.

If it be true that men are by nature free-born, and not to be governed without their own consents, and that self-preservation is to be regarded in the first place, it is not lawful for any government but self-government to be in the world. It were sin in the people to desire, or attempt to consent to any other government. If the fathers will promise for themselves to be slaves, yet for their children they cannot, who have always the same right to set themselves at liberty which their fathers had to enslave themselves.

To pretend that a major part, or the silent consent of any part, may be interpreted to bind the whole people, is both unreasonable and unnatural. It is against all reason for men to bind others where it is against nature for men to bind themselves. Men that boast so much of natural freedom are not willing to consider how contradictory and destructive the power of a major part is to the natural liberty of the whole people. The two grand favourites of the subjects, liberty and property (for which most men pretend to strive), are as contrary as fire to water, and cannot stand together. Though by human laws, in voluntary actions a major part may be tolerated to bind the whole multitude, yet in necessary actions—such as those of nature are—it cannot be so. Besides, if it were possible for the whole people to choose their representors, then either every each one of these representors ought to be particularly chosen by the whole people, and not one representor by one part, and another representor by another part of the people, or else it is necessary that continually the entire number of the representors be present—because otherwise the whole people is never represented.

Again, it is impossible for the people, though they might and would

62   1264[a] 1–5.

choose a government or governors, ever to be able to do it. For the people, to speak truly and properly, is a thing or body in continual alteration and change. It never continues one minute the same, being composed of a multitude of parts, whereof divers continually decay and perish, and others renew and succeed in their places. They which are the people this minute, are not the people the next minute. If it be answered that it is impossible to stand so strictly as to have the consent of the whole people, and therefore that which cannot be must be supposed to be the act of the whole people; this is a strange answer, first to affirm a necessity of having the peoples consent, then to confess an impossibility of having it. If but once that liberty—which is esteemed so sacred—be broken or taken away but from one of the meanest or basest of all the people, a wide gap is thereby opened for any multitude whatsoever that is able to call themselves, or whomsoever they please, the people.

Howsoever men are naturally willing to be persuaded that all sovereignty flows from the consent of the people, and that without it no true title can be made to any supremacy; and that it is so currant an axiom of late that it will certainly pass without contradiction, as a late exercitator[63] tells us; yet there are many and great difficulties in the point never yet determined, nor so much as disputed, all which the exercitator waives and declines, professing he will

> not insist upon the distinctions touching the manner of the people's passing their consent, nor determine which of them is sufficient, and which not to make the right or title; whether it must be antecedent to possession or may be consequent: express or tacit: collective or representative: absolute or conditioned: free or enforced: revocable or irrevocable.[64]

All these are material doubts concerning the people's title, and though the exercitator will not himself determine what consent is sufficient, and what not to make a right or title, yet he might have been so courteous as to have directed us to whom we might go for resolution in these cases. But the truth is that amongst all them that plead the necessity of the consent of the people, none of them hath ever touched upon these so necessary doctrines. It is a task, it seems, too difficult, otherwise surely it would not have been neglected, considering how necessary it is to resolve the conscience touching the manner of the people's passing their consent, and what is sufficient and what not to make or derive a right or title from the people.

63   Edward Gee.
64   Edward Gee, *An Exercitation Concerning Usurped Powers*, ch.1.

No multitude or great assembly of any nation, though they be all of them never so good and virtuous, can possibly govern. This may be evidently discovered by considering the actions of great and numerous assemblies, how they are necessitated to relinquish that supreme power which they think they exercise, and to delegate it to a few. There are two parts of the supreme power: the *legislative* and the *executive*. Neither of these can a great assembly truly act. If a new law be to be made it may in the general receive the proposal of it from one or more of the general assembly, but the forming, penning, or framing it into a law is committed to a few, because a great number of persons cannot without tedious and dilatory debates examine the benefits and mischiefs of a law. Thus in the very first beginning the intention of a general assembly is frustrated. Then after a law is penned or framed, when it comes to be questioned whether it shall pass or nay, though it be voted in a full assembly, yet by the rules of the assembly they are all so tied up and barred from a free and full debate that when any man hath given the reasons of his opinion, if those reasons be argued against, he is not permitted to reply in justification or explanation of them, but when he hath once spoken he must be heard no more—which is a main denial of that freedom of debate for which the great assembly is alleged to be ordained in the high point of *legislative* power.

The same may be said touching the *executive* power. If a cause be brought before a great assembly, the first thing done is to refer or commit it to some few of the assembly, who are trusted with the examining the proofs and witnesses, and to make report to the general assembly—who upon the report proceed to give their judgments without any public hearing or interrogating the witnesses, upon whose testimonies diligently examined every man that will pass a conscientious judgment is to rely. Thus the *legislative* and *executive* power are never truly practised in a great assembly. The true reason whereof is, if freedom be given to debate, never anything could be agreed upon without endless disputes. Mere necessity compels to refer main transactions of business to particular congregations and committees.

Those governments that seem to be popular are kinds of petty monarchies, which may thus appear: government is a relation between the governors and the governed, the one cannot be without the other, *mutuo se ponunt et auferunt* ["they rise and fall together"]. Where a command or law proceeds from a major part, there those individual persons that concurred in the vote are the governors, because the law is only their will in particular. The power of a major part being a contingent or casual thing, expires in the very act itself of voting, which power of a major part is grounded upon a supposition that they are the stronger part. When the vote is past, these voters—which are the major part—return again, and are incorporated into the whole assembly, and are buried as it were in that lump, and no otherwise considered. The act or law ordained by such a vote loseth the makers of it before it comes to be obeyed. For when it comes to be put in execution, it becomes the will of those who enjoin it and force obedience to it, not by virtue of any power derived from the makers of the law. No man can say, that during the reign of the late Queen Elizabeth, that King Henry VIII or Edward VI did govern, although that many of the laws that were made in those two former princes' times were observed and executed under her government. But those laws, though made by her predecessors, yet became the laws of her present government, who willed and commanded the execution of them, and had the same power to correct, interpret, or mitigate them, which the first makers of them had. Every law must always have some present known person in being, whose will it must be to make it a law for the present. This cannot be said of the major part of any assembly, because that major part instantly ceaseth as soon as ever it hath voted—an infallible argument whereof is this: that the same major part, after the vote given, hath no power to correct, alter, or mitigate it, or to cause it to be put in execution. So that he that shall act or cause that law to be executed makes himself the commander or willer of it, which was originally the will of others. It is said by Mr. Hobbes in his *Leviathan*, p. 141: 'Nothing is law where the legislator cannot be known', for there must 'be manifest signs that it proceedeth from the will of the sovereign; there is requisite not only a declaration of the law, but also sufficient signs of the author and the authority'.[65]

That senate or great council wherein it is conceived the supreme or legislative power doth rest, consists of those persons who are actually subjects at the very same time wherein they exercise their legislative power, and at the same instant may be guilty of breaking one law, whilst they are making another law. For it is not the whole and entire will of every particular person in the assembly, but that part only of his will which accidentally falls out to concur with the will of the greater part. So that the sharers of the legislative power have each of them perhaps not a hundredth part of the legislative power (which in itself is indivisible), and that not in *act* but in *possibility*, only in one particular point, for that moment whilst they give their vote. To close this point, which may seem strange and new to some, I will produce the judgment of Bodin. In his sixth book of a commonweal, and the fourth chapter, his words are,

---

65   Hobbes, *Leviathan*, p. 141.

The chief point of a commonweal, which is the right of sovereignty, cannot be nor subsist, to speak properly, but in monarchy. For none can be sovereign in a commonweal but one alone. If they be two, or three, or more, no one is sovereign, for that no one of them can give or take a law from his companion; and although we imagine a body of many lords or of a whole people to hold the sovereignty, yet hath it no true ground nor support if there be not a head with absolute power to unite them together, which a simple magistrate without sovereign authority cannot do. And if it chance that the lords or tribes of the people be divided (as it often falls out) then must they fall to arms one against another, and although the greatest part be of one opinion, yet may it so happen as the lesser part, having many legions and making a head, may oppose itself against the greater number and get the victory. We see the difficulties which are and always have been in popular estates, whereas they hold contrary parts and for divers magistrates. Some demand peace, others war; some will have this law, others that; some will have one commander, others another; some will treat a league with the king of France, others with the king of Spain; corrupted or drawn, some one way, some another, making open war—as hath been seen in our age amongst the Grisons, &c.[66]

Upon these texts of Aristotle fore-cited, and from the mutability of the Roman popularity, which Aristotle lived not to see, I leave the learned to consider whether it be not probable that these or the like paradoxes may be inferred to be the plain mind of Aristotle, viz:

1. That there is no form of government, but monarchy only.

2. That there is no monarchy, but paternal.

3. That there is no paternal monarchy, but absolute or arbitrary.

4. That there is no such thing as an aristocracy or democracy.

5. That there is no such form of government as a tyranny.

6. That the people are not born free by nature.

66 Bodin, *Six Bookes*, p. 715.

DIRECTIONS FOR
Obedience to GOVERNMENT
IN Dangerous or Doubtful Times.

All those who in these times so eagerly strive for an original power to be in the people do with one consent acknowledge that originally the supreme power was in the fatherhood; and that the first kings were fathers of families. This is not only evident and affirmed by Aristotle, but yielded unto by Grotius, Mr. Selden, Mr. Hobbs, Mr. Ascham, and all others of that party, not one excepted that I know of.

Now for those that confess an original subjection in children to be governed by their parents, to dream of an original freedom in mankind, is to contradict themselves. And to make subjects to be free, and kings to be limited. To imagine such pactions and contracts between kings and people as cannot be proved ever to have been made, or can ever be described or fancied, how it is possible for such contracts ever to have been is a boldness to be wondered at.

Mr. Selden confesseth that Adam,

> by donation from God, was made the general lord of all things, not without such a private dominion to himself as (without his grant) did exclude his children. And by donation, or assignation, or some kind of cession (before he was dead or left any heir to succeed him) his children had their distinct territories by right of private dominion. Abel had his flocks and pastures for them; Cain had his fields for corn and the land of Nod, where he built himself a city.[1]

It is confessed that in the infancy of the world the paternal government was monarchical; but when the world was replenished with multitude of people, then the paternal government ceased and was lost, and an elective kind of government by the people was brought into the world. To this it may be answered that the paternal power cannot be lost; it may either be transferred or usurped, but never lost, or ceaseth. God, who is the giver

---

1   John Selden, *Of the Dominion, or Ownership of the Sea*, p. 19.

of power, may transfer it from the father to some other; he gave to Saul a fatherly power over his father Kish. God also hath given to the father a right or liberty to alien his power over his children to any other, whence we find the sale and gift of children to have been much in use in the beginning of the world, when men had their servants for a possession and an inheritance as well as other goods: whereupon we find the power of castrating and making eunuchs much in use in old times. As the power of the father may be lawfully transferred or aliened, so it may be unjustly usurped. And in usurpation, the title of an usurper is before, and better than the title of any other than of him that had a former right; for he hath a possession by the permissive will of God, which permission, how long it may endure, no man ordinarily knows. Every man is to preserve his own life for the service of God and of his king or father, and is so far to obey an usurper as may tend not only to the preservation of his king and father, but sometimes even to the preservation of the usurper himself, when probably he may thereby be reserved to the correction or mercy of his true superior. Though by humane laws a long prescription may take away right, yet divine right never dies, nor can be lost or taken away.

Every man that is born is so far from being free born that by his very birth he becomes a subject to him that begets him. Under which subjection he is always to live, unless by immediate appointment from God, or by the grant or death of his father he become possessed of that power to which he was subject.

The right of fatherly government was ordained by God for the preservation of mankind. If it be usurped, the usurper may be so far obeyed as may tend to the preservation of the subjects, who may thereby be enabled to perform their duty to their true and right sovereign when time shall serve. In such cases, to obey an usurper is properly to obey the first and right governor, who must be presumed to desire the safety of his subjects. The command of an usurper is not to be obeyed in anything tending to the destruction of the person of the governor, whose being in the first place is to be looked after.

It hath been said that there have been so many usurpations by conquest in all kingdoms that all kings are usurpers or the heirs or successors of usurpers, and therefore any usurper, if he can but get the possession of a kingdom, hath as good a title as any other.

Answer: The first usurper hath the best title, being, as was said, in possession by the permission of God. And where an usurper hath continued so long that the knowledge of the right heir be lost by all the subjects, in such a case an usurper in possession is to be taken and reputed by such subjects for the true heir, and is to be obeyed by them as their father. As no man hath an infallible certitude but only a moral knowledge, which is no other than a probable persuasion grounded upon a peaceable possession, which is a warrant for subjection to parents and governors. For we may not say, because children have no infallible or necessary certainty who are their true parents, that therefore they need not obey because they are uncertain. It is sufficient, and as much as human nature is capable of, for children to rely upon a credible persuasion; for otherwise the commandment of 'honour thy father' would be a vain commandment, and not possible to be observed.

By human positive laws, a possession time out of mind takes away or bars a former right, to avoid a general mischief of bringing all right into a disputation not decidable by proof, and consequently to the overthrow of all civil government in grants, gifts, and contracts between man and man. But in grants and gifts that have their original from God or nature, as the power of the father hath, no inferior power of man can limit nor make any law of prescription against them. Upon this ground is built that common maxim, that *nullum tempus occurrit regi*, no time bars a king.

All power on earth is either derived or usurped from the fatherly power, there being no other original to be found of any power whatsoever; for if there should be granted two sorts of power without any subordination of one to the other, they would be in perpetual strife which should be supreme, for two supremes cannot agree. If the fatherly power be supreme, then the power of the people must be subordinate, and depend on it; if the power of the people be supreme, then the fatherly power must submit to it, and cannot be exercised without the licence of the people, which must quite destroy the frame and course of nature. Even the power which God himself exerciseth over mankind is by right of fatherhood; he is both the king and father of us all. As God hath exalted the dignity of earthly kings by communicating to them his own title by saying they 'are gods',[2] so on the other side he hath been pleased as it were to humble himself by assuming the title of a king to express his power, and not the title of any popular government. We find it is a punishment to have no king, Hosea 3:4, and promised as a blessing to Abraham, Genesis 17:6, that kings shall come out of thee.

Every man hath a part or share in the preservation of mankind in general. He that usurps the power of a superior thereby puts upon himself a necessity of acting the duty of a superior in the preservation of them over whom he hath usurped, unless he will aggravate one heinous crime by committing another more horrid. He that takes upon him the power of

2   Psalms 82:6.

a superior sins sufficiently, and to the purpose; but he that proceeds to destroy both his superior and those under the superior's protection goeth a strain higher, by adding murder to robbery. If government be hindered, mankind perisheth. An usurper by hindering the government of another brings a necessity upon himself to govern; his duty before usurpation was only to be ministerial or instrumental in the preservation of others by his obedience. But when he denies his own, and hinders the obedience of others, he doth not only not help, but is the cause of the distraction in hindering his superior to perform his duty. He makes the duty his own; if a superior cannot protract, it is his part to desire to be able to do it, which he cannot do in the future if in the present they be destroyed for want of government. Therefore it is to be presumed that the superior desires the preservation of them that should be subject to him. And so likewise it may be presumed that an usurper in general doth the will of his superior by preserving the people by government, and it is not improper to say that in obeying an usurper, we may obey primarily the true superior so long as our obedience aims at the preservation of those in subjection, and not at the destruction of the true governor. Not only the usurper, but those also over whom power is usurped may join in the preservation of themselves— yea, and in the preservation sometimes of the usurper himself.

Thus there may be a conditional duty or right in an usurper to govern. That is to say, supposing him to be so wicked as to usurp, and not willing to surrender or forgo his usurpation, he is then bound to protect by government, or else he increaseth and multiplieth his sin.

Though an usurper can never gain a right from the true superior, yet from those that are subjects he may; for if they know no other that hath a better title than the usurper, then as to them the usurper in possession hath a true right.

Such a qualified right is found at first in all usurpers, as is in thieves who have stolen goods, and during the time they are possessed of them, have a title in law against all others but the true owners; and such usurpers to divers intents and purposes may be obeyed.

Neither is he only an usurper who obtains the government, but all they are partakers in the usurpation who have either failed to give assistance to their lawful sovereign or have given aid either by their persons, estates or counsels for the destroying of that governor under whose protection they have been born and preserved. For although it should be granted that protection and subjection are reciprocal, so that where the first fails the latter ceaseth, yet it must be remembered that where a man hath been born under the protection of a long and peaceable government, he owes an assistance for the preservation of that government that hath protected him, and is the author of his own disobedience.

It is said by some that an usurped power may be obeyed in things that are lawful, but it may be obeyed not only in lawful things, but also in things indifferent. Obedience in things indifferent is necessary; not indifferent. For in things necessarily good, God is immediately obeyed, superiors only by consequence. If men command things evil, obedience is due only by tolerating what they inflict, not by performing what they require. In the first they declare what God commands to be done, in the latter what to be suffered; so it remains that things indifferent only are the proper object of humane laws. Actions are to be considered simply and alone, and so are good as being motions depending on the first mover; or jointly with circumstances, and that in a double manner: 1. In regard of the ability or possibility, whilst they may be done. 2. In the act when they be performed. Before they be done they be indifferent, but once breaking out into act, they become distinctly good or evil according to the circumstances which determine the same. Now an action commanded is supposed as not yet done (whereupon the Hebrews call the imperative mood the first future) and so remaineth many times indifferent.

Some may be of opinion that if obedience may be given to an usurper in things indifferent as well as to a lawful power, that then there is as much obedience due to an usurped power as to a lawful. But it is a mistake; for though it be granted that in things indifferent an usurper may be obeyed as well as a lawful governour, yet herein lieth a main difference, that some things are indifferent for a lawful superior which are not indifferent but unlawful to an usurper to enjoin. Usurpation is the resisting and taking away the power from him who hath such a former right to govern the usurper as cannot be lawfully taken away. So that it cannot be just for an usurper to take advantage of his own unlawful act or create himself a title by continuation of his own injustice, which aggravates and never extenuates his crime. And if it never can be an act indifferent for the usurper himself to disobey his lawful sovereign, much less can it be indifferent for him to command another to do that to which he hath no right himself. It is only then a matter indifferent for an usurper to command, when the actions enjoined are such as the lawful superior is commanded by the law of God to provide for the benefit of his subjects by the same or other like restriction of such indifferent things, and it is to be presumed, if he had not been hindered, would have commanded the same or the like laws.

THE Free-holder's GRAND INQUEST Touching Our Sovereign Lord the King, and His Parliament.

The Author's PREFACE.

There is a general belief that the Parliament of England was at first an imitation of the assembly of the three estates in France: therefore, in order to prepare the understanding in the research[1] we have in hand, it is proper to give a brief account of the mode of France in those assemblies: Scotland and Ireland being also under the dominion of the King of England; a touch of the manner of their Parliaments shall be by way of preface.

1. In France, the king's writ goeth to the bailiffs, seneschals, or stewards of liberties, who issue out warrants to all such as have fees and lands within their liberties, and to all towns, requiring all such as have any complaints, to meet in the principal city, there to choose two or three delegates, in the name of that province, to be present at the general assembly.

At the day appointed, they meet at the principal city of the bailiwick. The king's writ is read, and every man called by name, and sworn to choose honest men for the good of the king and commonwealth, to be present at the general assembly as delegates, faithfully to deliver their grievances and demands of the province. Then they choose their delegates and swear them. Next they consult what is necessary to be complained of, or what is fit to be desired of the king: and of these things they make a catalogue or index. And because every man should freely propound his complaint or demands, there is a chest placed in the town hall into which every man may cast his writing. After the catalogue is made and signed, it is delivered to the delegates to carry to the general assembly.

All the bailiwicks are divided into twelve classes. To avoid confusion,

---

1   "Recerche".

and to the end there may not be too great delay in the assembly by the gathering of all the votes, every classis compiles a catalogue or book of the grievances and demands of all the bailiwicks within that classis. Then these classes at the assembly compose one book of the grievances and demands of the whole kingdom. This being the order of the proceedings of the third estate, the like order is observed by the clergy and nobility. When the three books for the three estates are perfected, then they present them to the king by their presidents. First, the president for the clergy begins his oration on his knees, and the king commanding, he stands up bare-headed and proceeds. And so the next president for the nobility doth the like. But the president for the commons begins and ends his oration on his knees. Whilst the president for the clergy speaks, the rest of that order rise up and stand bare, till they are bid by the king to sit down and be covered, and so the like for the nobility. But whilst the president of the commons speaks, the rest are neither bidden to sit, or be covered. Thus the grievances and demands being delivered, and left to the king and his council, the general assembly of the three estates endeth, *atque ita totus actus concluditur* ["and the whole business is ended"].

Thus it appears the general assembly was but an orderly way of presenting the public grievances and demands of the whole kingdom to the consideration of the king: not much unlike the ancient usage of this kingdom for a long time, when all laws were nothing else but the king's answers to the petitions presented to him in parliament, as is apparent by very many statutes, parliament rolls, and the confession of Sir Edward Coke.

2. In Scotland, about twenty days before the parliament begins, proclamation is made throughout the kingdom to deliver into the king's clerk, or master of the rolls, all bills to be exhibited that sessions, before a certain day: then are they brought to the king and perused by him, and only such as he allows are put into the chancellor's hand to be propounded in parliament, and none others. And if any man in parliament speak of another matter than is allowed by the king, the chancellor tells him there is no such bill allowed by the king. When they have passed them for laws, they are presented to the king, who, with his scepter put into his hand by the chancellor, ratifies them, and if there be any thing the king dislikes, they raze it out before.

3. In Ireland, the parliament, as appears by a statute made in the tenth year of Henry VII, c. 4. Is to be after this manner:

> No parliament is to be holden but at such season as the king's lieutenant and council there do first certify the king, under the great seal of that land, the causes and consider-

ations, and all such acts as them seemeth should pass in the said parliament. And such causes and considerations, and acts affirmed by the king and his council to be good and expedient for that land: and his licence thereupon as well in affirmation of the said causes and acts, as to summon the parliament under his great seal of England had and obtained. That done, a parliament to be had and holden after the form and effect afore rehearsed, and if any parliament be holden in that land contrary to the form and provision aforesaid, it is deemed void, and of none effect in law.[2]

It is provided that all such bills as shall be offered to the parliament there shall be first transmitted hither under the great seal of that kingdom, and having received allowance and approbation here, shall be put under the great seal of this kingdom, and so returned thither to be preferred to the parliament. By a statute of 3 and 4 of Philip and Mary, for the expounding of Poyning's act, it is ordered for the king's 'passing of the said acts in such form and tenor as they should be sent into England, or else for the change of them, or any part of them'.[3]

After this shorter narrative of the usage of parliaments in our neighbour and fellow kingdoms, it is time the *inquisitio magna* of our own be offered to the verdict or judgment of a moderate and intelligent reader.

The Argument.

A presentment of divers statutes, records, and other precedents explaining the writs of summons to parliament: showing,

> I. That the Commons by their writ are only to perform and consent to the ordinances of parliament.

> II. That the Lords or common council by their writ are only to treat and give counsel in parliament.

> III. That the king himself only ordains and makes laws, and is supreme judge in parliament.

2   *Statutes of Ireland*, p. 55.
3   *Statutes of Ireland*, p. 253.

With the Suffrages of

Henry de Bracton	Henry Spelman
John Britton	John Glanvil
Thomas Egerton	William Lambard
Edward Coke	Richard Crompton
Walter Raleigh	William Camden
Robert Cotton	John Selden

THE Free-holder's GRAND INQUEST Touching Our
Sovereign Lord the King, and His Parliament.

Every freeholder that hath a voice in the election of knights, citizens, or
burgesses for the parliament ought to know with what power he trusts
those whom he chooseth, because such trust is the foundation of the power of the House of Commons.

A writ from the king to the sheriff of the county is that which gives authority and commission for the freeholders to make their election at the
next county court day after the receipt of the writ; and in the writ there is
also expressed the duty and power of the knights, citizens, and burgesses
that are there elected.

The means to know what trust or authority the country or freeholders
confer or bestow by their election is in this, as in other like cases, to have
an eye to the words of the commission or writ itself. Thereby it may be
seen whether that which the House of Commons doth act be within the
limit of their commission. Greater or other trust than is comprised in the
body of the writ, the freeholders do not, or cannot give if they obey the
writ. The writ being Latin and not extant in English, few freeholders understand it, and fewer observe it; I have rendered it in Latine and English.

Rex Vicecomiti salutem etc.

*Quia de advisamento et assensu concilii nostri pro quibusdam
arduis et urgentibus negotiis, nos, statum et defensionem regni
nostri Angliae, et ecclesiae Anglicanae concernentibus, quod-
dam parliamentum nostrum apud civitatem nostram West-
monasterii duodecimo die Novembris proxime futuro teneri
ordinavimus, et ibidem cum praelatis, magnatibus et proceribus dicti regni nostri colloquium habere et tractatum: tibi
praecipimus firmiter injungentes quod facta proclamatione
in proximo comitatu tuo post receptionem hujus brevis nostri
tenendo die et loco praedictis duos milites gladiis cinctos magis*

*idoneos et discretos comitatus praedicti, et de qualibet civitate
comitatus illius duos cives, et de quolibet burgo duos burgenses
de discretioribus et magis sufficientibus libere et indifferenter
per illos qui proclamationi hujusmodi interfuerint juxta formam statutorum inde editorum et provisiorum eligi, et nomi-
na eorundum militum, civium et burgensium, sic electorum in
quibusdam indenturis inter te et illos qui hujusmodi electioni
interfuerint, inde conficiendis sive hujusmodi electi praesentes
fuerint vel absentes, inseri: eosque ad dictos diem et locum
venire facias. Ita quod iidem milites plenam et sufficientem
potestatem pro se et communitate comitatus praedicti, ac dicti
cives et burgenses pro se et communitate civitatum et burgo-
rum praedictorum divisim ab ipsishabeant, ad faciendum et
consentiendum his quae tunc ibidem de communi consilio
dicti regni nostri (favente Deo) contigerint ordinari super negotiis ante dictis: Ita quod pro defectu potestatis hujusmodi,
seu propter improvidam electionem militum civium aut burgensium praedictorum, dicta negotia infecta non remaneant
quovismodo. Nolumus autem quod tu nec aliquis alius vice-
comes dicti regni nostri aliqualiter sit electus. Et electionem
illam in pleno comitatu factam, distincte et aperte sub sigillo
tuo et sigillis eorum qui electioni illi interfuerint, nobis in can-
cellariam nostram ad dictos diem et locum certifices indilate,
remittens nobis alteram partem indenturarum praedictarum
praesentibus consutam una cum hoc breve. Teste meipso apud
Westmonasterium.*

The king to the sheriff of _____ greeting.

Whereas, by the advice and consent of our council, for certain difficult and urgent businesses concerning us, the state
and defence of our kingdom of England and the English
church: we have ordained a certain parliament of ours to
be held at our city of _____ the _____ day of
_____ next ensuing, and there to have conference,
and to treat with the prelates, great men and peers of our said
kingdom. We command and straitly enjoin you, that making
proclamation at the next county court after the receipt of
this our writ, to be holden the day and place aforesaid: you
cause two knights, girt with swords, the most fit and discreet
of the county aforesaid: and of every city of that county two
citizens; of every borough, two burgesses of the discreeter

and most sufficient; to be freely and indifferently chosen by them who shall be present at such proclamation, according to the tenor of the statutes in that case made and provided: and the names of the said knights, citizens, and burgesses so chosen, to be inserted in certain indentures to be then made between you and those that shall be present at such election, whether the parties so elected be present, or absent: and shall make them to come at the said day, and place. So that the said knights for themselves and for the county aforesaid; and the said citizens and burgesses for themselves, and the commonalty of the aforesaid cities and boroughs, may have severally from them full and sufficient power to *perform* and to *consent* to those things which then by the favour of God shall there happen to be ordained by the common council of our said kingdom, concerning the businesses aforesaid. So that the business may not by any means remain undone for want of such power or by reason of the improvident election of the aforesaid knights, citizens, and burgesses. But we will not in any case you or any other sheriff of our said kingdom shall be elected; and at the day and place aforesaid, the said election made in the full county court, you shall certify without delay to us in our chancery, under your seal and the seals of them which shall be present at that election, sending back unto us the other part of the indenture aforesaid affiled to these presents, together with this writ. Witness our self at Westminister.

By this writ we do not find that the Commons are called to be any part of the common council of the kingdom, or of the supreme court of judicature, or to have any part of the legislative power, or to consult *de arduis regni negotiis*, of the difficult businesses of the kingdom. The writ only says the king would have conference and treat with the prelates, great men, and peers: but not a word of treating or conference with the Commons. The House of Commons, which doth not minister an oath, nor fine, nor imprison any but their own members (and that but of late in some cases) cannot properly be said to be a court at all, much less to be a part of the supreme court or highest judicature of the kingdom. The constant custom, even to this day, for the members of the House of Commons to stand bare, with their hats in their hands in the presence of the Lords while the Lords sit covered at all conferences, is a visible argument that the Lords and Commons are not fellow commissioners, or fellow counsellors of the kingdom.

The duty of knights, citizens, and burgesses mentioned in the writ is only *ad faciendum et consentiendum*, to perform and to consent to such things as should be ordained by the common council of the kingdom; there is not so much mentioned in the writ as a power in the commons to dissent. When a man is bound to appear in a court of justice, the words are *ad faciendum et recipiendum quod ei per curiam injungetur* ["to perform and to receive what is imposed on him by the court"], which shows that this word *faciendum* is used as a term in law, to signify to give obedience. For this, we meet with a precedent even as ancient as the parliament writ itself, and it is concerning proceedings in parliament 33 Edward I: *Dominus rex mandavit vicecom. quod, etc. summon' Nicolaum de Segrave et ex parte domini regis firmiter ei injungeret, quod esset coram domino rege in proximo parliamento etc., ad audiendum voluntatem ipsius domini regis, etc. et ad faciendum et recipiendum ulterius quod curia domini regis consideraret in praemissis.*

> Our lord the king commands the sheriff to summon Nicholas Segrave to appear before our lord the king in the next parliament, to hear the will of the lord our king himself, and to perform and receive what the kings court shall further consider of the premises.[4]

Sir Edward Coke, to prove the clergy hath no voice in parliament, saith that by the words of their writ their consent was only to such things as were ordained by the common council of the realm. If this argument of his be good, it will deny also voices to the Commons in parliament; for in their writ are the self-same words, viz. to consent to such things as were ordained by the common council of the kingdom. Sir Edward Coke concludes that the *procuratores cleri* have many times appeared in parliament as spiritual assistants, to consider, consult, and to consent, but never had voice there. How they could consult and consent without voices he doth not show, though the clergy (as he saith) oft appeared in parliament, yet was it only *ad consentiendum* ["to consent"], as I take it, and not *ad faciendum* ["to act"], for the word *faciendum* is omitted in their writ; the cause, as I conceive, is the clergy, though they were to assent, yet by reason of clerical exemptions, they were not required to perform all the ordinances or acts of parliament.

But some may think, though the writ doth not express a calling of the

---

4   *Rotuli Parliamentorum; ut et petitiones, et placita in Parliamento*, vol. i, p. 172.

knights, citizens, and burgesses to be part of the common council of the kingdom; yet it supposeth it a thing granted, and not to be questioned but that they are a part of the common council.

Indeed if their writ had not mentioned the calling of prelates, great men, and peers to council, there might have been a little better colour for such a supposition. But the truth is such a supposition doth make the writ itself vain and idle; for it is a senseless thing to bid men assent to that which they have already ordained, since ordaining is an assenting, and more than an assenting.

For clearing the meaning and sense of the writ, and satisfaction of such as think it impossible but that the Commons of England have always been a part of the common council of the kingdom, I shall insist upon these points: 1. That anciently the barons of England were the common council of the kingdom. 2. That until the time of Henry I the Commons were not called to parliament. 3. Though the Commons were called by Henry I, yet they were not constantly called, nor yet regularly elected by writ until Henry III's time.

For the first point, Mr. Camden in his *Britannia* doth teach us that 'in the time of the English Saxons and in the ensuing age a parliament was called *commune concilium* ["common council"],' which was, saith he, '*praesentia regis, praelatorum, procerumque collectorum*, the presence of the king, prelates, and peers assembled.'[5] No mention of the commons: the prelates and peers were all barons.

The author of the chronicle of the church of Lichfield, cited by Mr. Selden, saith '*postquam rex Edvardus, etc. concilio baronum Angliae*, etc. After King Edward was king; by the council of the barons of England he revived a law which had lain asleep three score & seven years: and this law was called the law of St. Edward the king.'[6]

In the same chronicle it is said that William the Conqueror, *anno regni sui quarto apud Londinias* ["in the fourth year of his reign, at London"], had *concilium baronum suorum*, a council of his barons. And of this parliament it is that his son Henry I speaks, saying, 'I restore you the laws of King Edward the Confessor, with those amendments wherewith my father amended them by the council of his barons.'[7]

In the fifth year, as Mr. Selden thinks, of the Conquerour, was a parliament, or *principum conventus*, an assembly of earls and barons at Pinen-

---

5 William Camden, *Britain, or a Chorographicall Description of the most flourishing Kingdomes, England, Scotland, and Ireland*, p. 177.
6 John Selden, *Eadmeri Monachi Cantuarensis Historiae Novorum*, p. 171.
7 John Selden, *Titles of Honor, 2nd ed*, p. 701.

den Heath in Kent, in the cause between Lanfranc the Archbishop of Canterbury, and Odo Earl of Kent. The king gave commission to Godfrid, then Bishop of Constance in Normandy, to represent his own person for hearing the controversy, as saith Mr. Lambarde:

> and caused Egelric the bishop of Chichester (an aged man, singularly commended for skill in the laws and customs of the realm) to be brought thither in a wagon for his assistance in council, commanded Haymo the sheriff of Kent, to summon the whole county to give in evidence: three whole days spent in debate. In the end Lanfranc and the bishop of Rochester were restored to the possession of Detling and other lands which Odo had withholden.[8]

There is mention of a parliament held under the same King William the Conqueror, wherein all the bishops of the land, earls and barons, made an ordinance touching the exemption of the Abby of Bury from the Bishops of Norwich.

In the tenth year of the Conqueror, *episcopi, comites et barones regni regia potestate ad universalem synodum pro causis audiendis et tractandis convocati* ["the bishops, earls, and barons of the kingdom were convoked by royal authority to hear and manage cases in a general assembly"], saith the book of Westminster.

In the second year of William II, there was a parliament *de cunctis regni principibus* ["of all the leading men of the kingdom"]; another which had *quosque regni proceres*: all the peers of the kingdom.

In the seventh year was a parliament at Rockingham Castle in Northamptonshire, '*episcopis, abbatibus cunctisque regni principibus una coeuntibus*' ["the bishops, abbots, and all the leading men of the kingdom assembled together"].[9]

A year or two after, the same king, *de statu regni acturus* ["to manage the state of the kingdom"], etc. 'called thither, by the command of his writ, the bishops, abbots, and all the peers of the kingdom.'[10]

'At the coronation of Henry I', all the people of the kingdom of England were called, and laws were then made; but it was '*per commune concilium baronum meorum*, by the common council of my barons.'[11]

In his third year, the peers of the kingdom were called without any men-

---

8   William Lambarde, *A Perambulation of Kent*, p. 222.

9   Selden, *Titles of Honor*, p. 702.

10 Selden, *Titles of Honor*, p. 702.

11 Selden, *Titles of Honor*, p. 702.

tion of the Commons; and another a while after, '*consensu comitum et baronum*, by the consent of earls and barons'.[12]

Florentius Wigorniensis saith these are statutes which Anselm and all the other bishops in the presence of King Henry by the assent of his barons ordained; and in his tenth year, of earls and peers; and in his twenty-third of earls and barons. In the year following, the same king held a parliament, or great council, with his barons spiritual and temporal.

King Henry II in his tenth year, had a great council or parliament at Clarendon, which was an assembly of prelates and peers.

22 Henry II saith Hovenden was a great council at Nottingham, and by the common council of the archbishops, bishops, earls and barons, the kingdom was divided into six parts. And again, Hovenden saith that the same king 'at Windsor (*apud Windeshores*) communi concilio ["by common council"] of bishops, earls, and barons, divided England into four parts'.[13] And in his twenty-first year a parliament at Windsor of bishops, earls, and barons. And another of like persons at Northampton.

King Richard I had a parliament at Nottingham, in his fifth year, of bishops, earls, and barons. This parliament lasted but four days, yet much was done in it: the first day the king disseiseth Gerard de Canvil of the sheriffwick of Lincoln, and Hugh Bardolph of the castle and sheriffwick of York. The second day he required judgment against his brother John, who was afterwards king, and Hugh de Novant, Bishop of Coventry. The third day was granted to the king of every ploughland in England two shillings. He required also the third part of the service of every knight's fee for his attendance into Normandy, and all the wool that year of the monks [of] Cisteaux, which, for that it was grievous and unsupportable, they fine for money. The last day was for hearing of grievances, and so the parliament broke up; and the same year held another at Northampton of the nobles of the realm.

King John, in his fifth year, he and his great men met, '*rex et magnates convenerunt*'. And the roll of that year hath '*commune concilium baronum meorum*, the common council of my barons at Winchester'.[14]

In the sixth year of King Henry III the nobles granted to the king, 'of every knight's fee, two marks in silver'.[15]

In the seventh year he had a parliament at London, an assembly of bar-

12 Selden, *Titles of Honor*, p. 703.
13 From Henry Savile, *Rerum Anglicarum post Bedam*, 312b.
14 Selden, *Titles of Honor*, p. 707.
15 Raphael Holinshed, *Holinshed's Chronicles of England, Scotland, and Ireland*, vol. *ii*, p. 351.

ons. In his thirteenth year an assembly of the Lords at Westminster. In his fifteenth year, of nobles, both spiritual and temporal.

Matthew Paris saith that 20 Henry III '*Congregati sunt magnates ad colloquium de negotiis regni tractaturi*, the great men were called to confer and treat of the business of the kingdom.'[16] And at Merton, 'our lord the king granted, by the consent of his great men, that hereafter usury should not run against a ward from the death of his ancestor.'[17]

21 Henry III. The king sent his 'royal writs commanding all belonging to his kingdom, that is to say, archbishops, bishops, abbots, and priors installed, earls and barons, that they should all meet at London to treat of the king's business touching the whole kingdom', and 'at the day prefixed, the whole multitude of the nobles of the kingdom met at London', saith Matthew Westminster.[18]

In his twenty-first year, 'at the request and by the council of the Lords',[19] the charters were confirmed.

22 Henry III at 'Winchester, the king sent his royal writs to archbishops, bishops, priors, earls and barons, to treat of business concerning the whole kingdom'.[20]

32 Henry III 'the king commanded all the nobility of the whole kingdom to be called to treat of the state of his kingdom'.[21] Matthew Westminster.

49 Henry III the king had a treaty at Oxford with the peers of the kingdom. Matthew Westminster.[22]

At a parliament at Marlborough, 55 Henry III, statutes were made by the assent of earls and barons.

Here the place of Bracton, chief justice in this king's time, is worth the observing; and the rather for that it is much insisted on of late to make for parliament's being above the king. The words in Bracton are, 'the king hath a superior, God; also the law by which he is made king; also his court, viz. the earls and barons'.[23] The court that was said in those days to be above the king was a court of earls and barons, not a word of the Commons, or the representative body of the kingdom being any part of the superior

16   Matthew Paris, *Matthaei Paris Historia Maior*, p. 429.

17   Paris, p. 422.

18   Matthew Westminster, *Matthaeus Westmonasteriensis, Florilegus dictis, praecipue de rebus Britannicus adb exorido mundi usque ad annum Domini*, p. 143.

19   Holinshed ii, p. 380.

20   Westminster, p. 228.

21   Westminster, p. 228.

22   Westminster, p. 330.

23   Henry de Bracton, *Henrici de Bracton De Legibus et Consuetudinibus Angliae, libri quinque*, 34a.

court. Now for the true sense of Bracton's words, how the law and the court of earls and barons are the king's superiors, they must of necessity be understood to be superiors so far only as to advise and direct the king out of his own grace and good will only, which appears plainly by the words of Bracton himself, where, speaking of the king, he resolves thus, '*nec potest ei necessitatem aliquis imponere quod injuriam suam corrigat et emendet, cum superiorem non habeat nisi Deum, et satis ei erat ad poenam, quod dominum expectat ultorem.* Nor can any man put a necessity upon him to correct and amend his injury unless he will himself, since he hath no superior but God; it will be sufficient punishment for him to expect the Lord an avenger'.[24] Here the same man, who speaking according to some men's opinion, saith the law and court of earls and barons are superior to the king, in this place tells us himself, the 'king hath no superior but God'. The difference is easily reconciled; according to the distinction of the schoolmen, 'the king is free from the coactive power of laws or counsellors, but may be subject to their directive power',[25] according to his own will: that is, God can only compel, but the law and his courts may advise him.

Rotuli parliamentorum, 1 Henry IV number 79. The Commons expressly affirm, judgement in parliament belongs to the king and Lords.[26]

These precedents show that from the Conquest until a great part of Henry III's reign (in whose days it is thought the writ for election of knights was framed), which is about two hundred years, and above a third part of the time since the Conquest, to our days, the barons made the parliament or common council of the kingdom; under the name of barons, not only the earls but the bishops also were comprehended, for the Conqueror made the bishops barons. Therefore it is no such great wonder that in the writ we find the Lords only to be the counsellors, and the Commons called only to perform and consent to the ordinances.

Those there be who seem to believe that under the word barons anciently the lords of court barons were comprehended, and that they were called to parliament as barons; but if this could be proved to have been at any time true, yet those lords of court barons were not the representative body of the commons of England, except it can be also proved that the commons or freeholders of the kingdom chose such lords of court barons to be present in parliament. The lords of manors came not at first by election of the

---

24   Bracton, 368b.
25   Sir Thomas Egerton, *The Speech of the Lord Chancellor or England, in the Eschequer chamber, touching the Post-nati*, p. 106.
26   *Rotuli*, p. 451.

people, as Sir Edward Coke, treating of the institution of court barons, resolves us in these words:

> By the laws and ordinances of ancient kings, and especially of King Alfred, it appeareth that the first kings of this realm had all the lands of England in demesne; and *les grand* manors and royalties they reserved to themselves, and of the remnant they, for the defence of the realm, enfeoffed the barons of the realm with such jurisdiction as the court baron now hath. Coke's *Institutes*, Part I, folio 58.

Here, by the way, I cannot but note that if the first kings had all the lands of England in demesne, as Sir Edward Coke saith they had, and if the first kings were chosen by the people (as many think they were), then surely our forefathers were a very bountiful (if not a prodigal) people to give all the lands of the whole kingdom to their kings, with liberty for them to keep what they pleased and to give the remainder to their subjects, clogged and encumbered with a condition to defend the realm. This is but an ill sign of a limited monarchy by original constitution or contract. But, to conclude the former point, Sir Edward Coke's opinion is that 'in the ancient laws, under the name of barons were comprised all the nobility'.[27]

This doctrine of the barons being the common council doth displease many, and is denied as tending to the disparagement of the Commons, and to the discredit and confutation of their opinion who teach that the Commons are assigned councillors to the king by the people. Therefore I will call in Mr. Prynne to help us with his testimony: he in his book of *Treachery and Disloyalty*, etc., proves that before the Conquest, by the laws of Edward the Confessor, chapter 17, the king by his oaths was 'to do justice by the council of the nobles of his realm'.[28] He also resolves that the 'earls and barons in parliament are above the king, and ought to bridle him',[29] when he exorbitates from the laws. He further tells us, 'the peers & prelates have oft translated the crown from the right heir',[30]

> 1. Electing and crowning Edward, who was illegitimate; and putting by Ethelred, the right heir, after Edgar's decease.
>
> 2. Electing and crowning Canutus, a mere foreigner, in op-

---

27   Sir Edward Coke, *The First Part of the Institutes*, folio 58.
28   William Prynne, *The Treachery and Disloyalty of Papists to their Sovereigns, in Doctrine and Practise*, p. 51.
29   Prynne, p. 37.
30   Prynne, p. 9.

position to Edmund, the right heir to king Ethelred.

3. Harold and Hardicanute, both elected kings successively without title; Edmund and Alfred the right heirs being dispossessed.

4. The English nobility, upon the death of Harold, enacted that none of the Danish blood should any more reign over them.

5. Edgar Atheling, who had best title, was rejected, and Harold elected and crowned king.

6. In the second and third year of Edward II the peers and nobles of the land, seeing themselves contemned, entreated the king to manage the affairs of the kingdom by the council of his barons. He gave his assent, and swore to ratify what the nobles ordained; and one of their articles was that he would thenceforward order all the affairs of the kingdom by the council of his clergy and lords.

7. William Rufus, finding the greatest part of the nobles against him, swore to Lanfranc that if they would choose him for king, he would abrogate their over-hard laws.

8. The beginning, saith Mr. Prynne, of the charter of Henry I is observable: 'Henry by the grace of God, of England, etc., know ye that by the mercy of God and common council of the barons of the kingdom, I am crowned king'.

9. Maud the Empress, the right heir, was put-by the crown by the prelates and barons, and Stephen Earl of Mortain, who had no good title, assembling the bishop and peers, promising the amendment of the laws according to all their pleasures and liking, was by them all proclaimed king.

10. Lewis of France crowned king by the barons, instead of King John.

All these testimonies from Mr. Prynne may satisfy that anciently the barons were the common council or parliament of England. And if Mr. Prynne could have found so much antiquity and proof for the knights, citizens, and burgesses being of the common council, I make no doubt but we should have heard from him in capital characters. But alas! he meets not with so much as these names in those elder ages. He dares not say the barons were assigned by the people, councillors to the king; for he tells us 'every baron in parliament doth represent his own person, and speaketh in behalf of himself alone; but in the knights, citizens, and burgesses are represented the commons of the whole realm.'[31] Therefore every one of the Commons hath a greater voice in parliament than the greatest earl in England. Nevertheless Mr. Prynne will be very well content if we will admit and swallow these parliaments of barons for the representative body of the kingdom; and to that purpose he cites them, or to no purpose at all. But to prove the treachery and disloyalty of popish parliaments, prelates, and peers to their kings, which is the main point that Mr. Prynne, by the title of his book, is to make good and to prove.

As to the second point, which is that until the time of Henry I, the Commons were not called to parliament, besides the general silence of antiquity which never makes mention of the Commons coming to parliament until that time, our histories say before his time only certain of the nobility were called to consultation about the most important affairs of the state; he caused the Commons also to be assembled by knights, citizens, and burgesses of their own appointment. Much to the same purpose writes Sir Walter Raleigh, saying it is held that the kings of England 'had no formal parliaments till about the eighteenth year of King Henry I. For in his third year, for the marriage of his daughter, the king raised a tax upon every hide of land, by the advice of his privy council alone.'[32] And 'the subjects,' saith he, 'soon after this parliament was established, began to stand upon terms with their king, and drew from him by strong hand and their swords their great charter; it was after the establishment of the parliament, by colour of it, that they had so great daring.'[33] If any desire to know the cause why Henry I called the people to parliament, it was upon no very good occasion, if we believe Sir Walter Raleigh. 'The grand charter,' saith he,

> was not originally granted regally and freely, for King Henry I did but usurp the kingdom, and therefore the better to secure himself against Robert his elder brother, he flattered the people with those charters. Yea, King John that confirmed them had the like respect: for Arthur duke of Britain[34] was the undoubted heir of the crown, upon whom John usurped: so these charters had their original from kings *de facto*, but not *de jure*.[35]

31 Prynne, p. 43.
32 Sir Walter Raleigh, *The Prerogative of Parliaments in England*, p. 2.
33 Raleigh, p. 3.
34 Arthur I, Duke of Brittany.
35 Raleigh, p. 4.

And then afterwards his conclusion is that the 'great charter had first an obscure birth by usurpation, and was fostered and showed to the world by rebellion'.[36] In brief, the king called the people to parliament and granted them Magna Charta that they might confirm to him the crown.

The third point consists of two parts. First, that the Commons were not called to parliament until Henry III's days; this appears by divers of the precedents formerly cited to prove that the barons were the common council. For though Henry I called all the people of the land to his coronation, and again in the fifteenth or eighteenth year of his reign, yet always he did not so; neither many of those kings that did succeed him, as appeareth before.

Secondly, for calling the commons by writ, I find it acknowledged in a book entitled *The Privilege and Practice of Parliaments*, in these words:

> In ancient times, after the king had summoned his parliament innumerable multitudes of people did make their access thereunto, pretending that privilege of right to belong to them. But King Henry III, having experience of the mischief and inconveniences by occasion of such popular confusion, did take order that none might come to his parliament but those who were specially summoned.

To this purpose it is observed by Mr. Selden that the first writs we find accompanied with other circumstances of a summons to parliament, as well for the Commons as Lords, is in the 49 of Henry III. In the like manner Mr. Camden, speaking of the dignity of barons, hath these words:

> King Henry III, out of a great multitude which were seditious and turbulent, called the very best by writ or summons to parliament; for he, after many troubles and vexations between the king himself and Simon de Montfort, with other barons, and after appeased, did decree and ordain that all those earls and barons unto whom the king himself vouchsafed to direct his writs of summons should come to his parliament, and no others. But that which he began a little before his death, Edward I and his successors constantly observed and continued. The said prudent King Edward summoned always those of ancient families, that were most wise, to his parliament; and omitted their sons after their death if they were not answerable to their parents in understanding.

36   Raleigh, p. 6.

Also Mr. Camden in another place saith that in the time of Edward I, select men for wisdom and worth among the gentry were called to parliament and their posterity omitted if they were defective therein.

As the power of sending writs of summons for elections was first exercised by Henry III, so succeeding kings did regulate the elections upon such writs as doth appear by several statutes, which all speak in the name and power of the kings themselves; for such was the language of our forefathers.

In 5 Richard II, c. 4, these be the words: 'the king willeth and commandeth all persons which shall have summons to come to parliament; and every person that doth absent himself (except he may reasonably and honestly excuse him to our lord the king) shall be amerced, and otherwise punished.'[37]

7 Henry IV, c. 15:

> Our lord the king, at the grievous complaint of his Commons of the undue election of the knights of counties, sometimes made of affection of sheriffs, and otherwise against the form of the writs, to the great slander of the counties, etc. Our lord the king, willing therein to provide remedy, by the assent of the Lords and Commons, hath ordained that election shall be made in the full county court, and that all that be there present, as well suitors as others, shall proceed to the election freely, notwithstanding any request or command to the contrary.[38]

11 Henry IV, c. 1: Our lord the king ordained that a sheriff that maketh an untrue return, etc. 'shall incur the penalty of one hundred pounds to be paid to our lord the king.'[39]

1 Henry V, c. 1:

> Our lord the king, by the advice and assent of the Lords and the special instance and request of the Commons, ordained that the knights of the shire be not chosen unless they be resident within the shire the day of the date of the writ, and that citizens and burgesses be resident, dwelling, and free in the same cities and boroughs, and no others in any wise.[40]

37   *The Statutes at Large*, p. 140.
38   *Statutes*, p. 194.
39   *Statutes*, p. 197.
40   *Statutes*, p. 200.

6 Henry VI, c. 4: 'Our lord the king, willing to provide remedy' for knights chosen for parliament, and sheriffs, 'hath ordained that they shall have their answer, and traverse to inquest of office found against them'.[41]

8 Henry VI, c. 7:

> Whereas elections of knights have been made by great out-
> rages and excessive number of people, of which most part
> was of people of no value, whereof every of them pretend
> a voice equivalent to worthy knights and esquires, whereby
> manslaughters, riots, and divisions among gentlemen shall
> likely be: our lord the king hath ordained that knights of
> shires be chosen by people dwelling in the counties, every of
> them having lands or tenements to the value of two pounds
> the year at the least, and that he that shall be chosen shall be
> dwelling and resident within the counties.[42]

10 Henry VI, [c. 2]: 'Our lord the king ordained that knights be chosen by people dwelling and having two pounds by the year within the same county'.[43]

11 Henry VI, c. 11:

> The king, willing to provide for the ease of them that come to
> the parliaments and councils of the king by his command-
> ment, hath ordained that if any assault or fray be made on
> them that come to parliament or other council of the king,
> the party which made any such affray or assault shall pay
> double damages, and make fine and ransom at the kings
> will.[44]

23 Henry VI, c. 15: The king, considering the statutes of 1 Henry V, c. 1. and 8 Henry VI, c. 7, and the defaults of sheriffs in returning knights, citizens, and burgesses, ordained:

> 1. That the said statutes should be duly kept.

> 2. That the sheriffs shall deliver precepts to mayors and bai-
> liffs to choose citizens and burgesses.

> 3. The penalty of one hundred pounds for a sheriff making

41 *Statutes*, p. 226.
42 *Statutes*, p. 230.
43 *Statutes*, p. 243.
44 *Statutes*, p. 248.

an untrue return concerning the election of knights, citizens, and burgesses.

4. The penalty of forty pounds for mayors or bailiffs making untrue returns.

5. Due election of knights must be in the full county court between the hours of eight and eleven before noon.

6. The party must begin his suit within three months after the parliament began.

7. Knights of the shire shall be notable knights of the county, or such notable esquires, or gentlemen born of the said counties as shall be able to be knights, and no man to be such knight which standeth in the degree of a yeoman and under.[45]

The last thing I observe in the writ for election of members for parliament is that, by the express words of the writ, citizens and burgesses for the parliament were eligible at the county court, as well as knights of the shire; and that not only freeholders but all others whosoever were present at the county court had voices in such elections: see the statute 7 Henry IV, c. 15.[46]

I have the longer insisted on the examination of the writ, because the power and actions of the House of Commons are principally justified by the trust which the freeholders commit unto them by virtue of this writ.

I would not be understood to determine what power the House of Commons doth or may exercise if the king please. I confine myself only to the power in the writ. I am not ignorant that King Henry VII in the cause of the Duke of Britain,[47] and King James in the business of the Palatinate, asked the council of the House of Commons. And not only the House of Commons, but every subject in particular by duty and allegiance, is bound to give his best advice to his sovereign when he is thought worthy to have his counsel asked.

13 Edward III, number 10: all the merchants of England were summoned by writ to appear at Westminster, in proper person, to confer upon great business concerning the king's honour, the salvation of the realm, and of themselves.

In passages of public counsel it is observable, saith Sir Robert Cotton,

45   *Statutes*, p. 271.
46   *Statutes*, p. 194.
47   Arthur I, Duke of Brittany.

that in ancient times the kings of England did 'entertain the Commons with weighty causes, thereby to apt and bind them to a readiness of charge; and the Commons to shun expense have warily avoided to give advice'.[48]

13 Edward III: The Lords and Commons were called to consult how the domestic quiet may be preserved, the marches of Scotland defended, and the sea secured from enemies. The peers and Commons having apart consulted, the Commons desired 'not to be charged to council of things of which they had no cognisance; *de queux ils n'ont pas de cognisance*'.[49]

21 Edward III: Justice Thorpe, declaring to the peers and Commons that the French war began by their advice, the truce after by their assent accepted and now ended: the king's pleasure was to have their counsel in the prosecution. The Commons, being commanded to assemble themselves, and when they were agreed, to give notice to the king and the lords of the council; after four days' consultation, 'humbly desire of the king that he would be advised therein by the lords and others of more experience than themselves in such affairs'.[50]

6 Richard II: The parliament was called to consult whether the king should go in person to rescue Gaunt or send an army. The Commons, after two days' debate, crave a conference with the Lords, and Sir Thomas Puckering (their speaker) protests that counsels for war did aptly belong 'to the king and his lords'; yet since the Commons were commanded to give their advice, 'they humbly wished a voyage by the king'.[51]

7 Richard II: At the second session, the Commons are willed to advise upon view of articles of peace with the French whether war or such amity should be accepted; they modestly excuse themselves as too weak to counsel in so weighty causes. But charged again, as they did tender their honour and the right of the king, they make their answer, giving their opinions rather for peace than war.

For fuller manifestation of what hath been said touching the calling, election, and power of the Commons in parliament, it is behooveful to observe some points delivered by Sir Edward Coke in his treatise of the jurisdiction of parliaments; where,

First, he fairly begins, and lays his foundation, that 'the high court of parliament consisteth of the king's majesty sitting there, and of the three estates':[52]

---

48 Robert Cotton, *Cottoni Posthuma: divers choice piece of that renowned antiquary, Sir Robert Cotton, Knight and Baronet, 3rd ed.*, p. 34.
49 *Rotuli*, p. 105.
50 *Rotuli*, p. 165.
51 *Rotuli*, p. 145.
52 Coke iv, p. 1.

1. The Lords spiritual.

2. The Lords temporal.

3. And the Commons.

Hence it is to be gathered that truly and properly it cannot be called the high court of parliament but whilst the king is sitting there in person. So that the question nowadays whether the parliament be above the king is either false or idle: false if you exclude, and idle if you include the king's person in the word parliament. The case truly put, and as it is meant, is whether the three estates (or, which is all one, the Lords and Commons) assembled in parliament be above the king, and not whether the king with the three estates be above the king. It appears also that they are much mistaken who reckon the king one of the three estates, as Mr. Prynne (p. 20) and many others do. For the three estates make the body, and the king is '*caput, principium, et finis parliamentorum*' ["head, beginning, and end of parliaments"], as confesseth Sir Edward Coke.[53]

Secondly, Sir Edward Coke delivers that 'certain it is both Houses at first sat together', and that it appears in Edward III's time, 'the Lords and Commons sat together, and the Commons had no continual speaker'.[54] If he mean the Lords and Commons did sit and vote together in one body, few there be that will believe it, because the Commons never were wont to loose or forego any of their liberties or privileges. And for them to stand now with their hats in their hands (which is no magistratical posture) there, where they were wont to sit and vote, is an alteration not imaginable to be endured by the Commons. It may be, in former times, when the Commons had no constant speaker, they were oft, and perhaps for the most part, in the same chamber, and in the presence of the Lords, to hear the debates and consultations of the great council, but not to sit and vote with them. For when the Commons were to advise among themselves, the chapter house of the abbey of Westminster was ofttimes their place to meet in before they had a settled House, and their meetings not being very frequent may be the reason, I conceive, why the name of the House of Commons is not of such great antiquity or taken notice of; but the House of Lords was only called the parliament house. And the treatise called *Modus Tenendi Parliamentum* speaks of the parliament as but of one House only. The House where now the Commons sit in Westminster is but of late use or institution. For in Edward VI's days, it was a chapel of the college of St. Stephen, and had a dean, secular canons, and chorists, who were the

---

53 Coke iv, p. 3.
54 Coke iv, p. 2.

king's quire at his palace at Westminster, and at the dissolution were translated to the king's chapel at Whitehall.

Also I read that Westminster Hall being out of repair, Richard II caused:

> a large house to be builded betwixt the clock tower and the
> gate of the great old hall in the midst of the palace court. The
> house was long and large, made of timber, covered with tiles,
> open on both sides that all might see and hear what was both
> said and done. Four thousand archers of Cheshire, which
> were the king's own guard, attended on that house, and had
> *bouche a court* ["food at court"], and sixpence by the day.[55]

Thirdly, he saith the 'Commons are to choose their Speaker, but seeing
after their choice the king may refuse him, the use is (as in the *conge d'es-
lire*[56] of a bishop) that the king doth name a discreet, learned man whom
the Commons elect [...] When the Commons have chosen, the king may
allow of his excuse, and disallow him, as Sir John Popham was',[57] saith his
margin.

Fourthly, he informs us that the first day of the parliament four justices'
assistants and two civilians (masters of the chancery) are appointed re-
ceivers of petitions, which are to be delivered within six days following;
and 'six of the nobility and two bishops, calling to them the king's learned
council, when need should be, to be tryers of the said petitions, whether
they were reasonable, good, and necessary to be offered and propounded
to the Lords'.[58] He doth not say that any of the Commons were either re-
ceivers or tryers of petitions, nor that the petitions were to be propounded
to them, but to the Lords.

Fifthly, he teacheth us that 'a knight, citizen, or burgess cannot make a
proxy because he is elected, and trusted by multitudes of people'.[59] Here a
question may be, whether a committee, if it be trusted to act anything, be
not a proxy, since he saith, 'the high power of parliament to be committed
to a few is holden to be against the dignity of parliaments, and that no such
commission ought to be granted'.[60]

Sixthly, he saith, 'the king cannot take notice of anything said or done

---

55   John Stow, *The Survey of London*, p. 415.
56   A licence from the Crown for a chapter of the cathedral church of a diocese
to elect a bishop or archbishop.
57   Coke iv, p. 8.
58   Coke iv, p. 10.
59   Coke iv, p. 12.
60   Coke iv, p. 42.

in the House of Commons, but by the report of the House'.[61] Surely if the Commons sat with the Lords and the king were present, he might take notice of what was done in his presence. And I read in Vowell that 'the old usage was that all the degrees of parliament sate together, and every man that had there to speak did it openly before the king and his whole parliament'.[62]

In the 35 Elizabeth there was a report that the Commons were against the subsidies, which was told the Queen. Whereupon, Sir Henry Knyvet said it should be a thing 'answerable at the bar for any man to report anything of speeches or matters done in the House'.[63] Sir John Wolley 'liked the motion of secrecy, except only the Queen, from whom, he said, there is no reason to keep anything': and Sir Robert Cecil did 'allow that the council of the House should be secretly kept, and nothing reported *in malam partem* ["with ill will"]. But, if the meaning be that they might not report anything done here to the Queen, he was altogether against it'.[64]

Seventhly, he voucheth 'an indictment or information in the king's bench against thirty-nine of the Commons for departing without licence from parliament, contrary to the kings inhibition. Whereof six submitted to their fines, and Edmund Plowden pleaded he remained continually from the beginning to the end of the parliament'.[65] Note, he did not plead to the jurisdiction of the court of king's bench, but pleaded his constant attendance in parliament, which was an acknowledgment and submitting to the jurisdiction of that court, and had been an unpardonable betraying of the privileges of parliament by so learned a lawyer, if his case ought only to be tried in parliament.

Eighthly, he resolves that 'the House of Lords in their House have power of judicature, and the Commons in their House, and both Houses together'.[66] He brings records to prove the power of judicature of both Houses together, but not of either of them by itself. He cites the 33 Edward I for the judicature of both Houses together: where Nicholas de Segrave was adjudged *per praelatos, comites, et barones, et alios de concilio*, by the prelates, earls, and barons, and others of the council. Here is no mention of the

61   Coke iv, p. 15.
62   John Vowell (AKA John Hooker), *The Order and Usage of the keeping of a Parliament*, p. 22.
63   Sir Simonds D'Ewes, *A Compleat Journal of the Votes, Speeches and Debates, both of the House of Lords and the House of Commons throughout the whole reign of Queen Elizabeth*, p. 487.
64   D'Ewes, *Journal*, p. 488.
65   Coke iv, p. 17.
66   Coke iv, p. 23.

judgment of the Commons. "Others of the council", may mean the king's privy council or his council learned in the laws, which are called by their writs to give counsel, but so are not the Commons. The judgment itself saith:

> Nicholas de Segrave confessed his fault in parliament, and submitted himself to the king's will. Thereupon the king, willing to have the advice of the earls, barons, great men, and others of his council, enjoined them by the homage, fealty, and allegiance which they owed, that they should faithfully counsel him what punishment should be inflicted for such a fact. Who all, advising diligently, say that such a fact deserves loss of life and members.[67]

Thus the Lords (we see) did but advise the king what judgment to give against him that deserted the kings camp to go fight a duel in France.

Ninthly, he saith, 'of later times, see divers notable judgments at the prosecution of the Commons by the Lords'.[68] Where the Commons were prosecutors, they were no judges, but (as he terms them) "general inquisitors", or the grand inquest of the kingdom. The judgments he cites are but in King James' days, and no elder.

Tenthly, also he tells us of the judicature in the House of Commons alone. His most ancient precedent is but in Queen Elizabeth's reign, of one 'Thomas Long, who gave the mayor of Westbury ten pounds to be elected burgess'.[69]

Eleventhly, he hath a section entitled, 'The House of Commons (to many purposes) a distinct court', and saith, '*Nota* ["note"], the House of Commons to many purposes, a distinct court'. Of those many purposes he tells but one, that is, 'it uses to adjourn itself'.[70] Commissioners that be but to examine witnesses may adjourn themselves, yet are no court.

Twelfthly, he handles the privileges of parliament, where the great wonder is that this great master of the law, who hath been oft a parliament-man, could find no other, nor more privileges of parliament but one, and that is, freedom from arrests. Which, he saith, holds, unless in three cases: treason, felony, and the peace. And for this freedom from arrests he cites ancient precedents for all those in the House of Lords, but he brings not one precedent at all for the Commons' freedom from arrests.

---

67   *Rotuli*, p. 173.
68   Coke iv, p. 23.
69   Coke iv, p. 23.
70   Coke iv, p. 28.

It is behooveful for a freeholder to consider what power is in the house of peers. For although the freeholder have no voice in the election of the Lords, yet if the power of that house extend to make ordinances that bind the freeholders, it is necessary for him to enquire what and whence that power is, and how far it reacheth. The chief writ of summons to the peers was in these words:

> *Carolus Dei gratia, etc. Reverendissimo in Christo patri G. eadem gratia Archiepiscopo Cantuariensi totius Angliae primati et metropolitano, salutem. Quia de advisamento et assensu concilii nostri, pro quibusdam arduis et urgentibus negotiis, nos et statum et defensionem regni nostri Angliae, et ecclesiae Anglicanae concernentibus, quoddam parliamentum nostrum apud W. etc. teneri ordinavimus, et ibidem vobiscum, et cum caeteris praelatis, magnatibus et proceribus dicti regni nostri Angliae colloquium habere, et tractatum: vobis in fide, et dilectione quibus nobis tenemini firmiter injungendo mandamus, quod consideratis dictorum negotiorum ardititate, et periculis imminentibus, cessante quacunque excusatione dictis die et loco personaliter intersitis. Nobiscum et cum caeteris praelatis, magnatibus, et proceribus praedictis, super dictis negotiis tractaturi, vestrumque concilium impensuri, et hoc sicut nos et honorem nostrum ac salvationem regni praedicti, ac ecclesiae sanctae, expeditionemque dictorum negotiorum diligitis, nullatenus omittatis; praemonentes decanum et capitulum ecclesiae vestrae Cantuariensis, ac archidiaconos, totumque clerum vestrae diocesis, quod idem decanus et archidiaconi in propriis personis suis, ac dictum capitulum per unum, idemque clerus per duos procuratores idoneos, plenam et sufficientem potestatem ab ipsis capitulo et clero habentes, praedictis die et loco personaliter intersint, ad consentiendum hiis quae tunc ibidem de commune concilio ipsius regni nostri, divina favente clementia, contigerint ordinari. Teste meipso apud Westmonasterium, etc.*

Charles by the grace of God, etc. To the most reverend father in Christ William, by the same grace Archbishop of Canterbury, primate and metropolitan of all England, health. Whereas by the advice and assent of our council, for certain difficult and urgent businesses concerning us, the state, and defence of our kingdom of England, and of the English church, we have ordained a certain parliament of ours to be holden at Westminster etc. and there to have conference, and to treat with you the prelates, great men, and peers of our said kingdom. We straitly charge and command, by the faith and love by which you are bound to us, that considering the difficulties of the businesses aforesaid, and the imminent dangers, and setting aside all excuses, you be personally present at the day and place aforesaid, to treat and give your counsel concerning the said businesses. And this, as you love us and our honour, and the safeguard of the foresaid kingdom and church, and the expedition of the said businesses, you must no way omit. Forewarning the dean and chapter of your church of Canterbury, and the archdeacons, and all the clergy of your diocese, that the same dean, and the archdeacon in their proper persons, and the said chapter by one, and the said clergy by two fit proctors, having full and sufficient power from them the chapter and clergy, be personally present at the foresaid day and place, to consent to those things which then and there shall happen by the favour of God, to be ordained by the common council of our kingdom. Witness ourself at Westminster.

The same form of writ, *mutatis mutandis*, concluding with, 'you must no way omit. Witness, etc.' is to the temporal barons. But whereas the spiritual barons are required by the faith and love, the temporal are required by their allegiance or homage.

The difference between the two writs is that the Lords are to treat and to give counsel; the Commons are to perform and consent to what is ordained.

By this writ the Lords have a deliberative or a consultive power to treat and give counsel in difficult businesses. And so likewise have the judges, barons of the exchequer, the king's council, and the masters of the chancery, by their writs. But over and besides this power, the Lords do exercise a decisive or judicial power which is not mentioned or found in their writ.

For the better understanding of these two different powers, we must carefully note the distinction between a judge and a counsellor in a monarchy. The ordinary duty or office of a judge is to give judgment and to command in the place of the king; but the ordinary duty of a counsellor is to advise the king what he himself shall do, or cause to be done. The judge represents the king's person in his absence, the counsellor in the king's presence gives his advice. Judges by their commission or institution are limited [in] their charge and power, and in such things they may judge, and cause their judgments to be put in execution; but counsellors have no power to command their consultations to be executed, for that were to take away the sovereignty from their prince, who by his wisdom is to weigh the advice of his council, and at liberty to resolve according to the judgment of the wiser part of his council, and not always of the greater. In a word, regularly a counsellor hath no power but in the king's presence, and a judge no power but out of his presence. These two powers thus distinguished, have yet such correspondency, and there is so near affinity between the acts of judging and counselling, that although the ordinary power of the judge is to give judgment, yet by their oath they are bound in causes extraordinary, when the king pleaseth to call them, to be his counsellors. And on the other side, although the proper work of a counsellor be only to make report of his advice to his sovereign, yet many times for the ease only, and by the permission of the king, counsellors are allowed to judge and command in points wherein ordinarily they know the mind of the prince. And what they do is the act of the royal power itself; for the council is always presupposed to be united to the person of the king, and therefore the decrees of the council are styled, by the king in his privy council.

To apply this distinction to the house of peers, we find originally they are called as counsellors to the king, and so have only a deliberative power specified in their writ, and therefore the Lords do only then properly perform the duty for which they are called when they are in the king's presence, that he may have conference and treat with them. The very words of the writ are, '*nobiscum ac cum praelatis, magnatibus et proceribus praedictis super dictis negotiis tractaturi vestrumque concilium impensuri*, with us and with the prelates, great men and peers, to treat and give your counsel'. The word *nobiscum* ['with us"] implieth plainly the king's presence. It is a thing in reason most absurd to make the king assent to the judgments in parliament, and allow him no part in the consultation; this were to make the king a subject. Counsel loseth the name of counsel, and becomes a command, if it put a necessity upon the king to follow it: such imperious counsels, make those that are but counsellors in name to be kings in fact, and kings themselves to be but subjects. We read in Sir Robert Cotton that 'towards the end of the Saxons and the first times of the Norman kings, parliaments stood in custom-grace fixed to Easter, Whitsuntide, and Christmas',[71] and that at the king's court or palace, parliaments sat in the presence or privy chamber. From whence he infers 'an improbability to believe the king excluded his own presence; and unmannerly for guests

---

71   Cotton, *Cottoni Posthuma*, p. 44.

to bar him their company who gave them their entertainment'.[72] And although nowadays the parliament sit not in the court where the king's household remains, yet still even to this day, to show that parliaments are the king's guests, the lord steward of the kings household keeps a standing table to entertain the peers during the sitting of parliament. And he alone, or some from or under him, as the treasurer or comptroller of the king's household takes the oaths of the members of the house of Commons the first day of the parliament.

Sir Richard Scroop, steward of the household of our sovereign lord the king, by the commandment of the Lords sitting in full parliament in the great chamber, put J. Lord Gomeniz and William Weston to answer severally to accusations brought against them.

The necessity of the king's presence in parliament appears by the desire of parliaments themselves in former times, and the practice of it Sir Robert Cotton proves by several precedents: whence he concludes that in the consultations of state and decisions of private plaints, it is clear from all times, the king was not only present to advise, but to determine also. Whensoever the king is present, all power of judging, which is derived from his, ceaseth. The votes of the lords may serve for matter of advice; the final judgment is only the king's. Indeed, of late years, Queen Mary and Queen Elizabeth, by reason of their sex, being not so fit for public assemblies, have brought them out of use, by which means it is come to pass that many things which were in former times acted by kings themselves have of late been left to the judgment of the peers, who, in quality of judges extraordinary, are permitted for the ease of the king, and in his absence to determine such matters as are properly brought before the king himself sitting in person, attended with his great council of prelates and peers. And the ordinances that are made there receive their establishment either from the king's presence in parliament, where his chair of state is commonly placed, or at least from the confirmation of him, who in all courts and in all causes is supreme judge. All judgment is by or under him; it cannot be without, much less against his approbation. 'The king only and none but he, if he were able, should judge all causes'[73] saith Bracton, that ancient chief justice in Henry III's time.

An ancient precedent I meet with cited by Mr. Selden, of a judicious proceeding in a criminal cause of the barons before the conquest, wherein I observe the king's will was that the lords should be judges in the cause wherein himself was a party, and he ratified their proceeding. The case was

---

72   Cotton, *Cottoni Posthuma*, p. 44.
73   Bracton, folio 107a.

thus, Earl Godwin having had a trial before the lords under King Hardicanute

touching the death of Alfred (son to king Ethelred and brother to him
who was afterward Edward the Confessor) had fled out of England. And
upon his return, with hope of Edward the Confessor's favour, he solicited
the lords to intercede for him with the king, who (consulting together)
brought Godwin with them before the king to obtain his grace and favour.
But the king presently, as soon as he beheld him, said, 'thou traitor Godwin, I do appeal thee of the death of my brother Alfred whom thou hast
most traitorously slain'. Then Godwin excusing it, answered, 'my lord the
king, may it please your grace, I neither betrayed nor killed your brother,
whereof I put myself upon the judgment of your court'. Then the king said,
'you noble lords, earls, and barons of the land, who are my liegemen now
gathered here together, and have heard my appeal, and Godwin's answer,
I will that in this appeal between us ye decree right judgment, and do true
justice'. The earls and barons treating of this among themselves were of
differing judgments. Some said that Godwin was never bound to the king,
either by homage, service, or fealty, and therefore could not be his traitor,
and that he had not slain Alfred with his own hands; others said that neither earl nor baron, nor any other subject of the king could wage his war
by law against the king in his appeal, but must wholly put himself into the
king's mercy, and offer competent amends. 'Then Leofric consul of Chester, a good man before God and the world, said, Earl Godwin, next to the
king, is a man of the best parentage of all England, and he cannot deny
but that by his counsel Alfred the king's brother was slain, therefore for
my part I consider that he and his son, and all we twelve earls who are his
friends and kinsmen, do go humbly before the king laden with so much
gold and silver as each of us can carry in our arms, offering him that for
his offence, and humbly praying for pardon; and he will pardon the earl,
and taking his homage and fealty, will restore him all his lands.' All they
in this form lading themselves with treasure, and coming to the king, did
shew the manner and order of their consideration, to which, the king not
willing to contradict, did ratify all that they had judged.[74]

23 Henry II:

> In Lent there was an assembly of all the spiritual and tem-
> poral barons at Westminster for the determination of that
> great contention between Alfonso, king of Castile, and San-
> cho, king of Navarre, touching divers castles and territories

---

74   Selden, *Titles of Honor*, p. 634.

in Spain, which was by comprise submitted to the judgment of the king of England. And the king, consulting with his bishops, earls, and barons determined it (as he saith) himself in the first person, in the exemplification of the judgment.

[...]

2 of King John also, that great controversy touching the barony that William of Mowbray claimed against William of Stuteville, which had depended from the time of King Henry II, was ended by the council of the kingdom, and will of the king: *concilio regni et voluntate regis.*[75]

The lords in parliament adjudge William de Weston to death for surrendering Berwick castle, but for that our lord the king was not informed of the manner of the judgment, the constable of the tower, Allen Buxhull, 'was commanded safely to keep the said William until he had other commandment from our lord the king,'[76] 4 Richard II.

Also the Lords adjudged John Lord of Gomeniz for surrendering the towns and castles of Arde, and for that he was a gentleman and banneret, and had served the late king, 'he should be beheaded, and for that our lord the king was not informed of the manner of the judgment, the execution thereof shall be respited until our lord the king shall be informed'. It is commanded to the 'constable of the tower safely to keep the said John until he hath other commandment from our lord the king'.[77]

In the case of Henry Spencer, Bishop of Norwich, 7 Richard II, who was accused for complying with the French, and other failings; the bishop complained, what was done against him did not pass by the assent and knowledge of the peers. Whereupon it was said in parliament that the cognisance and punishment of his offence did, of common right and ancient custom of the realm of England, solely and wholly belong to our lord the king, and no other. *Le cognisance et punissement de commune droit et auntienne custome de royalme de engleterre, seul et per tout apperteine au roy nostre seignieur, et a nul autre.*

In the case of the Lord de la Warr, the judgment of the lords was 'that he should have place next after the Lord Willoughby of Eresby', by consent of all, except the Lord Windsor; and the 'lord keeper was required to acquaint

---

75   Selden, *Titles of Honor*, pp. 706–707.
76   John Selden, *The Privileges of the Baronage of England*, p. 14.
77   Selden, *Privileges*, p. 28.

her majesty with the determination of the peers, and to know her pleasure concerning the same.[78]

The inference from these precedents is that the decisive or judicial power exercised in the chamber of peers is merely derivative, and subservient to the supreme power, which resides in the king, and is grounded solely upon his grace and favour. For howsoever the House of Commons do allege their power to be founded on the principles of nature, in that they are the representative body of the kingdom (as they say) and so being the whole, may take care, and have power by nature to preserve themselves; yet the house of peers do not, nor cannot make any such the least pretence, since there is no reason in nature why amongst a company of men who are all equal some few should be picked out to be exalted above their fellows, and have power to govern those who by nature are their companions. The difference between a peer and a commoner is not by nature, but by the grace of the prince, who creates honours, and makes those honours to be hereditary (whereas he might have given them for life only, or during pleasure, or good behaviour) and also annexeth to those honours the power of having votes in parliament, as hereditary counsellors, furnished with ampler privileges than the Commons. All these graces conferred upon the peers are so far from being derived from the law of nature, that they are contradictory and destructive of that natural equality and freedom of mankind which many conceive to be the foundation of the privileges and liberties of the House of Commons. There is so strong an opposition between the liberties of grace and nature that it had never been possible for the two houses of parliament to have stood together without mortal enmity and eternal jarring, had they been raised upon such opposite foundations. But the truth is, the liberties and privileges of both houses have but one and the self-same foundation, which is nothing else but the mere and sole grace of kings.

Thus much may serve to show the nature and original of the deliberative and decisive power of the peers of the kingdom.

The matter about which the deliberative power is conversant is generally the consulting and advising upon any urgent business which concerns the king, or defence of the kingdom, and more especially sometimes in preparing new laws; and this power is grounded upon the writ.

The decisive power is exercised in giving judgment in some difficult cases; but for this power of the peers, I find no warrant in their writ.

Whereas the parliament is styled the supreme court, it must be under-

78   D'Ewes, p. 528.

stood properly of the king sitting in the house of peers in person, and but improperly of the Lords without him. Every supreme court must have the supreme power, and the supreme power is always arbitrary; for that is arbitrary which hath no superior on earth to control it. The last appeal in all government must still be to an arbitrary power, or else appeals will be *in infinitum*, never at an end. The legislative power is an arbitrary power, for they are *termini convertibiles* ["convertible terms"].

The main question in these our days is where this power legislative remains or is placed. Upon conference of the writs of summons for both houses, with the bodies and titles of our ancient acts of parliament, we shall find the power of making laws rests solely in the king. Some affirm that a part of the legislative power is in either of the houses; but besides invincible reason from the nature of monarchy itself, which must have the supreme power alone, the constant ancient declaration of this kingdom is against it. For howsoever of later years in the titles and bodies of our acts of parliament it be not so particularly expressed who is the author and maker of our laws, yet in almost all our elder statutes it is precisely expressed that they are made by the king himself. The general words used of later times, that laws are made by authority of parliament, are particularly explained in former statutes to mean that the king ordains, the Lords advise, the Commons consent, as by comparing the writs with the statutes that expound the writs will evidently appear.

Magna Carta begins thus, 'Henry by the grace of God, know ye, that we of our mere and free will have given these liberties'.

In the self-same style runs *Carta de Foresta*, and tells us the author of it.

The statute *de scaccario*, 41 Henry III, begins in these words, 'the king commandeth that all bailiffs, sheriffs, and other officers,' etc. And 'concerning the justices of Chester, the king willeth,' etc. And again, he 'commandeth the treasurer and barons of the exchequer upon their allegiance'.[79]

The statute of Marlborough, 52 Henry III, goeth thus: 'the king hath made these acts, ordinances, and statutes, which he willeth to be observed of all his subjects, high and low'.[80]

3 Edward I: the title of this statute is, 'These are the acts of King Edward', and after it follows, 'the king hath ordained these acts', and in the first chapter, 'the king forbiddeth and commandeth that none do hurt, damage, or grievance to any religious man or person of the church' and in the

---

79   *Statutes*, p. 7.
80   *Statutes*, p. 9.

thirteenth chapter, 'the king prohibiteth that none do ravish or take away by force any maid within age'.[81]

6 Edward I: it is said, 'our sovereign lord the king hath established these acts, commanding they be observed within his realm', and in the fourteenth chapter the words are, 'the king of his special grace granteth, that the city of London shall recover in an assise, damage with the land'.[82]

The statute of Westminster II saith, 'our lord the king hath ordained, that the will of the giver be observed' and in the third chapter, 'our lord the king hath ordained, that a woman after the death of her husband shall recover by a writ of entry'.[83]

The statute of *Quo Warranto* saith, 'our lord the king at his parliament, of his special grace, and for affection which he beareth to his prelates, earls, and barons, and others, hath granted', that they that have liberties by prescription shall enjoy them.[84]

In the statute *de finibus levatis*, the king's words are, 'we intending to provide remedy in our parliament, have ordained',[85] etc.

28 Edward I, c. 5: 'The king wills, that the chancellor, and the justices of the bench shall follow him, so that he may have at all times some near unto him that be learned in the laws',[86] and in chapter twenty-four the words are, 'our lord the king, after full conference and debate had with his earls, barons, nobles, and other great men, by their whole consent, hath ordained', etc.

The statute *de tallagio* (if any such statute there be) speaks in the kings person, 'no officer of ours; no tallage shall be taken by us; we will and grant'.[87]

1 Edward II begins thus, 'our lord the king willeth and commandeth'.[88]

The statute of 9 the same king saith, 'our lord the king, by the assent of the prelates, earls, and other great states, hath ordained'.[89]

10 Edward II: 'It is provided by our lord the king and his justices'.[90]

81   *Statutes*, p. 17.
82   *Statutes*, pp. 23–25.
83   *Statutes*, pp. 28–29.
84   *Statutes*, p. 44.
85   *Statutes*, p. 48.
86   *Statutes*, p. 51.
87   *Statutes*, p. 56.
88   *Statutes*, p. 57.
89   *Statutes*, p. 59.
90   *Statutes*, p. 59.

The statute of Carlisle saith, 'we have sent our command in writing firmly to be observed'.[91]

1 Edward III begins thus, 'King Edward III, at his parliament at the request of the commonalty by their petition before him, and his council in parliament, hath granted', etc. And in the fifth chapter, 'the king willeth, that no man be charged to arm himself otherwise than he was wont'.[92]

5 Edward III: 'Our lord the king, at the request of his people, hath established these things, which he wills to be kept'.[93]

9 of the same king there is this title, 'our lord the king by the assent etc., and by the advice of his councel being there, hath ordained',[94] etc.

In his tenth year it is said, 'because our lord King Edward III hath received by the complaint of the prelates, earls, barons, also at the showing of the knights of the shires, and his commons by their petition put in his parliament, etc. Hath ordained, by the assent, etc. at the request of the said knights and commons',[95] &c.

The same year in another parliament you may find, 'these be our articles accorded by our lord the king, with the assent, etc. at the request of the knights of the shires, and the commons by their petition put in the said parliament'.[96]

In the Year Book 22 Edward III, 3. pl. 25, it is said, 'the king makes the laws by the assent of the peers and commons; and not the peers and commons'.

The statute of 1 Richard II hath this beginning, 'Richard II, by the assent of the prelates, dukes, earls and barons, and at the instance and special request of the commons, ordained'.[97]

There being a statute made 5 Richard II, c. 5, against Lollards, in the next year the Commons petition him, '*supplient les Commons que come un estatute fuit fait*, etc. The Commons beseech that whereas a statute was made in the last parliament, etc. which was never assented to or granted by the Commons, but that which was done therein was done without their assent',[98] in this petition the Commons acknowledge it a statute, and so call it, though they assented not to it.

17 Richard II, number 44: The Commons desire, some pursuing to make

91   *Statutes*, p. 61.
92   *Statutes*, pp. 66–67.
93   *Statutes*, p. 72.
94   *Statutes*, p. 74.
95   *Statutes*, p. 76.
96   *Statutes*, p. 76.
97   *Statutes*, p. 129.
98   *Statutes*, p. 140.

a law which they conceive hurtful to the commonwealth, that his majesty will not pass it.

As for the parliaments in Henry IV's, Henry V's, Henry VI's, Edward IV's, and Richard III's reigns, the most of them do agree in this one title, 'our lord the king, by the advice and assent of his lords, and at the special instance and request of the commons, hath ordained'. The precedents in this point are so numerous, that it were endless to cite them.

The statutes in Henry VII's days do for the most part agree, both in the titles and bodies of the acts, in these words: 'our lord the king by the assent of the lords spiritual and temporal, and the commons in parliament assembled, and by the authority of the same hath ordained'.

Unto this king's time we find the Commons very often petitioning, but not petitioned unto. The first petition made to the Commons that I meet with among the statutes is but in the middle of this King Henry VII's reign, which was so well approved that the petition itself is turned into a statute: it begins thus, 'to the right worshipful Commons in this present parliament assembled: showeth to your discreet wisdoms, the wardens of the fellowship of the craft of Upholsters within London', etc. This petition, though it be directed to the Commons in the title, yet the prayer of the petition is turned to the king, and not to the Commons; for it concludes, 'therefore it may please the king's highness, by the advice of the Lords spiritual and temporal, and his Commons in parliament', &c.

Next for the statutes of Henry VIII, they do most part agree both in their titles and the bodies of the acts with those of his father King Henry VII.

Lastly, in the statutes of Edward VI, Queen Mary, Queen Elizabeth, King James, and of our sovereign lord the king that now is, there is no mention made in their titles of any assent of Lord and Commons, or of any ordaining by the king, but only in general terms it is said, 'acts made in parliament', or thus, 'at the parliament were enacted'. Yet in the bodies of many of these acts of these last princes, there is sometimes mention made of consent of Lord and Commons, in these or the like words: 'it is enacted by the king with the assent of the Lord and Commons'; except only in the statutes of our lord King Charles, wherein there is no mention that I can find of any consent of the Lord and Commons, or ordaining by the king. But the words are, 'be it enacted by authority of parliament', or else, 'be it enacted by the king, the lords spiritual and temporal, and Commons'; as if they were all fellow-commissioners.

Thus it appears that even till the time of King Edward VI, who lived but in our fathers' days, it was punctually expressed in every king's laws that the statutes and ordinances were made by the king. And withal we may see by what degrees the styles and titles of acts of parliament have been varied, and to whose disadvantage. The higher we look, the more absolute we find the power of kings in ordaining; nor do we meet with at first so much as the assent or advice of the Lords mentioned. Nay, if we cast our eye upon many statutes of those that be of most antiquity, they will appear as if they were no laws at all, but as if they had been made only to teach us that the punishments of many officers were left to the mere pleasure of kings. The punitive part of the law, which gives all the vigour and binding part to the law, we find committed by the statutes to the king's mere will and pleasure, as if there were no law at all. I will offer a few precedents to the point.

3 Edward I, c. 9 saith, 'that sheriffs, coroners, and bailiffs, for concealing of felonies shall make grievous fines at the king's pleasure'.[99]

Chapter thirteen ordains that 'such as be found culpable of ravishing of women, shall fine at the kings pleasure'.[100]

Chapter fifteen saith the penalty for detaining a prisoner that is mainpernable,[101] is a fine at the king's pleasure, or a grievous amercement to the king; and he that shall take reward for deliverance of such shall be at the great mercy of the king.

Chapter twenty: Offenders in parks or ponds shall make fines at the king's pleasure.[102]

Chapter twenty-five: Committers of champerty, and extortioners are to be punished at the king's pleasure.[103]

Chapter thirty-one: Purveyors, not paying for what they take, shall be grievously punished at the king's pleasure.[104]

Chapter thirty-two: The king shall punish grievously the sheriff, and him that doth maintain quarrels.[105]

Chapter thirty-seven: The king shall grant attaint in plea of land where it shall seem to him necessary.[106]

7 Edward I saith,

> whereas of late, before certain persons deputed to treat upon debates between us and certain great men, it was accorded that in our next parliament provision shall be made by us and the common assent of the prelates, earls, and barons,

99   *Statutes*, p. 16.
100   *Statutes*, p. 17.
101   Able to be bailed.
102   *Statutes*, p. 18.
103   *Statutes*, p. 19.
104   *Statutes*, p. 19.
105   *Statutes*, p. 19.
106   *Statutes*, p. 20.

that in all parliaments forever, every man shall come without force and armour. And now in our next parliament the prelates, earls, barons, and commonalty have said that to 'us it belongeth, through our royal signory, straitly to defend force of armour at all times, when it shall please us, and to punish them which shall do otherwise, and hereunto they are bound to aid us their sovereign lord at all seasons when need shall be'.[107]

13 Edward I: 'Takers away of nuns from religious houses, fined at the king's will'.[108]

'If by the default of the lord that will not avoid the dyke, underwoods, and bushes in highways, murder be done, the lord shall make fine at the king's pleasure'.[109]

28 Edward I: 'If a goldsmith be attainted for not assaying, touching, and working vessels of gold, he shall be punished by a ransom at the king's pleasure'.[110]

2 Henry IV:

> The Commons desire they may have answer of their petitions before the gift of any subsidy; to which the king answers, he would confer with the Lords and do what should be best according to their advice; and the last day of parliament he gave this answer, that that manner of doing had not been seen nor used in no time of his progenitors or predecessors, that they should have any answer of their petitions or knowledge of it before they have shewed and finished all their other business of parliament, be it of any grant, business, or otherwise, and therefore the king would not in any ways change the good customs and usages made and used of ancient times.[111]

5 Henry IV, c. 6: Whereas one Savage did beat and maim one Richard Cheddar esquire, menial servant to Thomas Brook, knight of the shire for

---

107   *Statutes*, p. 25.
108   *Statutes*, p. 37.
109   *Statutes*, p. 41.
110   *Statutes*, p. 52.
111   *Rotuli*, p. 458.

Somersetshire, the statute saith Savage 'shall make fine and ransom at the king's pleasure'.[112]

8 Henry IV: It is said, '*potestas principis non est inclusa legibus*, the power of the prince is not included in the laws'.

13 Henry IV, number 20: we read of a 'restitution in blood and lands of William Lasenby, by the king, by the assent of the Lords spiritual, and Commons';[113] omitting the lords temporal.

2 Henry V: In a law made, there is a clause that it 'is the king's regality to grant or deny such of their petitions as pleaseth himself'.

6 Henry VI, c. 6: An ordinance was made for to endure 'as long as it shall please the king'.[114]

11 Henry VII, c. 1, hath this law,

> The king our sovereign lord, calling to his remembrance the duty of allegiance of his subjects of this his realm, and that by reason of the same they are bound to serve their prince and sovereign lord for the time being in his wars, for the defence of him and the land against every rebellion, power, and might reared against him, and with him to enter and abide in service in battle if case so require; and that for the same service, what fortune ever fall by chance in the same battle against the mind and will of the prince (as in this land some time past hath been seen) that it is not reasonable, but against all laws, reason, and good conscience that the said subjects, going with their sovereign lord in wars, attending upon him in his person, or being in other places by his commandment within the land, or without, anything should lose or forfeit for doing their true duty and service of allegiance. Be it therefore enacted that no person that shall attend upon the king and do him true service shall be attainted therefore of treason or any other offence by act of parliament or otherwise.[115]

Also the eighteenth chapter of the same year saith,

> Where every subject by the duty of his allegiance is bounden to serve and assist his prince and sovereign lord at all

112   *Statutes*, p. 189.
113   *Rotuli*, p. 655.
114   *Statutes*, p. 254.
115   *Statutes*, p. 356.

seasons, when need shall require, and bound to give attendance upon his royal person, to defend the same when he shall fortune to go in person in war for defence of the realm or against his rebels and enemies, for the subduing and repressing of them and their malicious purpose.[116]

Christopher Wray, serjeant-at-law, chosen speaker 13 Elizabeth, in his speech to her majesty, said that for the orderly government of the commonwealth three things were necessary:

1. Religion.

2. Authority.

3. Law.

By the first, we are taught not only our duty to God, but to obey the queen, and that not only in temporals but in spirituals, in which her power is absolute.[117]

Mr. Greville in the 35 Elizabeth said in parliament, he wished not the making of many laws, since 'the more we make, the less liberty we have ourselves,'[118] her majesty not being bound by them.

For further proof that the legislative power is proper to the king, we may take notice that in ancient time, as Sir Edward Coke saith, 'all acts of parliament were in form of petitions.'[119] If the petitions were from the Commons and the answer of them the king's, it is easy thereby to judge who made the act of parliament. Also Sir John Glanville affirms that,

in former times the course of petitioning the king was this: the Lords and Speaker, either by words or writing, preferred their petition to the king. This then was called the bill of Commons, which being received by the king, part he received, part he put out, and part he ratified; for as it came from him, it was drawn into a law.[120]

---

116   *Statutes*, p. 367.
117   D'Ewes, p. 141.
118   D'Ewes, p. 490.
119   Coke iv, p. 25.
120   Sir John Glanville, *The Copies of two Speeches in Parliament. The one by Iohn Glanville Esquire. The other by Sir Henry Martin Knight. At a General Committee of both Houses, the 22. of May. 1628*, p. 3.

Also it appears that provisions, ordinances, and proclamations made heretofore out of parliament have been always acknowledged for laws and statutes.[121] We have amongst the printed statutes one called the statute of Ireland, dated at Westminster, 9 February, 14 Henry III, which is nothing but a letter of the king to Gerard son of Maurice, justiciar of Ireland.

The explanations of the statute of Gloucester made by the king and his justices only were received always for statutes, and are still printed with them.[122]

Also the statute made for the correction of the twelfth chapter of the statute of Gloucester was signed under the great seal and sent to the justices of the bench after the manner of a writ patent, with a certain writ closed, dated by the king's hand at Westminster, 2 May, 9 Edward I, requiring that 'they should do and execute all and everything contained in it, though the same do not accord with the statute of Gloucester in all things'.[123]

The provisions of Merton, made by the king at an assembly of prelates and the greater part of the earls and barons for the coronation of the king and his Queen Eleanor, are in the form of a proclamation, and begin, '*provisum est in curia domini regis apud Merton*'[124] ["it is provided in the court of the lord king at Merton"].

19 Henry III: A provision was made, *de assisa ultimae praesentationis*, which 'was continued and allowed for a law until the statute of Westminster II, which provides the contrary in express words'.[125]

In the old statutes it is hard to distinguish what laws were made by kings in parliament, and what out of parliament. When kings called peers only to parliament, and of those how many or whom they pleased (as it appears anciently they did), it was no easy matter to put a difference between a council table and a parliament, or between a proclamation and a statute. Yet it is most evident that in old times there was a distinction between the king's especial or privy council and his common council of the kingdom; and his special council did sit with the peers in parliament and were of great and extraordinary authority there.

In the statute of Westminster I it is said, 'these are the acts of King Edward I made at his first parliament by his council, and by the assent of bishops, abbots, priors, earls, barons, and all the commonalty of the realm'.[126]

The statute of Acton Burnell hath these words, 'the king for himself, and

121   Egerton, pp. 12–16.
122   Egerton, p. 15.
123   *Statutes*, p. 26.
124   Egerton, p. 14.
125   Egerton, p. 15.
126   *Statutes*, p. 15.

by his council, hath ordained and established'.[127]

In *articulis super chartas*, when the great charter was confirmed at the request of the prelates, earls, and barons, are found these two provisions:

> 1. Nevertheless the king and his council do not intend by reason of this statute to diminish the king's right.[128]

> 2. Notwithstanding all these things before-mentioned, or any part of them, both the king and his council, and all they that were present, will and intend that the right and prerogative of his crown shall be saved to him in all things.[129]

The statute of escheators hath this title, 'at the parliament of our sovereign lord the king, by his council it was agreed, and also by the king himself commanded'.[130]

1 Edward III, where Magna Charta was confirmed, this Preamble is found, 'at the request of the commonalty, by their petition made before the king and his council in parliament, by the assent of the prelates, earls, and barons',[131] etc.

The statute made at York 9 Edward III goeth thus:

> Whereas the knights, citizens, and burgesses desired our sovereign lord the king in his parliament by their petition, etc. our sovereign lord the king, desiring the profit of his people, by the assent of his prelates, earls, barons, and other nobles of his realm, and by the advice of his council being there, hath ordained.[132]

25 Edward III, in the statute of purveyors, where 'the king, at the request of the lords and commons, made a declaration what offences should be adjudged treason', it is there further said, 'if per-case any man ride armed with men of arms against any other to slay him or rob him, it is not the mind of the king or of his council that in such cases it shall be adjudged treason'. By this statute it appears that even in the case of treason, which is the kings own cause, as, 'whereas a man doth compass or imagine the death of our lord the king, or a man do wage war against our lord the king

---

127   *Statutes*, p. 27.
128   *Statutes*, p. 50.
129   *Statutes*, p. 52.
130   *Statutes*, p. 52.
131   *Statutes*, p. 54.
132   *Statutes*, p. 74.

in his realm, or be adherent to the king's enemies in his realm, giving to them aid or comfort in the realm, or elsewhere'; in all these cases it is the 'king's declaration only' that makes it to be treason. And though it be said that difficult points of treason shall be brought and showed to the king, and his parliament, yet it is said it is the mind of the king and his council that determines what shall be adjudged treason, and what felony or trespass.[133]

27 Edward III: The Commons presenting a petition to the king which the king's council did mislike, were content thereupon to amend and explain their petition. The petition hath these words:

> To their most redoubted sovereign lord the king, praying, your said Commons, that whereas they have prayed him to be discharged of all manner of articles of the eyre, etc. which petition seemeth to his council to be prejudicial unto him, and in disinherison of his crown if it were so generally granted. His said Commons not willing nor desiring to demand things of him or of his crown perpetually, as of escheats, etc. but of trespasses, misprisions, negligences, ignorances, etc.[134]

And as in parliaments the king's council were of supereminent power, so out of parliament kings made great use of them.

'King Edward I, finding that Bogo de Clare was discharged of an accusation brought against him in parliament, commanded him nevertheless to appear before him and his council, *ad faciendum et recipiendum quod per regem et ejus concilium fuerit faciendum* ["to perform and to receive what was decreed by the king and his court"], and so proceeded to the examination of the whole cause, 18 Edward I'.[135]

Edward III, in the Star Chamber (which was the ancient council-table at Westminster) upon the complaint of Elizabeth Audley, commanded James Audley to appear before him and his council, and determined a controversy between them touching land contained in her jointure, *rotulo clauso de anno* ["in the close roll of the year"] 41 Edward III.

Henry V: 'In a suit before him and his council, for the titles of the manors of Serre and St. Lawrence in the Isle of Thanet in Kent, took order for the sequestering the profits till the right were tried'.[136]

---

133 *Statutes*, p. 96.
134 *Statutes*, p. 119.
135 Lambarde, p. 73.
136 Lambarde, p. 75

Henry VI 'commanded the justices of the bench to stay the arraignment of one Verney in London, till they had other commandment from him and his council, 34 Henry VI. *rotulo 37 in banco* ["in roll 37 in the king's bench"]'.[137]

Edward IV and his council, in the Star Chamber,

> heard the cause of the master and poor brethren of Saint Leonard's in York, complaining that Sir Hugh Hastings and others withdrew from them a great part of their living, which consisted chiefly upon the having of a thrave of corn of every plowland within the counties of York, Westmorland, Cumberland, and Lancashire, *rotulo patente de anno* ["in the patent roll of the year"] 8 Edward IV, part three, membrane 14.[138]

Henry VII and his council, in the Star Chamber,

> decreed that Margery and Florence Becket should sue no further in their cause against Alice Radley, widow, for lands in Woolwich and Plumsted in Kent, forasmuch as the matter had been heard first before the council of Edward IV, after that before the president of the Requests of that King Henry VII, and then lastly before the council of the said king, 1 Henry VII.[139]

In the time of Henry III an order or provision was made by the king's council, and it was pleaded at the common law in bar to a writ of dower. 'The plaintiff's attorney could not deny it, and thereupon the judgment was *ideo sine die*'.[140] It seems in those days an order of the king's council was either parcel of the common law, or above it.

Also we may find, the judges have had regard that before they would resolve or give judgment in new cases, they consulted with the king's privy council.

In the case of Adam Brabson who was assaulted by R.W. in the presence of the justices of assize at Westminster, the judges would have 'the advice of the king's council. For in a like case, because R.C. did strike a juror at Westminster which passed against one of his friends, it was adjudged by all the council that his right hand should be cut off and his lands and goods

---

137 Lambarde, p. 75
138 Lambarde, p. 75
139 Lambarde, p. 76.
140 Egerton, p. 13.

forfeited to the king'.[141]

'Green and Thorpe were sent by the judges to the kings council to demand of them whether by the statute of 14 Edward III, c. 16, a word may be amended in a writ. And it was answered that a word may be well amended, although the statute speaks but of a letter or syllable'.[142]

In the case of Sir Thomas Ughtred, who

> brought a formedon against a poor man and his wife; they came and yielded to the demandant, which seemed suspicious to the court. Whereupon judgment was stayed, and Thorpe said that in the like case of Giles Blacket it was spoken of in parliament, and we were commanded that when any like should come, we should not go to judgment without good advice.[143]

Therefore the judge's conclusion was, *sues au counseil et comment ils voilent que nous devomus faire, nous volums faire, et autrement nient en cest case*; sue to the councel, and as they will have us to do, we will do; and otherwise not in this case, 39 Edward III.

Thus we see the judges themselves were guided by the king's council, and yet the opinions of judges have guided the Lords in parliament in point of law.

'All the judges of the realm, barons of exchequer, of the quoif; the king's learned council, and the civilians, masters of chancery', are called 'temporal assistants' by Sir Edward Coke, and though he deny them voices in parliament, yet he confesseth that by their writ they have power both to 'treat, and to give counsel'.[144] I cannot find that the Lords have any other power by their writ; the words of the Lords' writ are, 'that you be present with us the prelates, great men, and peers, to treat and give your counsel'. The words of the judges' writ are, 'that you be present with us, and others of the council (and sometimes with us only) to treat and give your counsel'.

The judges usually joined in committees with the Lords in all parliaments, even in Queen Elizabeth's reign, until her 39th year. And then upon the 7th of November, the judges were appointed to attend the Lords. And whereas the judges have liberty in the upper house itself, upon leave given them by the Lord Keeper, to cover themselves, now at committees they sit always uncovered.

---

141 Egerton, p. 50.
142 Egerton, p. 52.
143 Egerton, p. 52.
144 Coke iv, p. 4.

The power of judges in parliament is best understood if we consider how the judicial power of peers hath been exercised in matter of judicature: we may find it hath been the practice that though the Lords in the king's absence give judgment in point of law, yet they are to be directed and regulated by the king's judges, who are best able to give direction in the difficult points of the law, which ordinarily are unknown to the Lords. And therefore, if any error be committed in the king's bench, which is the highest ordinary court of common law in the kingdom, that error must be redressed in parliament. And the manner is, saith the lord chancellor Egerton,

> if a writ of error be sued in parliament upon a judgment given by the judges in the king's bench, the Lords of the higher house alone (without the Commons) are to examine the errors. The Lords are to proceed according to the law, and for their judgments therein they are to be informed by the advice and counsel of the judges, who are to inform them what the law is, and to direct them in their judgment; for the Lords are not to follow their own discretion or opinion otherwise.[145]

28 Henry VI:

> The Commons made suit that William de la Pole, Duke of Suffolk, should be committed to prison for many treason, and other crimes. The lords of the higher house were doubtful what answer to give. The opinion of the judges was demanded; their opinion was that he ought not to be committed, for that the Commons did not charge him with any particular offence, but with general reports and slanders. This opinion was allowed.[146]

31 Henry VI: A parliament being prorogued, in the vacation the Speaker of the House of Commons

> was condemned in a thousand pounds damages in an action of trespass, and committed to prison in execution for the same. When the parliament was re-assembled, the Commons made suit to the king and Lords to have their Speaker delivered. The Lords demanded the opinion of the judges,

---

145   Egerton, p. 22.
146   Egerton, p. 19.

whether he might be delivered out of prison by privilege of parliament.

Upon the judges' answer it was concluded that the Speaker

> should remain in prison according to the law, notwithstanding the privilege of parliament, and that he was Speaker. Which resolution was declared to the Commons by Moyle, the king's serjeant-at-law, and the Commons were commanded in the Kings name by the Bishop of Lincoln (in the absence of the Archbishop of Canterbury, then chancellor) to choose another Speaker.[147]

7 Henry VIII: A question was moved in parliament,

> whether spiritual persons might be convented before temporal judges for criminal causes? There Sir John Fineux and the other judges delivered their opinion that they might and ought to be; and their opinion allowed and maintained by the king and Lords. And Dr. Standish, who before had holden the same opinion, was delivered from the bishops.[148]

I find it affirmed that in causes which receive determination in the House of Lords, the king hath no vote at all, no more than in other courts of ministerial jurisdiction. True it is, the king hath no vote at all if we understand by vote a voice among others; for he hath no partners with him in giving judgement. But if by no vote is meant he hath no power to judge, we despoil him of his sovereignty: it is the chief mark of supremacy to judge in the highest causes and last appeals. This the children of Israel full well understood when they petitioned for a king to judge them; if the *dernier resort* ["last resort"] be to the Lords alone, then they have the supremacy. But as Moses by choosing elders to judge in small causes did not thereby lose his authority to be judge himself when he pleased—even in the smallest matters, much less in the greatest, which he reserved to himself—so kings by delegating others to judge under them do not hereby denude themselves of a power to judge when they think good.

There is a distinction of these times that kings themselves may not judge, but they may see and look to the judges, that they give judgment according to law. And for this purpose only (as some say) kings may sometimes sit in the courts of justice. But it is not possible for kings to see the laws

147 Egerton, p. 21.
148 Egerton, p. 22.

executed, except there be a power in kings both to judge when the laws are duly executed, and when not; as also to compel the judges if they do not their duty. Without such power a king sitting in courts is but a mockery, and a scorn to the judges. And if this power be allowed to kings, then their judgments are supreme in all courts. And indeed our 'common law to this purpose doth presume that the king hath all laws within the cabinet of his breast, *in scrinio pectoris*', saith Crompton's *Jurisdiction* p. 108.

When several of our statutes leave many things to the pleasure of the king, for us to interpret all those statutes of the will and pleasure of the king's justices only, is to give an absolute arbitrary power to the justices in those cases wherein we deny it to the king.

The statute of 5 Henry IV, c. 2, makes a difference between the king and the kings justices, in these words, 'divers notorious felons be indicted of divers felonies, murders, rapes: and as well before the kings justices, as before the king himself, arraigned of the same felonies'.[149]

I read that in *anno* 1256, Henry III sat in the 'exchequer, and there set down order for the appearance of sheriffs, and bringing in their accounts; there was five marks set on every sheriff's head for a fine, because they had not distrained every person that might dispend fifteen pounds lands by the year, to receive the order of knighthood, according as the same sheriffs were commanded'.[150]

In Michaelmas Term, 1462, Edward IV sat three days together in open court in the king's bench.

For this point there needs no further proofs, because Mr. Prynne doth confess that kings themselves have sat in person in the king's bench and other courts, and there given judgment, p. 32. *Treachery and Disloyalty*, &c.

Notwithstanding all that hath been said for the legislative and judicial power of kings, Mr. Prynne is so far from yielding the king a power to make laws, that he will not grant the king a power to hinder a law from being made; that is, he allows him not a negative voice in most cases, which is due to every other, even to the meanest member of the House of Commons in his judgment.

To prove the king hath not a negative voice, his main, and in truth, his only argument insisted on, is a coronation oath, which is said anciently some of our kings of England have taken, wherein 'they grant to defend and protect the just laws and customs, which the vulgar hath, or shall

149   *Statutes*, p. 189.
150   Holinshed ii, p. 439.

choose: *justas leges et consuetudines quas vulgus elegerit*.[151] Hence Mr. Prynne concludes that the king cannot deny any law which the Lords and Commons shall make choice of; for so he will have *vulgus* to signify.

Though neither our king nor many of his predecessors ever took this oath, nor were bound to take it, for ought appears, yet we may admit that our king hath taken it, and answer, we may be confident, that neither the bishops, nor privy council, nor parliament, nor any other, whosoever they were, that framed or penned this oath, ever intended in this word *vulgus* the Commons in parliament, much less the Lords. They would never so much disparage the members of parliament as to disgrace them with a title both base and false. It had been enough, if not too much, to have called them *populus*, the people; but *vulgus* the vulgar, the rude multitude (which hath the epithet of *ignobile vulgus*) is a word as dishonourable to the composers of the oath to give, or for the king to use, as for the members of the parliament to receive, it being most false. For the peers cannot be *vulgus*, because they are the prime persons of the kingdom. Next, the knights of the shires are or ought to be notable knights, or notable esquires, or gentlemen born in the counties, as shall be able to be knights. Then the citizens and burgesses are to be most sufficient, none of these can be *vulgus*. Even those freeholders that choose knights are the best and ablest men of their counties; there being for every freeholder above ten of the common people to be found to be termed the vulgar. Therefore it rests that *vulgus* must signify the vulgar or common people, and not the Lords and Commons.

But now the doubt will be, what the common people, or *vulgus*, out of parliament, have to do to choose laws? The answer is easy and ready; there goeth before *quas vulgus* the antecedent *consuetudines*, that is, the customs which the vulgar hath, or shall choose. Do but observe the nature of custom, and it is the *vulgus* or common people only who choose customs. Common usage time out of mind creates a custom; and the commoner an usage is, the stronger and the better is the custom. Nowhere can so common an usage be found as among the vulgar, who are still the far greatest part of every multitude. If a custom be common through the whole kingdom, it is all one with the common law in England, which is said to be common custom. Thus in plain terms, to protect the customs which the vulgar choose, is to swear to protect the common laws of England.

But grant that *vulgus* in the oath signifies Lords and Commons, and that *consuetudines* doth not signify customs, but statutes, as Mr. Prynne, for a desperate shift affirms. And let *elegerit* be the future, or preterperfect tense, even which Mr. Prynne please, yet it cannot exclude the king's neg-

151 Prynne, p. 56.

ative voice; for as *consuetudines* goeth before *quas vulgus*, so doth *justas* stand before *leges et consuetudines*: so that not all laws, but only all just laws are meant. If the sole choice of the Lords and Commons did oblige the king to protect their choice without power of denial, what need, or why is the word *justas* put in, to raise a scruple that some laws may be unjust? Mr. Prynne will not say that a decree of a general council or of a pope is infallible, nor (I think) a bill of the Lords and Commons is infallible, just, and impossible to err. If he do, Sir Edward Coke will tell him that parliaments have been utterly deceived, and that in cases of greatest moment, even in case of high treason; and he calls the statute of 11 Henry VII an unjust and strange act. But it may be Mr. Prynne will confess that laws chosen by the Lords and Commons may be unjust, so that the Lords and Commons themselves may be the judges of what is just or unjust. But where the king by oath binds his conscience to protect just laws, it concerns him to be satisfied in his own conscience that they be just, and not by an implicit faith, or blind obedience; no man can be so proper a judge of the justness of laws as he whose soul must lie at the stake for the defence and safeguard of them.

Besides, in this very oath the king doth swear, 'to do equal and right justice and discretion, in mercy and truth in all his judgments: *facies fieri in omnibus judiciis tuis aequam et rectam justitiam et discretionem in misericordia et veritate*'. If we allow the king discretion and mercy in his judgments, of necessity he must judge of the justness of the laws.

Again, the clause of the oath, *quas vulgus elegerit*, doth not mention the assenting unto or granting any new laws, but of holding, protecting, and strengthening with all his might the just laws that were already in being. There were no need of might or strength if assenting to new laws were there meant.

Some may wonder why there should be such labouring to deny the king a negative voice, since a negative voice is in itself so poor a thing that if a man had all the negative voices in the kingdom it would not make him a king; nor give him power to make one law. A negative voice is but a privative power, that is, no power at all to do or act anything, but a power only to hinder the power of another. Negatives are of such a malignant or destructive nature that if they have nothing else to destroy, they will, when they meet, destroy one another, which is the reason why two negatives make an affirmative, by destroying the negation which did hinder the affirmation. A king with a negative voice only is but like a syllogism of pure negative propositions, which can conclude nothing. It must be an affirmative voice that makes both a king, and a law, and without it there can be no imaginable government.

The reason is plain why the king's negative voice is so eagerly opposed; for though it give the king no power to do anything, yet it gives him a power to hinder others: though it cannot make him a king, yet it can help him to keep others from being kings.

For conclusion of this discourse of the negative voice of the king, I shall oppose the judgment of a chief justice of England to the opinion of him that calls himself an utter barrister of Lincoln's inn, and let others judge who is the better lawyer of the two. The words are Bracton's, but concern Mr. Prynne to lay them to heart:

> Concerning the charters and deeds of kings, the justices nor private men neither ought, nor can dispute; nor yet if there rise a doubt in the king's charter can they interpret it; and in doubtful and obscure points, or if a word contain two senses, the interpretation and will of our lord the king is to be expected, seeing it is his part to interpret who makes the charter.[152]

Full well Mr. Prynne knows, that when Bracton writ, the laws that were then made and strived for were called the king's charters, as Magna Carta, *Charta de Foresta*, and others: so that in Bracton's judgment the king hath not only a negative voice to hinder, but an affirmative to make a law, which is a great deal more than Mr. Prynne will allow him.

Not only the lawmaker, but also the sole judge of the people is the king, in the judgment of Bracton. These are his words: '*rex et non alius debet judicare, si solus ad id sufficere possit*: the king and no other ought to judge, if he alone were able'.[153]

> Much like the words of Bracton speaketh Britton, where, after that he had showed that the king is the viceroy of God, and that he hath distributed his charge into sundry portions because he alone is not sufficient to hear all complaints of his people, then he addeth these words in the person of the king: '*nous volons que nostre jurisdiction soit sur touts jurisdictions*, etc. We will that our jurisdiction be above all the jurisdictions of our realm, so as in all manner of felonies, trespasses, contracts, and in all other actions personal or real, we have power to yield, or cause to be yielded, such judgments as do appertain without other process, wheresoever we know the

152   Bracton, folio 34a.
153   Bracton, folio 107a.

right truth as judges'.[154]

Neither was this to be taken, saith Mr. Lambarde,

> to be meant of the king's bench, where there is only an imaginary presence of his person, but it must necessarily be understood of a jurisdiction remaining and left in the king's royal body and breast, distinct from that of his bench and other ordinary courts. Because he doth immediately after, severally set forth by themselves as well the authority of the king's bench, as of the other courts.[155]

'And that this was no new made law', Mr. Lambarde puts us in mind of a Saxon law of King Edgar's:

> '*Nemo in lite regem appellato*', etc. 'Let no man in suit appeal unto the king unless he cannot get right at home, but if that right be too heavy for him then let him go to the king to have it eased'. By which it may evidently appear that even so many years ago there might be appellation made to the king's person whensoever the cause should enforce it.[156]

'The very like law in effect is to be seen in the laws of Canutus the Dane, sometimes king of this realm', out of which law Mr. Lambarde gathers 'that the king himself had a high court of justice, wherein it seemeth he sat in person; for the words be *let him not seek to the king*, and the same court of the king did judge not only according to mere right and law, but also after equity and good conscience'.[157]

For the close, I shall end with the suffrage of our late antiquary Sir Henry Spelman, in his glossary, he saith,

> *Omnis regni justitia solius regis est*, etc. All justice of the kingdom is only the king's, and he alone, if he were able, should administer it; but that being impossible, he is forced to delegate it to ministers, whom he bounds by the limits of the laws. The positive laws are only about generals; in particular cases, they are sometimes too strict, sometimes too remiss, and so, oft wrong instead of right will be done, if we stand

154 Lambarde, p. 56.
155 Lambarde, p. 56.
156 Lambarde, p. 58.
157 Lambarde, pp. 16–17.

to strict law. Also causes hard and difficult daily arise which are comprehended in no law books; in those there is a necessity of running back to the king, the fountain of justice, and the vicegerent of God himself, who in the commonwealth of the Jews took such causes to his own cognisance, and left to kings not only the example of such jurisdiction but the prerogative also.[158]

Of Privilege of Parliaments.

What need all this ado, will some say, to sift out what is comprised in the writ for the election of the Commons to parliament, since it is certain, though the writ do not, yet privilege of parliament gives sufficient power for all proceedings of the two Houses? It is answered that what slight esteem soever be made of the writ, yet in all other cases the original writ is the foundation of the whole business or action, and to vary in substance from the writ makes a nullity in the cause, and the proceedings thereupon. And where a commissioner exerciseth more power than is warranted by his commission, every such act is void and in many cases punishable. Yet we will lay aside the writ and apply ourselves to consider the nature of privilege of parliament. The task is the more difficult, for that we are not told what the number of privileges are, or which they be; some do think that as there be dormant articles of faith in the Roman church which are not yet declared, so there be likewise privileges dormant in the House of Commons, not yet revealed; we must therefore be content in a generality to discourse of the quality or condition of privilege of parliament, and to confine ourselves to these three points:

1. That privilege of parliament gives no power, but only helps to the execution of the power given by the writ.

2. That the freeholders by their elections give no privilege.

3. That privilege of parliament is the gift of the king.

First, the end or scope of privilege of parliament is not to give any power to do any public act not warranted by the writ, but they are intended as helps only to enable to the performance of the duty enjoined, and so are subservient to the power comprised in the writ. For instance, the grand privilege

---

158 Henry Spelman, *Henrici Spelmanni Equit. Anglo-Brit. Archeologus. In modum Glossarii ad rem antiquam posteriorem*, p. 129.

of freedom from arrests doth not give any power at all to the House of Commons to do any act, but by taking away from the freeholders and other subjects the power of arrests, the Commons are the better enabled to attend the service to which they are called by the king.

In many other cases the servants or ministers of the king are privileged and protected much in the same nature. The servants in household to the king may not be arrested without special licence; also the officers of the king's courts of justice, having a privilege not to be sued in any other court but where they serve and attend, and to this purpose they are allowed a writ of privilege. Likewise all such as serve the king in his wars, as are employed on foreign affairs for him, are protected from actions and suits. Nay the king's protection descends to the privileging even of laundresses, nurses, and midwives if they attend upon the camp, as Sir Edward Coke saith, *quia lotrix, seu nutrix, seu obstetrix*.[159] Besides the king protects his debtors from arrests of the subject till his own debts be paid.

These sorts of protections are privileges the common law takes notice of and allows, and hath several distinctions of them; and some are protections, *quia profecturus* ["because (he is) about to depart"], and others are *quia moraturus* ["because (he is) about to be delayed"]. Some are with a clause of *volumus* for stay of suits, others with a clause of *nolumus* for the safety of men's persons, servants, and goods; and the king's writs do vary herein according to the nature of the business.

But none of these privileges or protections do give any power; they are not positive, but privative: they take away and deprive the subject of the power or liberty to arrest, or sue, in some cases only. No protection or privilege doth defend in point of treason, felony, or breach of the peace. Privileges are directly contrary to the law, for otherwise they should not be privileges, and they are to be interpreted in the strictest manner as being odious and contrary to law. We see the use of privileges; they do but serve as a dispensation against law, intended originally and principally for the expediting of the king's business; though secondarily and by accident there do sometimes redound a benefit by them to the parties themselves that are protected. Strictly and properly, every privilege must be against a public or common law, for there is no use or need of a private law to protect where there is no public law to the contrary. Favours and graces which are only besides and not against the law, do not properly go under the name of privileges, though common use do not distinguish them. I know no other privilege that can be truly so called, and to belong to the House of Commons, which is so vast and great as this privilege of their persons, servants,

159 Coke i, folio 396.

and goods. This being indeed against the common law, and doth concern the whole kingdom to take notice of it, if they must be bound by it.

Touching this grand privilege of freedom from arrests, I read that in the 33 Henry VIII, the Commons did not proceed to the punishment of offenders for the breach of it until the Lords referred the punishment thereof to the lower house. The case is thus reported: George Ferrers, gentleman, servant to the king, and burgess for Plymouth, going to the parliament house was arrested in London by process out of the king's bench for debt, wherein he had before been condemned as surety for one Welden, at the suit of one White. Which arrest, signified to Sir Thomas Moyle, Speaker, and to the rest, the serjeant (called St. John) was sent to the Counter in Bread Street to demand Ferrers. The officer of the Counter refused to deliver him and gave the serjeant such ill language that they fall to an affray. The sheriff coming, taketh the officer's part, the serjeant returned without the prisoner. This being related to the Speaker and burgesses, they would sit no more without their burgess, and rising, repaired to the upper house, where the case was declared by the Speaker before Sir Thomas Audley, chancellor, and the lords and judges there assembled, who judging the contempt to be very great, referred the punishment thereof to the House of Commons itself.

This privilege of freedom from arrests is the only privilege which Sir Edward Coke finds to belong to the House of Commons. He cannot, or at least he doth not, so much as name any other in his section of the privileges of parliament. Neither doth he bring so much as one precedent for the proof of this one privilege for the House of Commons, which may cause a doubt that this sole privilege is not so clear as many do imagine. For in a parliament in the 27 Elizabeth, Richard Coke, a member, being served with a subpoena of chancery, the lord chancellor thought the House had no such privilege for subpoenas as they pretended; neither would he allow of any precedents of the House committed unto them, formerly used in that behalf, unless the House of Commons could also prove the same to have been likewise thereupon allowed and ratified also by precedents in the court of chancery.

In the 39 of Elizabeth, Sir Edward Hoby and Mr. Brograve, attorney of the duchy, were sent by the House to the lord keeper,

> in the name of the whole House, to require his lordship to revoke two writs of subpoenas which were served upon Mr. Thomas Knyvet, a member of the House, since the beginning of parliament. The lord keeper demanded of them whether they were appointed by any advised consider-

ation of the House, to deliver this message unto him with the word required in such manner as they had done, or no. They answered his lordship, yea. His lordship then said, as he thought reverently and honourably of the House and of their liberties and privileges of the same, so to revoke the said subpoenas in that sort was to restrain her majesty in her greatest power, which is justice in the place wherein he serveth under her,[160]

and therefore he concluded, as they had required him to revoke his writ, so he did require to deliberate.

Upon the 22nd of February, being Wednesday, 18 Elizabeth,

report was made by Mr. Attorney of the duchy, upon the committee for the delivering of one Mr. Hall's man, that the committee found no precedent for setting at large by the mace any person in arrest but only by writ. And that by divers precedents of records perused by the said committee, it appeareth that every knight, citizen, or burgess which doth require privilege hath used in that case to take a corporal oath before the lord chancellor or lord keeper, that the party for whom such writ is prayed came up with him and was his servant at the time of the arrest made.[161]

Thereupon Mr. Hall was moved by the house to repair to the lord keeper and make oath, and then take a warrant for a writ of privilege for his servant.

It is accounted by some to be a privilege of parliament to have power to examine misdemeanours of courts of justice and officers of state. Yet there is not the meanest subject but hath liberty, upon just cause, to question the misdemeanour of any court or officer if he suffer by them. There is no law against him for so doing, so that this cannot properly be called a privilege, because it is not against any public law. It hath been esteemed a great favour of princes to permit such examinations; for, when the lords were displeased with the greatness of Piers Gaveston, it is said that in the next parliament, the whole assembly obtain of the king to draw articles of their grievances, which they did. Two of which articles were, first, that 'all strangers should be banished the court and kingdom', of which Gaveston

---

160   D'Ewes, p. 554.
161   D'Ewes, p. 249.

was one. Secondly, that 'the business of the state should be treated of by the council of the clergy and nobles'.

In the reign of King Henry VI, one Mortimer, an instrument of the Duke of York, by promising the Kentish men a reformation and freedom from taxations, wrought with the people that they drew to a head, and made this Mortimer (otherwise Jack Cade) their leader, who styled himself Captain Mend-all. He presents to the parliament the complaints of the Commons, and he petitions that the Duke of York and some other lords might be received by the king into favour, by the undue practices of Suffolk and his complices commanded from his presence, and that all their opposites might be banished the court and put from their offices, and that there might be a general amotion of corrupt officers. These petitions are sent from the lower house to the upper, and from thence committed to the lords of the king's privy council, who, having examined the particulars, explode them as frivolous, and the authors of them to be presumptuous rebels.

Concerning liberty or freedom of speech, I find that at a parliament at Blackfriars in the 14 of Henry VIII, Sir Thomas More being chosen speaker of the House of Commons, he first disabled himself, and then petitioned the king that 'if in communication and reasoning any man in the Commons House should speak more largely than of duty they ought to do, that all such offences should be pardoned, and to be entered of record, which was granted'. It is observable in this petition that liberty or freedom of speech is not a power for men to speak what they will or please in parliament, but a privilege not to be punished but pardoned for the offence of speaking 'more largely than in duty ought to be',[162] which in an equitable construction must be understood of rash, unadvised, ignorant, or negligent escapes and slips in speech, and not for wilful, malicious offences in that kind. And then the pardon of the king was desired to be upon record, that it might be pleaded in bar to all actions. And it seemeth that Richard Strode and his complices were not thought sufficiently protected for their free speech in parliament unless their pardon were confirmed by the king in parliament; for there is a printed statute to that purpose in Henry VIII's time.

Touching the freedom of speech, the Commons were warned in Queen Elizabeth's days not to meddle with the queen's person, the state, or church government. In her time the discipline of the church was so strict that the litany was read every morning in the House of Commons during the

---

162 Holinshed ii, p. 682.

parliament, and when the Commons first ordered to have a fast in the Temple upon a Sunday, the queen hindered it.

21 January, Saturday, 23 Elizabeth, the case is thus reported: Mr. Paul Wentworth moveth for a public set fast, and for a preaching every morning at 7 of the clock before the House sat. The House was divided about the fast, one hundred and fifteen were for it, and one hundred against it. It was ordered that as

> many of the House as conveniently could, should on Sunday fortnight after, assemble and meet together in the Temple church, there to hear preaching and to join together in prayer with humiliation and fasting for the assistance of God's spirit in all their consultations, during this parliament, and for the preservation of the queen's majesty and her realms. And the preachers to be appointed by the privy council that were of the House, that they may be discreet, not meddling with innovation or unquietness.[163]

This order was followed by a message from her majesty to the House, declared by Mr. Vice-chamberlain, that her highness had a great admiration of the rashness of this House in committing such an apparent contempt of her express command as to put in execution such an innovation, without her privity or pleasure first known. Thereupon Mr. Vice-chamberlain moved the House to make humble submission to her majesty, acknowledging the said offence and contempt, craving a remission of the same, with a full purpose to forbear the committing of the like hereafter. And by the consent of the whole House, Mr. Vice-chamberlain carried their submission to her majesty.

35 Elizabeth,

> Mr. Peter Wentworth and Sir Henry Bromley delivered a petition to the lord keeper desiring the lords of the upper house to be suppliants with them of the lower house unto her majesty, for entailing the succession of the crown. Whereof a bill was ready drawn by them. Her majesty was highly displeased herewith as contrary to her former strait command, and charged the council to call the parties before them. Sir Thomas Heneage sent for them, and after speech with them, commanded them to forbear the parliament and not to go out of their several lodgings. After, they were

---

163   D'Ewes, p. 282.

called before the lord treasurer, the Lord Buckhurst, and Sir Thomas Heneage. Mr. Wentworth was committed by them to the tower, Sir Henry Bromley, with Mr. Richard Stephens, to whom Sir Henry Bromley had imparted the matter, were sent to the Fleet, as also Mr. Welch, the other knight for Worcestershire.[164]

In the same parliament, 'Mr. Morrice, attorney of the court of wards, moved against the hard courses of the bishops, ordinaries, and other ecclesiastical judges in their courts, used towards sundry learned, and godly ministers and preachers,'[165] and spake against subscriptions and oaths, and offered a bill to be read against imprisonment for refusal of oaths. Mr. Dalton opposed the reading of it, as a thing expressly against her majesty's command to meddle in. Dr. Lewin showed that subscription was used even at Geneva. At two of the clock the same day, the speaker, Mr. Coke, (afterwards Sir Edward Coke) was sent for to the court, where the queen herself gave him in command a message to the house. She told him:

> It being wholly in her power to call, to determine, to assent, or dissent to anything done in parliament, that the calling of this was only that the majesty of God might be more religiously observed, by compelling, by some sharp laws, such as neglect that service; and that the safety of her majesty's person and the realm might be provided for. It was not meant they should meddle with matters of state or causes ecclesiastical (for so her majesty termed them). She wondered that any could be of so high commandment to attempt (they were her own words) a thing so expressly contrary to that which she had commanded. Wherefore with this she was highly offended; and because the words spoken by my lord keeper are not now perhaps well remembered, or some be now here that were not then present. Her majesty's present charge and express command is that no bill touching the said matter of state, or reformation in causes ecclesiastical, be exhibited. And upon my allegiance (saith Mr. Coke), I am charged, if any such bill be exhibited, not to read it.[166]

---

164   D'Ewes, p. 470.
165   D'Ewes, p. 474.
166   D'Ewes, p. 478.

I have been credibly informed that the queen sent a messenger, or serjeant-at-arms, into the House of Commons, and took out Mr. Morrice, and committed him to prison. Within few days after, I find Mr. Wroth moved in the House, that they might be humble suitors to her majesty, that she would be pleased to set at liberty those members of the House that were restrained. To this it was answered by the privy counsellors that her majesty had committed them for causes best known to herself, and to press her highness with this suit would but hinder them whose good is sought; that the House must not call the queen to account for what she doth of her royal authority, that the causes for which they are restrained may be high and dangerous, that her majesty liketh no such questions; neither doth it become the House to search into such matters.

In the 39 Elizabeth, the Commons were told their privilege was *yea*, and *no*, and that her majesty's pleasure was that if the Speaker perceived any idle heads which would not stick to hazard their own estates, which will meddle with reforming the church and transforming the commonweal, and do exhibit bills to that purpose, the Speaker should not receive them till they were viewed and considered by those whom it is fitter should consider of such things, and can better judge of them. And at the end of this parliament, the queen refused to pass forty-eight bills which had passed both Houses.

In the 28 of Elizabeth, the queen said, 'she was sorry the commons meddled with choosing and returning knights of the shire for Norfolk, a thing impertinent for the House to deal withal, and only belonging to the office and charge of the lord chancellor, from whom the writs issue and are returned'.[167]

4 Henry IV:

> The 10th of October, the chancellor before the king declared the Commons had sent to the king, praying him that they might have advice and communication with certain lords about matters of business in parliament for the common good of the realm. Which prayer our lord the king graciously granted, making protestation, he would not do it of duty, nor of custom, but of his special grace at this time. And therefore our lord the king charged the clerk of the parliament that this protestation should be entered on record upon the parliament roll,

---

167   D'Ewes, p. 393.

which the king made known to them by the Lord Say and his secretary,

> how that neither of due nor of custom, our lord the king
> ought to grant any lords to enter into communication with
> them of matters touching the parliament. But by his special
> grace at this time, he hath granted their request in this par-
> ticular. Upon which matter the said steward and secretary
> made report to the king in parliament that the said Com-
> mons knew well that they could not have any such lords to
> commune with them of any business of parliament without
> special grace and command of the king himself.[168]

It hath heretofore been a question whether it be not an infringing and prejudice to the liberties and privileges of the House of Commons for them to
join in conference with the Lords in cases of benevolence or contribution
without a bill.

In the 35 Elizabeth, on Tuesday the 1st of March, Mr. Egerton, attorney
general, and Dr. Cary came with a message from the Lords. Their lordships
desired to put the House in remembrance of the speech delivered by the
lord keeper, the first day, for consultation and provision of treasure to be
had against the great and imminent dangers of the realm. Thereupon their
lordships did look to have something from the Houses touching those
causes before this time (and yet the parliament had sat but three days, for
it began February 26th), and therefore their lordships had hitherto omitted
to do anything therein themselves. And thereupon their lordships desired
that according to former laudable usages between both Houses in such
like cases, a committee of Commons may have conference with a committee of Lords touching provision of treasure against the great dangers of
the realm, which was presently resolved by the whole House, and they signified to their lordships the willing and ready assent of the whole House.
At the meeting, the Lords negatively affirm not to assent to less than three
subsidies, and do insist for a second conference. Mr. Francis bacon yielded
to the subsidy, but opposed the joining with the Lords as contrary to the
privileges of the House of Commons. Thereupon the House resolved to
have no conference with the Lords, but

> to give their lordships most humble and dutiful thanks with
> all reverence for their favourable and courteous offer of con-
> ference, and to signify that the Commons cannot in those
> cases of benevolence or contribution join in conference with

168   *Rotuli*, p. 486.

their lordships without prejudice to the liberties and privileges of the House; and to request their lordships to hold
the members of this House excused in their not assenting
to their lordships said motion for conference, for that so to
have assented without a bill had been contrary to the liberties and privileges of this House, and also contrary to the
former precedents of the same House in like cases had.[169]

This answer delivered to the Lords by the chancellor of the exchequer,
their lordships said they well hoped to have had a conference according
to their former request, and desired to see those precedents by which the
Commons seem to refuse the said conference. But in conclusion it was
agreed unto, upon the motion of Sir Walter Raleigh, who moved that without naming a subsidy it might be propounded in general words, to have a
conference touching the dangers of the realm and the necessary supply of
treasure to be provided speedily for the same, according to the proportion
of the necessity.

In the 43 Elizabeth, Serjeant Heal said in parliament,

he marvelled the House stood either at the granting of a subsidy or time of payment, when all we have is her majesty's,
and she may lawfully at her pleasure take it from us; and
that she had as much right to all our lands and goods as to
any revenue of the crown; and he said he could prove it by
precedents in the time of Henry III, King John, and King
Stephen.[170]

The ground upon which this serjeant-at-law went may be thought the
same Sir Edward Coke delivers in his *Institutes*, where he saith, 'the first
kings of this realm had all the lands of England in demesne, and the great
manors and royalties they reserved to themselves, and of the remnant for
the defence of the kingdom enfeoffed the barons'. From whence it appears
that no man holds any lands but under a condition to defend the realm;
and upon the self-same ground also the kings prerogative is raised as being a pre-eminence in cases of necessity, above and before the law of property or inheritance. Certain it is, before the Commons were ever chosen to
come to parliament, taxes or subsidies were raised and paid without their
gift. The great and long continued subsidy of Danegeld was without any
gift of the Commons or of any parliament at all that can be proved. In the

169   D'Ewes, p. 486.
170   D'Ewes, p. 633.

8 Henry III a subsidy of two marks in silver upon every knight's fee was granted to the king by the nobles, without any Commons. At the passing of a bill of subsidies, the words of the king are, 'the king thanks his loyal subjects, accepts their good will, and also will have it so: *le roy remercie ses loyaux subjects, accept leur benevolence, et ausi ainsi le vault*', which last words of *ainsi le veult*, 'the king wills it to be so', are the only words that makes the act of subsidy a law to bind every man to the payment of it.

In the 39 Elizabeth, the Commons, by their Speaker, complaining of monopolies, the queen spake in private to the lord keeper, who then made answer touching monopolies, that 'her majesty hoped her dutiful and loving subjects would not take away her prerogative, which is the chiefest flower in her garland, and the principal and head pearl in her crown and diadem'; but 'that they will rather leave that to her disposition'.[171]

The second point is that the freeholders or counties do not nor cannot give privilege to the Commons in parliament. They that are under the law cannot protect against it, they have no such privilege themselves as to be free from arrests and actions; for if they had, then it had been no privilege, but it would be the common law. And what they have not, they cannot give; *nemo dat quod non habet*. Neither do the freeholders pretend to give any such privilege, either at their election or by any subsequent act. There is no mention of any such thing in the return of the writ, nor in the indentures between the sheriff and the freeholders.

The third point remains that privilege of parliament is granted by the king. It is a known rule: that which gives the form gives the consequences of the form. The king by his writ gives the very essence and form to the parliament. Therefore privileges, which are but consequences of the form, must necessarily flow from kings.

All other privileges and protections are the acts of the king; and by the king's writ. Sir Edward Coke saith that the protection of men's persons, servants, and goods is done by a writ of grace from the king. At the presentment of the speaker of the House of Commons to the king upon the first day of parliament, the speaker in the name and behoof of the Commons humbly craveth that his majesty would be graciously pleased to grant them their accustomed liberties and privileges; which petition of theirs is a fair recognition of the primitive grace and favour of kings in bestowing of privilege, and it is a shrewd argument against any other title. For our ancestors were not so ceremonious nor so full of complement as to beg that by grace which they might claim by right. And the renewing of this petition every parliament argues the grant to be but temporary during only the present parliament, and that they have been accustomed, when they have been accustomably sued, or petitioned for. I will close this point with the judgment of King James, who in his *Declaration Touching His Proceedings in Parliament*, 1621, resolves 'that most privileges of parliament grew from precedents which rather shew a toleration than an inheritance'. Therefore he 'could not allow of the style, calling it their ancient and undoubted right and inheritance, but could rather have wished that they had said their privileges were derived from the grace and permission of his ancestors and him'. And thereupon he concludes, he cannot 'with patience endure his subjects to use such antimonarchical words concerning their liberties, except they had subjoined that they were granted unto them by the grace and favours of his predecessors'. Yet he promiseth 'to be careful of whatsoever privileges they enjoy by long custom and uncontrolled and lawful precedents'.

Sources and Editions

The following is a list of editions used by Filmer in his quotations, and where specified, editions used specifically in ths volume. Not included are classical works, which generally have been referenced in the standard form.

Aristotle, *Politics*. Quotations sourced from *Aristotle's Politica*. ed. W. D. Ross, Oxford: Clarendon Press. 1957.

Aristotle, *Nicomachean Ethics*. Quotations sourced from *Aristotle's Ethica Nicomachea*, ed. J. Bywater, Oxford: Clarendon Press, 1894.

Bodin, Jean, *The Six Bookes of a Commonweale*, tr. Richard Knolles, London: 1606.

Botero, Giovanni, *Relations of the Most Famous Kingdoms and Commonwealthes throwout the World*, London: 1630.

Bracton, Henry de, *Henrici de Bracton De Legibus et Consuetudinibus Angliae, libri quinque.*, London: 1640.

Camden, William, *Britain, or a Chorographicall Description of the most flourishing Kingdomes, England, Scotland, and Ireland*, London: 1637.

Coke, Sir Edward, *The First Part of the Institutes*, London: 1628.

Coke, Sir Edward, *The Fourth Part of the Institutes*, London: 1644.

Cotton, Robert, *Cottoni Posthuma: divers choice piece of that renowned antiquary, Sir Robert Cotton, Knight and Baronet*, London: 1679.

D'Avity, Pierre, *The Estates, Empires, and Principalities of the World.*, tr. Edward Grimstone, London: 1615.

Decreti prima pars, in *Corpus Iuris Canonici*, Halle: 1747.

Discourse upon the Questions in debate between the King and Parliament, A, London, 1642.

D'Ewes, Sir Simonds, *A Compleat Journal of the Votes, Speeches and Debates, both of the House of Lords and the House of Commons throughout the whole reign of Queen Elizabeth*, London: 1693.

Digestorum et Pandectorum, in *Corpus Iuris Civilis,* ed. Krueger, Paul. Mommsen, Theodor. Schoell, Rudolf, Berlin: 1895. Republished 1954.

Egerton, Sir Thomas, *The Speech of the Lord Chancellor or England, in the Eschequer chamber, touching the Post-nati*, London: 1609.

Ferne, Henry, *A Reply unto Severall Treatises pleading for the Armes now taken up by Subjects*, Oxford: 1643.

Gee, Edward, *An Exercitation Concerning Usurped Powers*, London: 1650.

Glanville, Sir John, *The Copies of two Speeches in Parliament. The one by Iohn Glanville Esquire. The other by Sir Henry Martin Knight. At a General Committee of both Houses, the 22. of May. 1628*, London: 1628.

Grotius, Hugo de, *De Jure Belli et Pacis*, Paris: 1625.

Hobbes, Thomas, *Leviathan or the Matter, Forme and Power of a Commonwealth Ecclesiastical and Civil*, London: 1651.

Hobbes, Thomas, *De Cive*, Paris: 1642.

Holinshed, Raphael, *Holinshed's Chronicles of England, Scotland, and Ireland*, London: 1577.

Richard Hooker, *Of the Laws of Ecclesiastical Polity*, London: 1648.

Hunton, Philip, *A Treatise of Monarchie*, London: 1643.

James I, *A Speech to the Lords and Commons of the Parliament at White-Hall, on Wednesday the XII of March, Anno 1609*, London: 1610.

James I, *The True Law of Free Monarchies*, London: 1598.

Lambarde, William, *A Perambulation of Kent*, London: 1635.

Milton, John, *Pro Populo Anglicano Defensio*, London: 1651.

Milton, John, *The Tenure of Kings and Magistrates*, London: 1649.

Paris, Matthew, *Matthaei Paris Historia Maior*, London: 1640.

Parker, Henry, *Observations upon some of his Majesties late Answers and Expresses*, London: 1642.

Prynne, William, *The Treachery and Disloyalty of Papists to their Sovereigns, in Doctrine and Practise*, London: 1643.

Raleigh, Sir Walter, *The Prerogative of Parliaments in England*, London: 1628.

Rotuli Parliamentorum; ut et petitiones, et placita in Parliamento, London: 1783.

Salmasius, Claudius, *De Usuris Liber*, Leiden: 1638.

Savile, Henry, *Rerum Anglicarum post Bedam*, London: 1596.

Selden, John *Eadmeri Monachi Cantuarensis Historiae Novorum*, London: 1623.

Selden, John, *Of the Dominion, or Ownership of the Sea*, London: 1652 (*Mare Clausum Seu De Dominio Maris Libri Duo*, London: 1635). Filmer translated the Latin edition for the excerpts in this volume.

Selden, John, *The Privileges of the Baronage of England*, London: 1642.

Selden, John, *Titles of Honor*, London: 1631.

Spelman, Henry, *Henrici Spelmanni Equit. Anglo-Brit. Archeologus. In modum Glossarii ad rem antiquam posteriorem*, London: 1626.

Statutes at Large, The, London: 1618.

Statutes of Ireland, Dublin: 1621.

Stow, John, *The Survey of London*, London: 1598.

Suarez, Francisco, *Tractatus de Legibus ac Deo Legislatore*, Ciombra: 1612.

Vowell, John (AKA John Hooker), *The Order and Usage of the keeping of a Parliament*, London: 1575.

Westminster, Matthew, *Matthaeus Westmonasteriensis, Florilegus dictis, praecipue de rebus Britannicus adb exorido mundi usque ad annum Domini*, London: 1570.

Bibliography

BACKGROUND

Peter Laslett. **"Sir Robert Filmer: The Man versus the Whig Myth."** In The William and Mary Quarterly. Third Series, Vol. 5, No. 4 (Williamsburg: Early American History and Culture, 1948).

Peter Laslett. **"The gentry of Kent in 1640."** In The Cambridge Historical Journal, Vol. 9, Issue 2 (Cambridge: Cambridge University Press, 1948).

Johann Sommerville. **Politics and Ideology in England 1603-1640** (London and New York: Longman, 1986).

Quentin Skinner. **"History and Ideology in the English Revolution."** In The Historical Journal Vol. 8, Issue 2 (Cambridge: Cambridge University Press, 1965).

MANUSCRIPTS

John M. Wallace. **"The Date of Sir Robert Filmer's Patriarcha."** In The Historical Journal, Vol. 23, No. 1 (Cambridge: Cambridge University Press, 1980).

Corinne Comstock Weston. **"The Authorship of the Freeholders Grand Inquest."** In The English Historical Review, Vol. 95, No. 374 (Oxford: Oxford University Press, 1980).

James Daly. **"Some Problems in the authorship of Sir Robert Filmer's works."** In *The English Historical Review*, Vol. 98, Issue 389 (Oxford: Oxford University Press, 1983).

POLITICAL THOUGHT

John Neville Figgis. **The Divine Right of Kings** (Cambridge: Cambridge University Press, 1914).

James Daly. **Sir Robert Filmer and English Political Thought** (Toronto:

University of Toronto Press, 1979).

John W. Robbins. **"The Political Thought of Sir Robert Filmer."** Ph.D thesis, Johns Hopkins University, 1973.

J. G. A. Pocock. **The Ancient Constitution and the Feudal Law: a study of English Historical Thought in the Seventeenth Century** (Cambridge: Cambridge University Press, 1987).

Gordon J. Schochet. **Patriarchalism in Political Thought: The Authoritarian Family and Political Speculation and Attitudes Especially in Seventeenth-Century England** (New York: Basic Books, 1975).

CONTEMPORARIES

Edmund Bohun. **A defence of Sir Robert Filmer, against the mistakes and misrepresentations of Algernon Sidney, esq.** (London: W. Kettilby, 1684).

Edward Hyde, Earl of Clarendon. **A brief view and survey of the dangerous and pernicious errors to church and state, in Mr. Hobbes's book, entitled Leviathan** (Oxon: Printed at the Theater, 1676).

Nathaniel Johnston. **The excellency of monarchical government** (London: for Robert Clavel, 1686).

Matthew Wren. **Monarchy asserted, or, The state of monarchicall & popular government in vindication of the consideration upon Mr. Harrington's Oceana** (Oxford: F. Bowman, 1659).

INFLUENCES

Constance Smith. **"Filmer, and the Knolles Translation of Bodin."** In The Philosophical Quarterly, Vol. 13, No. 52, (Oxford: Oxford University Press, 1963).

Julian H. Franklin. **Jean Bodin and the Rise of Absolutist Theory** (London and New York: Cambridge University Press, 1973).

Index